Creative Shakespeare

Related titles from the Arden Shakespeare

Shakespeare for Young People, Abigail Rokison
Springboard Shakespeare: Hamlet, Ben Crystal
Springboard Shakespeare: King Lear, Ben Crystal
Springboard Shakespeare: A Midsummer Night's Dream, Ben Crystal
Springboard Shakespeare: Macbeth, Ben Crystal

Creative Shakespeare

The Globe Education Guide to practical Shakespeare

FIONA BANKS

B L O O M S B U R Y
LONDON • NEW DELHI • NEW YORK • SYDNEY

Bloomsbury Arden Shakespeare
An imprint of Bloomsbury Publishing Plc

50 Bedford Square
London
WC1B 3DP
UK

1385 Broadway
New York
NY 10018
USA

www.bloomsbury.com

Bloomsbury is a registered trade mark of Bloomsbury Publishing Plc

British Library Cataloguing-in-Publication Data
A catalogue record for this book is available from the British Library.

ISBN: PB: 978-1-4081-5684-1
ePDF: 978-1-4081-5685-8
ePub: 978-1-4081-5683-4

Library of Congress Cataloging-in-Publication Data
A catalog record for this book is available from the Library of Congress.

Typeset by Fakenham Prepress Solutions, Fakenham, Norfolk NR21 8NN
Printed and bound in Great Britain

For my parents, Gwen and Ray Banks – who took me to see my first Shakespeare play.

I can no other answer make but thanks, And thanks, and ever thanks;

Twelfth Night 3:3 14–15

CONTENTS

ACKNOWLEDGEMENTS

I would like to thank everyone at Bloomsbury/Arden who worked on this book. In particular Margaret Bartley for all her support and care throughout. Also Faye Clarke, Emily Hockley and Molly Yarn. This book is the result of years of creative experiment and practice by Globe Education. My thanks to all Globe Education staff and Globe Education Practitioners, past and present: for their work, creativity and dedication to exploring Shakespeare's plays with young people. This book is a reflection of all our endeavours. Particular thanks to Rosemary Linnell, who began the process of training arts educators at the Globe. Grateful thanks are also due to all of the contributors, in particular the group of Globe Education Consultants whose work and creative practice forms the basis for this book: Giles Block, Bill Buckhurst, Adam Coleman, Colin Hurley, Patricia Kerrigan, Glynn MacDonald, Chris Stafford and Yolanda Vazquez. Special thanks to Adam and Chris for their invaluable support and advice and to the simply amazing Yolanda for sharing her extensive knowledge, expertise and cooking. Thank you to Tony Howard for contributing his expertise on Shakespeare on Film and to Isobel Durrant, Jon David, Frankie and the children of Gosden House School for providing their personal insights into learning through Shakespeare.

I would like to thank my colleagues: Patrick Spottiswoode, Neil Constable, Dominic Dromgoole, Farah Karim-Cooper, Paul Shuter, Maggie Tildesley, Alex Massey, Georghia Ellinas, Robert Norman, Claire Godden and Joanna Philpotts for all they have done to support and nurture this book; Amy Kenny and Lana Harper for their research; Pete Le May for his photographs; and Phil Brooks for his diagrams. Special thanks to Madeline Knights for her invaluable support in bringing the book together in the final stages. Thank you also to Kate Jamie and to the indomitable Julia Blades for their thoughtfulness and insights. Finally, a massive thank you to my wonderful family, John and Teddy, who now know a lot about *Creative Shakespeare*!

LIST OF ILLUSTRATIONS

THE BEGINNING: A GUIDE TO USING *CREATIVE SHAKESPEARE*

The Globe is a space of experiment and discovery. This book seeks to share some of Globe Education's discoveries since it was founded in 1989. In our work we endeavour to capture the spirit of creative exploration found in the rehearsal room and bring it into our daily work with young people. Here I share what has worked well for Globe Education, and the ideas that inform our practice – our learning, from exploring Shakespeare's plays with young people – in the UK and around the world, during the last twenty-four years.

I'm aware that teachers reading this book will have a wide range of skills and differing experience. This book does not seek to prescribe, in any way, but simply to share Globe Education's process; to make it as transparent as possible. When writing this book I was continually struck by its similarity to a cookery book. Writing some of the activities in particular felt like putting together a recipe. I hope you will use this book as I use a cookery book – pretty irreverently: scribbling notes in the margin, adjusting quantities and cooking times until I find what produces the best result for me. Drama activities are also like recipes in the sense that they are often evolutions of an existing method or approach. There are many different versions of similar exercises. The activities shared here are described as they are used by Globe Education, as they came to us. There may be different versions in existence, of which I am unaware.

All the activities in this book are creative, active approaches. I believe they are approaches that can be integrated into the everyday teaching of Shakespeare. Most of them do not require a special space and many do not require cleared desks. Whole group references assume there is c 30 in a group.

Structure

Deciding how to structure this book has been one of the greatest challenges. I'm aware that it could have been structured in a number of different ways. The structure ultimately used reflects the areas that concern us most at the Globe. Chapters 1 and 2 provide the ideas and contextual knowledge that inform Globe Education's work, while the following chapters are broken down into different areas of focus. Chapter 3: *Core approaches to Creative Shakespeare* is the foundation stage of activities. Everything featured in that section forms the basis of our work. Chapters 4, 5 and 6 focus on particular areas of language, staging and performance. Finally Chapter 7 provides an insight into the potential for Shakespeare to be used as a tool for learning. A great many of the activities could be featured in several chapters, as they work on a multi-dimensional level. It's worth noting that although we are used to divisions such as themes, character, language plot etc., actors tend not to think about plays in this way. Rehearsals explore a scene and look at it as a whole. Similarly the majority of activities in this book can be used to facilitate learning about any area of a play. All areas inform and affect the other; thinking about how they work together in performance is an excellent starting point for exploring the plays and the way they are constructed.

Age groups

The majority of the activities in this book work well with students from 11 years to adults. Many of them can also be used with younger students. They mostly started life in the rehearsal room where they are largely used with adults. We have adapted them, where necessary, to be appropriate for young people. We use the majority of these activities across all age groups. In order to differentiate for age and level we mostly change the complexity of the text used (see *Cutting Text* page 32–3). We also consider the stage to which we develop the activity. Students vary so much from group to group that which activity you use, and how you use it, really only depends on what you think is appropriate for your group. There are some activities we do only use with more advanced groups and these are denoted with the letter A.

Text

Text is central to every activity or activity sequence. The purpose of all activities is ultimately to explore text. Examples of possible text to use for an activity are given either within or at the end of an activity. Text is denoted by the letter T.

A word about writing

Sometimes on our training days for teachers the spectre of writing can be the elephant in the room. Even if an activity works well, how can students translate this experience into a piece of writing about the play? All of the activities in this book can provide ways into writing. They can be both catalysts for writing and methods of collecting ideas and discoveries that can be put together in a written response to the play. The questions used throughout the activities can be triggers for writing. The possibilities are so limitless and so group and learning objective dependant, that it is impossible to produce exhaustive lists here for possible written outcomes from activities.

If a written outcome is the desired goal of a session, plan and select activities with this in mind from the outset. Change them if necessary to ensure students explore the areas they will need for their written responses. Build key points into the activity where you can pause and harvest material for written work. This can be simply on post-it notes, or in a more structured student log book. If this happens at regular intervals, possibly around answers to clear key questions, students can quickly build up a list of points and quotations that can be used in a written response. When questioning, always bring students back to the text to illustrate and/or make their point. This is, of course, everyday practice for teachers. The activities are simply a tool to help you achieve a learning objective and should be used as you see fit for purpose.

Background

Historically, I wish to acknowledge the work of Rex Gibson and his contribution to the Globe in the early days. His work on practical approaches to Shakespeare was groundbreaking, and is the ground on which any practical Shakespeare educator stands. Rex Gibson was the first recipient of the Shakespeare's Globe Sam Wanamaker Award in 1994.

Globe Education began developing work for young people in 1989, long before the Globe theatre opened. Some of the activities in this book stem from this time, created by an early team of pioneer actor/teachers (as they were then known). This team, working without the Globe, often talked about the potential for incorporating discoveries made in the reconstructed Globe into approaches to Shakespeare with young people. Since the Globe opened in 1997 this is exactly what our team of Globe Education Practitioners have worked to achieve. They are a diverse and talented team, largely of actors and directors, trained as arts educators, who daily bring approaches from the rehearsal room and Globe stage into their work with young people. Their work is the basis and inspiration for this book.

In the summer of 2006 Globe Education was approached by the National Strategies to create training for their team of consultants working in schools across the UK. A team of Globe Education's most experienced and innovative practitioners came together in the 'attic', the area directly above the Globe stage, for a very hot week in July to create the training programme. A great many of the activities, or approaches to activities, in this book have come out of that attic! Largely the team that created that training are the team featured in this book.

Meet the Globe Education Consultants

Below are the biographies of the creative team whose practice particularly informs activities as they appear in the chapters which follow. All of them (except for myself) are consultants for Globe Education. With the exception of Glynn and Giles (who are our movement and voice experts, respectively), they train, or have trained, theatre artists to work as practitioners with young people at the Globe. I've included them simply because the individuals who create the work determine the type of work created. If a different group of people had come together on those hot summer days the activities in this book would be different activities. As you will see, each of this team have different strengths and interests and it is the diversity of their skills and approaches that is so valuable in their work. They feature throughout the book and in the *Tips* section after activities, giving their individual perspective on why an activity does or doesn't work for them, and how it can be most effectively used in the classroom. *Tips* appear most prolifically in Chapter 3: *Core approaches to Creative Shakespeare* – this is simply because these activities form the foundation of much of our work and require most comment as a result.

Fiona Banks

Fiona Banks is an Arts Educator and Producer of theatre for young people. She began her career as a stage manager and agent before training and working as a teacher in London secondary schools. Fiona joined the Globe in 1997 to develop Globe Education's work and partnerships with schools and the education sector. She went on to create and lead Globe Education's diverse and extensive programming for young people and teachers. These programmes now reach over

100,000 people each year – in Southwark, across the UK and around the world.

Fiona pioneered the training of arts educators at the Globe, building a team of over 70 theatre artists (largely actors and directors) who bring their expertise in creating theatre into their work with young people. In 2006 Fiona created the annual *Playing Shakespeare with Deutsche Bank* project, making theatre specifically for young people at the Globe. The partnership has so far provided access to theatre at the Globe for over 100,000 young people who might otherwise not experience Shakespeare in performance. Fiona specializes in the use and development of creative approaches to learning. She founded the Globe/Kings MA in *Creative Arts in the Classroom* and MEd module *Teaching Shakespeare Through Performance* with Cambridge University. She has acted as an adviser to the DFE, National strategies and QCA, creating with QCA the first creative assessment tasks for Shakespeare. She is a member of the advisory panel for the Cultural Learning Alliance.

Fiona is a general and series editor of the *Globe Education Shakespeare* play editions and author of *Creative Shakespeare: The Globe Education Guide to teaching Shakespeare* for Arden/Bloomsbury. She is Senior Advisor: Creative Programmes for Globe Education.

I'm interested in the journey from the rehearsal room to the classroom. How a technique used to create performance can equally become a catalyst for learning.

Giles Block (Globe Associate – Text)

When Giles was four he appeared in a show at the Stanley Halls in South Norwood. He thinks there might have been some tap dancing involved, but all he remembers is his costume, waving to his parents from the stage, and being refused orange juice because apparently he had upset a little girl. Despite all these things he is now uncertain about, it was from that day onwards that he decided to become an actor. By the time he left university in 1963 and started life as a professional actor, he'd appeared in about a dozen of Shakespeare's plays. By 1970 he had also begun directing, and in 1977 he joined the National Theatre as a Staff Director and went on to direct two main-house productions, *The Fawn* (John Marston) and *She Stoops to Conquer* in 1983/4. Between 1982 and 2003 he regularly visited Japan, directing, for the Japanese theatre company Shochiku, some twenty plays, including productions of *Macbeth*, *King Lear*, *Hamlet* and *Richard III*.

By the early 1990s he was increasingly drawn to wondering why Shakespeare's writing developed in the way it did, and why his verse contained so many irregularities. He felt that the answer had to be that this was exactly how Shakespeare 'heard' his characters speaking, and in 1995 Richard Eyre, then Artistic Director at the National Theatre, invited him to run some workshops to investigate this further. It was these workshops that, indirectly, led him in 1999 to taking up a post at Shakespeare's Globe theatre leading the Globe Company's text work. He has taught Shakespeare to countless groups in the UK and abroad, running workshops in America, Canada and Japan. In 2008 he was Shakespeare Consultant on the film *Me and Orson Welles*, directed by Richard Linklater. In 2011 he received the Sam Wanamaker Award in recognition of his work at the Globe.

Working with young people makes me feel young. I love the way they can surprise me and teach me things about the work I do which otherwise I wouldn't have alighted upon.

Bill Buckhurst

Bill's directing credits include: *King Lear, Hamlet* (Shakespeare's Globe); *A Midsummer Night's Dream*, *Macbeth*, *Romeo and Juliet* (Shakespeare's Globe/UAE tour, Playing Shakespeare); *Barbarians*, *Tinderbox* (Tooting Arts Club); *Hamlet*, *Much Ado About Nothing*, *A Midsummer Night's Dream* (Stafford Festival Shakespeare); *Riff Raff* (Arcola); *The Vegemite Tales* (West End/Riverside Studios); *Normal* (The Union); *Penetrator*, *The Night Before Christmas* (Theatre503). As assistant director, his credits include *Get Santa!* and *Aunt Dan and Lemon* (Royal Court). As an actor, his theatre credits include: seasons at the RSC, Royal Court, Shakespeare's Globe, Propeller, Chichester, Northampton and Oxford Stage Company. His film and television credits include: *Skyfall*, *World War Z*, *New Tricks*, *Spooks*, *Collision*, *Murphy's Law*, *EastEnders*, *Coronation Street*, *Holby*, *Bad Girls* and *As If*.

I hope that the young people who come to the Globe to see a play have a really positive experience and leave with an understanding that Shakespeare wrote these extraordinary stories for them as much as anyone else – that these plays are here to be enjoyed and engaged with, not just written about for an exam question.

Adam Coleman

Adam Coleman is an actor, writer and arts education practitioner. Adam trained at Mountview Conservatoire. In 1997 Adam became involved with Mark Rylance and Richard Olivier and their early developmental work at Shakespeare's Globe. It was then that he heard of the remarkable and extensive work of Globe Education. He has been the Senior Practitioner for Globe Education since 2003, where his responsibilities include the training and professional development of theatre practitioners and teachers, as well as the creation and delivery of projects and workshops for all ages. Adam has worked with more than 70,000 students and encourages the use of imagination, emotional intelligence, physical and vocal awareness to develop self-expression.

Adam represents Globe Education internationally and has delivered workshops, projects and lectures for young people and teachers in Mongolia, across California, New York and North Carolina. He has worked with partners such as the British Council and the English Speaking Union in Beirut, as well as working for Service Children's Education (the educational arm of the Armed Forces) in Germany, Cyprus and Gibraltar. He has worked for Cranfield School of Management and Oliver Mythodrama facilitating sessions for the business community, specifically focusing on inspirational leadership and presentation skills.

Adam is also the successful author of twenty children's books published by Oxford University Press and has sold over three million copies worldwide. In 2009, Adam formed a communications company which works specifically with young people creating bespoke programmes to develop communication skills.

I am especially interested in the connection between imagination, thought, emotion and speech and am inspired when students discover these connections. My particular interest is SEN and Primary as this is where these discoveries and connections are at their strongest and most transparent.

Colin Hurley

Colin has been a professional actor for over thirty years, mainly working in theatre, with a strong bias towards plays by Shakespeare. Repertory work around the country includes *Henry V*, *Hamlet*, *Macbeth*, *The Comedy of Errors* and *The Tempest*, then *Richard III* and *King Lear* at the National, and *Hamlet* and *Troilus and Cressida* with the RSC. Since 2001 Colin has worked extensively at Shakespeare's Globe. Productions include *Macbeth*, *Twelfth Night*, *The Golden Ass*, *The Winter's Tale*, an original pronunciation production of *Troilus and Cressida*, *Measure For Measure*, *In Extremis*, *Henry VIII*, *Anne Boleyn*, *All's Well That Ends Well*, and most recently *Richard III* and a revival of *Twelfth Night*. Colin also works with a group called The Factory, who inspired a lot of the exercises he uses in his workshops. Colin has taught at drama schools and has worked as a freelance education practitioner since 2003, leading workshops and courses for teachers, university students, drama students, secondary school groups and primary school students.

Even though I was a clever Grammar School boy, when I read Shakespeare I felt stupid. I think his words seem to land in the ears much more effectively than the eyes.

Patricia Kerrigan

Patricia trained at the Drama Centre London and worked as an actor for over twenty years. Patricia worked with Cheek by Jowl, the RSC, at the Almeida, the National Studio, the Bush, the Royal Exchange, Soho Theatre, the Traverse, Hampstead Theatre, Glasgow Citizens and at Shakespeare's Globe. TV appearances included Lady Macbeth in *Macbeth*, *The Crow Road*, *Flowers of the Forest*, *Sherlock Holmes*, *Dalziel and Pascoe*, *Playing for Real*, *A Fatal Inversion*, *Imaginary Friends*, *Waking the Dead*, *Inspector Linley* and *Silent Witness*. Films included *Joyriders*, *The Magic Toyshop*, *The Find*, *Big Pants*, *Age of Treason*, *To Kill a King* and *Miss Potter*.

Patricia was involved with Shakespeare's Globe Education between

2001and 2008. She ran courses for young people, teachers, undergraduates and drama students, teaching practical approaches to Shakespeare. While some of the work was on site at the Globe, the majority took place in primary, secondary and special needs schools across London. Patricia specialized in working with students with a range of special needs including autism and behavioural and emotional difficulties. Patricia created and led community projects aimed at specific groups in the area local to the Globe theatre. She helped train a pool of sixty-three Globe Education Practitioners to run workshops with young people of diverse backgrounds, ages and abilities and also trained consultant teachers in practical approaches to Shakespeare in the classroom.

In 2008 Patricia retrained and currently works as a Child and Adolescent Psychotherapist at the Brent Centre for Young People.

My main focus when working as a Globe Education Practitioner was to help young people make an emotional connection to the material in order to create a space where the student could explore their own preoccupations within the safety of playing a Shakespearean character.

Glynn MacDonald (Globe Associate – Movement)

Glynn trained in the Alexander Technique at the Constructive Teaching Centre in 1972. She has worked in the Actors' Centre and the Field Day Theatre Company in Ireland, *Dramaten* in Stockholm, *Norskspillersforbund* in Norway, *Holback Engstheatre* in Denmark, Bremen Opera Company in Germany, in Poland, Switzerland, Japan, Australia and the USA.

Since 1997 she has been resident Director of Movement at Shakespeare's Globe on all theatre productions. In 2002 she directed *Transforming September 11th* at the Linbury Studio, Royal Opera House for Peace Direct. She works for Globe Education giving movement workshops for schools, undergraduates and Continuing Professional Development for teachers. For the last six years she has worked on *Playing Shakespeare with Deutsche Bank*, which 16,000 students attend annually. She heads the Movement Department for the Conservatory Training Programme for Rutgers University at Shakespeare's Globe. She also works on the Jette Parker Young Artists Programme at the Royal Opera House.

I work to enable students to be free enough in their own physicality for their emotion to flow through their movement.

Chris Stafford

Chris is a Theatre Producer and Arts Consultant. He is a graduate of the Central School of Speech and Drama and began his career at Shakespeare's Globe, where he spent eight years leading and developing projects for schools, young people and teachers. Chris is currently a Learning Consultant and Producer for Globe Education and has produced all of the Globe's professional productions for young people to date, including several productions for the Globe stage and tours to Barbados, Abu Dhabi, Qatar and Dubai.

Since leaving his full-time position at the Globe, Chris has provided arts consultancy for the Donmar Warehouse and Bristol Old Vic, where he was responsible for the interim management of a £20 million capital campaign and produced Bristol Jam with Tom Morris. In December 2011, Chris was appointed Executive Director for dreamthinkspeak, one of the UK's leading producers of site-responsive theatre.

Chris is a 2009/10 Clore Fellow of the Clore Leadership Programme and a Fellow of the Royal Society of Arts.

My main area of interest at the Globe is making exciting and accessible theatre for young people.

Yolanda Vazquez

Yolanda Vazquez is an actor and theatre practitioner. She was born in the province of Cadiz in the south of Spain and moved to England with her parents when she was ten. Yolanda is a graduate of the Drama Centre, London and began her career in the role of Juliet at the Royal Theatre, Northampton. Since then she has enjoyed a long career in theatre, television, film and radio. Credits include: Gertrude in *Hamlet* (Teatro Español), Titania in *A Midsummer Night's Dream* (RSC), Mother in *Six Actors Looking for an Author* (Young Vic), *Children Of Men*, *The Air Up There*, *Notting Hill*, *Top Boy*, *Any Human Heart*, *Pinochet in Suburbia*, *Ashes to Antarctica (*BBC4), *Catherine of Aragon* (Book of the Week, BBC4).

She first joined the Globe in 1999 to play Adriana in *A Comedy Of Errors* and Bertha in *Augustine's Oak* and continued working in many productions, including *The Winter's Tale* (Hermione), *Much Ado About Nothing* (Beatrice), *Richard III* (Queen Elizabeth) until 2005. In 2003 she was asked to join the Education Department as a freelance Globe Education Practitioner and since then has had the privilege of working with and directing many students, teachers, actors and directors, as well as developing Globe Education's portfolio of work nationally and internationally.

Yolanda works at many leading drama schools including Central School of Speech and Drama and the Guildford School of Acting, as well as running drama workshops internationally. Her main body of work is still in performance both in Spain and in the UK.

My focus is to allow the students to discover their own interpretation of the text through rhythm, movement and activities gleaned from my experience in the rehearsal room.

CHAPTER ONE

Key principles and ideas for Creative Shakespeare

Keep it personal

There is no right way to teach Shakespeare. Just as there is no right interpretation of the plays or 'correct' reading of a character or scene. This is one of the reasons that Shakespeare can be so exciting, the potential for discoveries so potent, the possibilities for learning so great. It is also, of course, one of the reasons that it can be challenging. I'm often asked, what is Globe Education's standard workshop for 14–16 year-olds (or indeed any particular age group)? The answer is always that we don't have one; each one is particular to the group leader and the group in question. This is because if we did have a standard workshop I don't think it would be very good. The key to teaching Shakespeare well is the recognition that there is no formula or approach that will bring unfailing 'success', but that every session relies on the interaction between teacher, students and play. This is true of the teaching of any subject, but just as painting a 'fiddly' area requires a greater application of skill and focus as a painter, so teaching a subject so potentially challenging and demanding as Shakespeare requires all our skill and expertise as teachers. When a session goes well it feels like the easiest thing in the world to teach. We are helped by great material, amazing stories and words that enliven our imaginations and emotions. But we also know that these words and the stories they tell can feel alien and mountainous to students. We need always to find ways to interpret and access the plays that are best for each particular group, and to create a journey into the world of the play that is structured to facilitate maximum learning, challenge and discovery.

I've said that each session relies on the interaction between teacher, students and play. It is no accident that 'teacher' is first on this list. I've noticed, though, that teachers rarely think about themselves, and if they do it's certainly not first. We all have different feelings and attitudes towards teaching Shakespeare. These vary from play to play. Some plays we like and feel comfortable with, while the thought of teaching others is perhaps not so welcome! It's important to recognize these feelings when thinking of approaches to the play and planning sessions.

Everyone has different strengths and interests. In our Globe Education Practitioner team we employ people with a wide range of skills, from backgrounds as actors and directors to clowns and writers. We always try to pick the person with the most appropriate skills and attributes for the group. It's also an issue of personality. Who we are and our own personal life experiences affect the way we connect with and approach teaching any particular play. Teachers daily face the challenge of finding a wide range of skills within themselves. There is not the luxury of a large team within each classroom. Nevertheless, it is important to consider your strengths and weakness, likes, dislikes and style preferences. Not all the approaches in this book will be right for you, while others will need changing and developing to suit your personal style and approach. When we train our Globe Education Practitioners, one of the greatest challenges we face is trying to help them develop the confidence to be themselves and teach to their strengths, rather than use an activity they find difficult and don't connect with simply because they saw it work well for another practitioner. Throughout the activities in this book there are comments and *Tips* from Globe Education's team of consultants. They all use the activities differently to fit with their preferred teaching style and as they do so, the activities themselves evolve and develop. Their comments are intended to offer different windows onto an activity and to highlight the importance Globe Education places on individuality of approach – the value that each teacher as an individual brings to their teaching of Shakespeare.

No student is a 'blank canvas'

Every group of students is different, with varying interests and needs. What works for one group may not work for another. Knowledge of the group and its needs is central to session planning. Some of the active approaches in this book work well with groups with little prior experience of active approaches to Shakespeare, while others are more complex and will probably work best with a group which is used to working together in this manner.

It's rare to encounter a child post-11, but to a large extent, of almost any age, without some prior exposure to Shakespeare. Usually students have strong existing ideas, perceptions and experiences, both positive and negative. If a child has watched *The Lion King* they are familiar with the basic story of *Hamlet*. Strong Primary school engagement with Shakespeare means that students arrive at Secondary school with a developed knowledge and already have made a personal response to the plays. The (then DFES) publication *Shakespeare for all ages and stages* provided a framework for teaching Shakespeare from Early Years Foundation stage to Post-16 and captured and promoted excellent practice across all levels of education. It reminds us that as secondary level educators we are building on existing knowledge rather than starting with a 'blank canvas'.

Dr Anton Franks, Associate Professor, Faculty of Social Sciences, University of Nottingham often encourages his trainee teachers to approach any engagement with Shakespeare's plays (with a new group) by asking the question 'What does Shakespeare mean to you?'. This approach, with its intrinsic reminder that all learning and teaching of Shakespeare is to some extent contingent on prior experience or perception, is one Globe Education returns to in its work again and again. It doesn't matter whether the answer to this question is positive, negative or indifferent. The knowledge it gives us about our students can be invaluable.

Creative Shakespeare, active learning

Shakespeare was an actor and playwright who wrote plays to be played, on a stage and to be seen and heard by an audience. He wrote many of them for playhouses, such as the Globe, that were large social spaces. Reading his plays without any form of active engagement, without his words in our mouths and emotions and actions in our bodies, is like trying to engage with a piece of music by looking at the notes on the page but not listening to the music itself, or like reading a television script without watching the programme that was made.

There is nothing new about the idea that Shakespeare wrote plays to be performed and that his work is best taught actively. Shakespeare's plays were not printed in any format we would recognize during his lifetime. The first folio was printed in 1623, so his audiences would not have enjoyed the access to the plays as texts that we know today. Early publishers of early modern drama were all too aware of the potential pitfalls of doing so. In the preface to his play *The Malcontent* John Marston apologizes 'that Scenes invented, merely to be spoken, should be enforcively published to be read' and asks that the play 'be pardoned, for the pleasure it once afforded you, when it was presented with the soul of lively action'. It was rare to read a play, commonplace to see it. An English Association pamphlet of 1908 on *The Teaching of Shakespeare in Schools* warns that 'There is a serious danger in the classroom with text books open before us of our forgetting what drama really means'. The pamphlet goes on to recommend acting out of scenes and seeing the play in performance as good practice.

Shakespeare did not give his own actors a text, a complete written play, and expect them to learn or understand it. He provided them with parts containing their lines and cue only. They explored the play by playing: by acting it for an audience, by speaking the words, by experiencing their characters' emotions, actions, reactions and their relationships with those around them. Simply reading a Shakespeare play is like watching a 3D film without the glasses. We get the story, we read the words, but we miss the richness and depth of the art form. We cannot engage with the film in the way that its creators intended. In his book *Teaching Shakespeare* Rex Gibson wrote simply:

> Shakespeare was essentially a man of the theatre who intended his words to be spoken and acted out on stage. It is in that context of dramatic realisation that the plays are most appropriately understood and experienced. The consequence for teaching is clear: treat the plays as plays, for imaginative enactment in all kinds of different ways.
>
> Active methods comprise a wide range of expressive, creative and physical activities. They recognise that Shakespeare wrote his plays for performance and that his scripts are completed by enactment of some kind.[1]

Approaches from the Globe

Many of the approaches in this book started life in the rehearsal room at the Globe. They are based on the way an actor engages with a play as a script. They have, in some cases, evolved and been adapted to work for young people, although in other cases they have not changed at all and are used with students just as a director would with an actor. When actors talk about the rehearsal process they often talk about 'putting a play on its feet' – in other words, exploring the text actively, discovering aspects of the play by 'playing'. Playing their character but also being playful and experimental in their approach. Being inspired by the language of the plays, trying different ideas until they find the right one for their particular interpretation. Rehearsals are not about right answers but asking questions and exploring possibility. Actors are text detectives, looking for clues in the language – the words of the play. As actors become experienced in playing Shakespeare they develop a range of different ways into text. They select a particular technique or a combination of approaches to help them best play a character or moment. It's these that we share in this book.

What is Creative Shakespeare?

A creative approach to Shakespeare can take many forms. It can mean physical activity; students discovering and exploring language through action – the type of exercise that can require an empty space where students can move freely. Equally it can be an exercise that can be performed at a desk with no particular space or circumstances required. Creative approaches can involve students in large and small group work, but can also require them to work on their own and in pairs. This diversity of approach mirrors a day in the rehearsal room.

Creative approaches are active, physically and/or intellectually. They require students to engage fully with the moment they are exploring, to analyse based on the evidence of their actual experience and to make informed critical responses to the play. They can enable and deepen a student's insight and his/her analysis of any given moment or character. They challenge any notion that academic understanding and physical, vocal and emotional engagement with a text do not go hand in hand. Creative approaches invariably draw on, and value, imaginative engagement and response. They ask students to suspend judgement, to ask 'what if?'. Creative approaches often require students, like actors, to turn detective and to try different approaches to exploring and analysing any given scene, character or situation.

Key benefits

Creative approaches to Shakespeare not only ensure students meet Shakespeare's plays in the form in which they were created, as plays, but have been shown to deliver key benefits for learning and teaching. They offer us an opportunity to engage students with a range of different learning styles and can be adapted for all abilities. Often students who find Shakespeare daunting or difficult benefit most from these methods. In recent Globe Education research, boys made the most significant development after using a range of the creative approaches in this book – some climbing two attainment levels more than predicted during one Shakespeare unit.

This work is experiential. Students feel the emotions of a character and argue for their point of view. They are required to connect the physical and intellectual parts of themselves. This is the most natural state of learning. It's how we learn as babies, trying everything physically – exploring what works. The creation of a physical and emotional memory of the play empowers students and can allow them to reach deeper and lasting levels of understanding. This idea is not new; it can be found as early as 551 BC in the work of Chinese philosopher and reformer Confucius, who said: 'I hear and I forget. I see and I remember. I do and I understand.'

Through engaging actively with text, students gain ownership of it. Shakespeare ceases to be high art, a dead unapproachable cultural icon whose value and meaning is set in stone. By creating their own interpretations of a play or scene, students make it relevant to themselves, and in doing so play a part in reinventing Shakespeare for the current age, making the plays worth studying.

The benefits of creative approaches to Shakespeare are probably best expressed by the students themselves. The comments below are typical.

> Before we started the new work, all the sitting and reading out was boring. And I couldn't see the point of Shakespeare at all. First time we did the active work I felt a bit silly but I became more confident. I thought people would mess about but they were taking it seriously and it made me want to do it properly.
>
> I used to get embarrassed about the language because I was worried I would say the words wrong. But now we have looked at the words in detail and done 'hook, probe' (see page 48–52) I don't worry about saying them out. Now I can think about what they mean.
>
> These were my best lessons in school, ever. I think this work benefits because with just writing, you don't get into the words. I think I understand why Shakespeare uses his words. The language is different and active work has helped me to understand the language.
>
> I enjoyed the tasks and activities we had to do ... they helped me understand Shakespeare more. Understanding the words was difficult but the activities helped me. I did well. I thought the lessons were brilliant. I would like to do more of this work because of GCSE. I could get high grades.

The text is central to learning

All we know for certain about Shakespeare's plays are contained in the words of the plays themselves. Everything else, including many of the stage directions which were added later by editors of play editions, is conjecture or a 'best guess'. All we have are the words, and they are all we need, for everything that is necessary to know about the play is found in the text itself. For this reason activities in this book centre around text, either working with the text directly or through a series of exercises that will help students to access text. Engagement with the text at all times remains the primary goal. In a rehearsal room actors may have spent some time researching their role, but in the rehearsals themselves they are focused on interpreting the words of the play and how their character relates to those around them. This is how they create or discover meaning. The text here is not passive. In a rehearsal the function of language is not to be beautiful or poetic (although it may be both). Language here is physical. Characters speak because they want to communicate a desire or idea – to get something, or to make something happen.

When we study a play with students we often often talk about it in terms of divisions, e.g. plot, character, language. While these can be useful they are, to an extent, artificial. Everything is in the language of the play and it should always be at the centre of any study. This does not mean that it is sacred in any way – in fact, quite the opposite. While Globe Education never changes the actual words or meaning of the text for an exercise, it is frequently cut to maximize learning, or to achieve a particular learning objective. The importance of language and the freedom to cut text lie at the heart of all the approaches in the book. Ways of cutting text are explored in detail on pages 31–6.

The importance of the text does not mean it is always the starting point of sessions. Globe Education Consultant Chris Stafford always maintains 'the words are the last thing' when planning an exercise for young people. His point is that it is important to engage with why a character speaks before they speak. Exploring the story of the play is a powerful tool and central to many of the approaches in this book. The universal power of the stories and characters' dilemmas and choices are one of the reasons Shakespeare has endured and are often a good way to gain students' interest. Where the text comes in an activity is a matter of individual preference and will depend on the particular structure of each session. Quite often each activity in a session builds to the introduction of some text. An activity at the beginning of the session may culminate in simple text, e.g. one word or phrase, while typically activities towards the end of a session contains more text of greater complexity. What is important is that the physical and intellectual exploration of text informs the structure and objective of any activity.

Experience the play as player and audience

Performing Shakespeare can bring a whole range of benefits to young people, from fresh insights and perspectives into text, to confidence-building and the development of core literacy skills. These are explored fully in Chapter 6, along with approaches to creating different types of performances of Shakespeare's plays with young players. This type of performance is quite different, however, from the everyday active approaches to Shakespeare we use in the classroom.

Creative approaches to Shakespeare in the classroom enable students to begin to experience the play as actors do. They do not typically produce performance, although some activities can be extended and developed to do so. The focus is not on how a student might speak a line or lines, but on how they engage with them. Many of the activities are private ones that involve students working in pairs or individually. Most activities do not require any form of group sharing, although obviously teachers may wish to ask students to share their work at times, if they feel it is appropriate.

The aim of all activities is to enable students to engage in an active process which mirrors that used by actors creating a play for performance; to put them into a position where they begin to experience a play from the inside as a creative interpreter – a player in all senses of the word – rather than stare at it from without. It is not to create a product for consumption or judgement.

Equally important is the opportunity for young people to experience a Shakespeare play in performance as an audience member. This performance could be of any kind, from student performance to professional production, and in any setting from school hall to large theatre. Each type of performance has its own particular merits. The issues around seeing Shakespeare in performance are explored fully in Chapter 6. It is crucial that this experience should be active rather than passive. In the Globe theatre the audience are exposed to the light and the sounds of the world outside the theatre. They stand in the yard or sit on wooden benches. They can see each other. It is an active experience. This is different from the opportunity to be a passive audience member, sitting comfortably in the dark, focused on the bright light on stage that is offered by indoor theatres. Being an audience member at the Globe theatre requires us to be engaged, and reminds us how important it is for young people to feel able to be an active audience. This simply means that they are engaged by the production and that they feel able and equipped to make a critical response to the play.

Not every production of a Shakespeare play is suitable for young people, particularly if it is their first, or an early encounter with Shakespeare in performance. This is not necessarily about the subject matter of the play itself, or the theatre or theatre company that produce it, but about the production. Productions of the same play, even by the same company, vary greatly. This is a strength, but it is important to ensure as far as possible that the production in question will 'speak to' the particular group. In a world of the sound bite and the pause button we should not assume that young people possess an existing schema through which to process early experiences of theatre.

Arts organizations have a responsibility to create work that seeks to embrace and serve its young audience. Some companies, like Globe Education, create Shakespeare productions for young people. Usually shorter than an average production in length and directed and designed for a young audience, these can provide a good first experience. It's worth remembering that most cinema created for young people is usually a maximum of 1 hour 45 mins long. We wouldn't attempt a marathon on our first day as a runner and there is no reason why a first encounter with Shakespeare in performance should be a production of three-plus hours in length which makes no concessions to the needs of a younger audience.

Becoming an engaged, critical audience member for most young people is a journey. The challenge for a teacher is to find the most appropriate productions for each group that enable them to move forward on their journey, building on their experience and knowledge as critical, reflective audience members.

Shakespeare's plays as a teaching tool

Shakespeare's plays provide an excellent teaching tool as well as being a subject to teach. We can learn through Shakespeare's plays as much, if not more, than we can learn about Shakespeare's plays. This subject is explored in Chapter 7. It is possible to create units of work for a range of subjects using the plays, particularly those that are concerned with students' personal and social development, or address particular issues around subjects such as transition, group division/conflict or friendship. However, it is important to remember that learning through the plays has a place in our everyday Shakespeare.

In Globe Education workshops, learning through Shakespeare is integrated into every session. Every character and every scene teaches us something about ourselves as human beings, as well as about the craft of the playwright who created them. This is one of the main reasons why the plays remain worth studying, for their 'mirror' held 'up to nature', their insight into the human condition. If students engage with this, with how the situations they experience in the plays relate to their own lives and dilemmas, they not only develop as human beings but are more likely to be interested in the stories and enabled to develop greater insights into the plays themselves. Activities which develop experiential understanding and connection with a character or situation are often a starting point in sessions. If students can empathize with how a character behaves, they are more likely to understand why they speak and the language through which they choose to express themselves. In this way they develop the skills necessary to make original interpretations of the play and demonstrate individual critical insights.

Why teach Shakespeare?

If you have bought this book, the chances are you don't need convincing that it is a good idea to teach Shakespeare. The case for teaching his work has been made eloquently throughout the ages, in a variety of different formats. For this reason I don't intend to spend a great deal of time on this question here. It is, however, a question I often ask our Globe Education Practitioners to think about in their training sessions. I hope that this questioning will help keep our teaching practice fresh and focused. Recent research for the World Shakespeare Festival showed that 50 per cent of the world's children – at least 64 million children worldwide – are studying Shakespeare at school.[2] Whatever we think about these figures and their implications for international cultural learning, it's worth taking a moment to think about why this should be the case. Particularly in the face of such overwhelming acceptance, we do need to question the status quo, the seemingly widespread assumption that Shakespeare is good for our young people, and ask ourselves: why do we teach Shakespeare in school?

The shortest and most prosaic answer to this question would be: because it's on the curriculum. Not just, the World Shakespeare's Festival research indicates, in the UK but in 65 per cent of countries around the world. In the UK, it seems likely that this will be the case for the foreseeable future. Shakespeare has become such a cultural icon, such a symbol of 'Britishness', that it seems unlikely that a government of any political hue would remove him. At present an English teacher in a UK school is likely to spend more time teaching Shakespeare than any other single subject or author. I once met a teacher (a member of our Globe Education Academy at UC Davis California) who had taught *A Midsummer Night's Dream* fifty-three times. For this reason we need to find own own reasons to teach Shakespeare that go beyond the demands of curriculum fulfilment. Which reasons are most important to us will evolve over time and will vary for each individual teacher and group. The reasons that broadly motivate Globe Education's teaching follow below, in no particular order.

The plays are full of amazing, stimulating and challenging stories that captivate the imagination. They are universal stories, often taken by Shakespeare from existing classical sources. The characters that people them are complex and diverse. Their dilemmas are of their time but simultaneously modern. The stories are timeless and enable students to gain perspective, a sense of themselves and of the universality of the human condition. Simply, these plays contain stories worth 'hearing'. They do not patronize, but challenge a young audience and provide access to a range of complex human emotions and situations. The stories of the plays provide a frame, a safe place, within which young people can explore their own emotions and issues which concern them. Thus exploration of a Shakespeare play can deepen a student's moral understanding and development. This knowledge can then be applied to his or her own relationships and experiences. Rex Gibson best summed up these benefits when he stated simply that 'Shakespeare develops understanding of the human heart'.[3]

On a practical level, the stories provide opportunities for the acquisition of knowledge in a range of different subjects and areas, from history and geography to philosophy. They can help young people understand the mechanisms by which society is governed and engage with such concepts as individual and state, public and private, and in doing so examine their own key relationships and role in society. The stories resonate with young people from a wide range of cultural backgrounds and provide opportunities for a varied personal response to the plays.

The language of the plays is both challenging and familiar. It is alien in many ways to young people today and yet when they experience speaking it for themselves the rhythm and construction of the verse can make it surprisingly accessible. Shakespeare's language can be simultaneously beautiful, practical and playful. It opens a window onto a world of expression that can can enable young people to experience the power of the word and encourage them to play with language themselves, to extend their vocabulary and forms of expression. Shakespeare wrote for theatres without lighting, revolves or sound systems – none of the technical specifications we take for granted today. Most of his lighting and sound cues are in the words of the plays themselves. This subject is explored in Chapter 2. The physical role of language in Shakespeare's plays requires students to develop their imaginations and to consider the power and potential of words to paint pictures in the minds of the audience.

Shakespeare is a cultural icon. Playwright and plays take a central role in most mainstream perspectives of high art and 'Britishness'. Simultaneously he is part of our everyday culture. In our pub names, our street names, in the names of footballers' children, in the plots of our TV soap operas, he and his plays are there. He is quoted by everyone from politicians to royalty, to TV presenters, to us all in our everyday speech when we use, maybe unknowingly, some of the words he invented that have become part of our language. If we do not introduce young people to Shakespeare's plays we deny them some of the tools they need to decode and critique the world around them; we deny them cultural capital.

Shakespeare is often perceived to be difficult. Young people of all academic abilities know this. When they achieve in a Shakespeare session, when they feel they have understood or have a light bulb moment where they connect with a character, or are enthralled by a moment of drama, they feel good. Their confidence as a learner grows. This feeling is increased by the knowledge that Shakespeare can be challenging – the reward is greater because of the perceived complexity of the challenge. For a large number, although by no means all students, Shakespeare will be a subject recognized by family and carers. His study can present opportunity for social discourse between generations and a point of shared experience of education. One of the best moments during our *Playing Shakespeare with Deutsche Bank* productions of Shakespeare's plays is always the family performances when young people bring their family to the play, more often than not explaining the story to the adults in their party.

If a young person feels able to be a critical interpreter of Shakespeare then they know that they are able to access great art. Whether they feel this is something they wish to pursue is irrelevant. What is important is that they feel they have a choice, and that choice is based on engagement rather than alienation. A young person's experience of studying Shakespeare at school plays a part in how they go on to define themselves in relationship to culture and literature in general, throughout their lives.

Studying Shakespeare enables young people to engage with great work, with genius, and they deserve no less.

CHAPTER TWO

Context: Learning from the Globe

Background

When the Globe theatre opened its doors in 1997 there had not been a playhouse like it for over 400 years. It was built because of the tenacity and vision of founder Sam Wanamaker and his architect Theo Crosby. When Sam Wanamaker, a veteran of many Shakespearean roles, visited London in 1949 he was amazed to find no lasting memorial to the original Globe theatre, or any playing space that could help him locate Shakespeare's plays within the architecture that Shakespeare would have known and written for. He set out to build the Globe, using all early modern sources and contemporary scholarship available, to create the best possible reconstruction of Shakespeare's playhouse. This was a long and loving process that celebrated craft and craftsmanship. It resulted in the creation of a playhouse, a playing space, that was new and alien to actors, directors and audiences alike.

The opening of the Globe theatre enabled actors and theatre-makers to experience, for the first time, the playing conditions of an early modern playhouse; to play Shakespeare's plays in the theatre for which many of them were written. Mark Rylance, the Globe's first artistic director, described the theatre as a 'tool' in which he was challenged to mount early modern plays. In *Shakespeare's Globe A Theatrical Experiment* he elaborates on this idea:

> In my mind it is a bit like someone discovering the original cello, or the original violin and saying 'Mozart wrote for the instrument, not the modern one we're using, so who will take up the challenge to try and play his music on this instrument?' and that seemed a very exciting challenge.[1]

Everything in and about the Globe theatre was, and remains, an experiment. It is a theatre laboratory, in which artists and educators hypothesize, try, test, fail, 'fail better' and learn. Learning at the Globe is a physical necessity, a daily reality, if we are to move forward in our knowledge of this reconstructed playhouse and what it can tell us about Shakespeare's plays – how we play them, understand them and interpret them in the classroom. This learning is a physical, visceral experience. Staff at the Globe *have* to learn by doing and this experience has been central to Globe Education's work.

The Globe theatre is like a massive classroom where actor can be both student and teacher. In the opening theatre season at the Globe actors in the green room could often be heard discussing the demands of playing in the theatre, as they explored, and sometimes struggled with, the implications of playing to an audience that they could see, and which could see them. What's more, this audience could see each other and could easily be distracted if the actor's playing was not strong enough. Some of this audience could move around and were 'present' throughout the performance in a way that an audience in a dark auditorium were not. How should this be played or managed, they asked? Playing in the Globe theatre, they concluded, was hard work, but when actor and audience came together in a shared moment of theatrical experience, the feeling was like no other. Their experience bore a striking resemblance to a teacher's in a classroom. Actors entered the Globe stage with a script, just a teacher enters a classroom with a lesson plan. How well the performance went, actors soon learnt, relied on the quality of interaction between themselves, the play, the audience and the

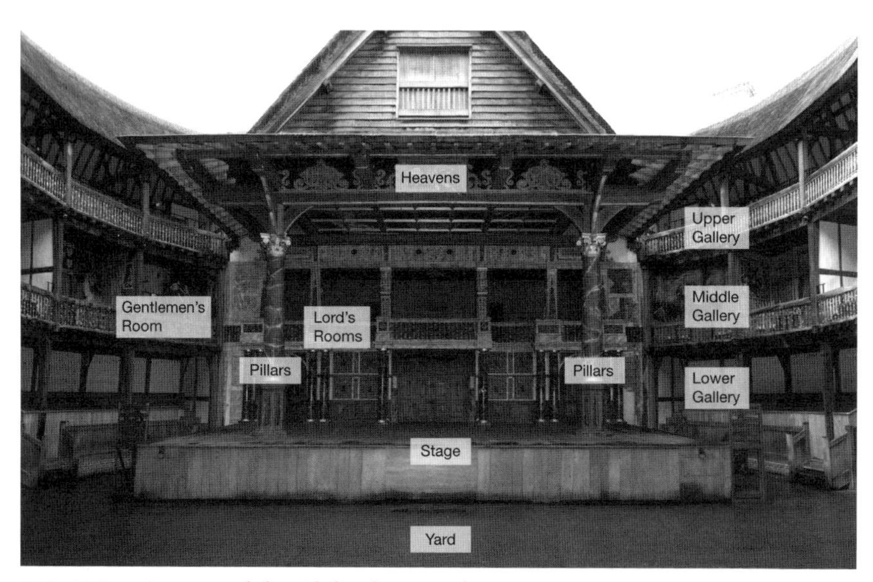

FIGURE 1 *Interior of the Globe theatre – front view.*

FIGURE 2 *Interior of the Globe theatre in performance. From the Globe stage. Macbeth.* Playing Shakespeare with Deutsche Bank *2010.*

playhouse itself, just as a session in the classroom relies on the quality of interaction between students, teacher and the environment or circumstances under which the session takes place.

Architecture

It's important to reflect, in the simplest terms, on what makes the architecture of the Globe different from a standard proscenium arch theatre. The following paragraphs should be read in conjunction with the picture and diagram on pages 14 and 15. First, and most obviously, the Globe theatre is round in shape (technically it is a many-sided polygon). It has no roof over its centre and is open to daylight and the elements. A thatched roof runs around the circumference, covering the gallery seating. A roof, known as the 'heavens', covers the stage. This means that plays are performed in daylight and that, crucially, the actor and audience share the same light. There is no stage lighting, no sound system, audience and actor can see one other.

The stage itself thrusts out into the yard. The audience can sit around all sides and above the rear of the stage in the musicians' gallery or Lords' rooms. They surround the actors, not just on all sides but on three levels, as seating is arranged in three tiered galleries: lower, middle and upper. The heavens are supported by two pillars on either side. The position of the pillars and the seating structure means that there is no point on stage where a single actor can be seen by every member of the audience. This has key implications for the way scenes and speeches are played. Early modern audiences often talked about going to 'hear' a play. They wanted to see it as well – the costumes, for example, were one of the key components of early modern theatre production. But this emphasis on hearing reflects the way in which people in Shakespeare's time were accustomed to receiving much of their information or stories. It also highlights to us the importance of hearing the words of the play in the Globe. It was a practical necessity, as no audience member would be able to see the action all the time and at some point during the play had to rely on what they heard in order to know what was taking place onstage.

The audience in the yard in the middle of the theatre stood throughout the performance. They were, and are, known as 'groundlings', so named after small river fishes which live at the bottom of the water. Groundlings are not protected from the elements by a roof. The remainder of the audience sit on wooden benches in the three covered galleries around the theatre. This is not the comfortable experience offered by a padded seat in a darkened auditorium, where bright lights focus the audience's attention on the key part of the action, and actors can be visible at all times, highlighted by spotlights when necessary.

This experimental new reconstruction of an old space has generated discoveries and ideas that have shed new light on our understanding of Shakespeare's plays. They inform all of our approaches to teaching Shakespeare's plays to young people.

The three A's

Theatre artists working on early theatre seasons at the Globe soon began to talk about the importance of 'the three A's': Actor, Audience and Architecture, and their impact on the way we understand and play in the theatre. All of these components are crucially important in their own right, but it is how the three work together during performance at the Globe that have led to the most interesting discoveries about playing Shakespeare and have the greatest implications for teaching. When we look at any moment or scene we need to ask ourselves what role the actor, audience and architecture are playing in that particular moment. How does each affect what is said, by who, to whom?

Yolanda Vazquez feels that the Globe architecture and audience are the 'missing components' of the play. She believes that architecture, audience, play and actor (in that order of importance) are the core elements that must be put together, both in theatre production and in the teaching of Shakespeare. She elaborates:

> When a play leaves the rehearsal room it is the actor's interpretation of the play. When it goes into technical and dress rehearsal in the Globe the architecture makes sense of the play on a whole new level. Then performances begin and the audience add another level to the play and it makes sense in a way it did not before. It is only when architecture, audience, play and actor come together that our experience and understanding of the play is whole.

The architecture of the Globe forces the audience into a more physical place, their senses are engaged and they are asked to respond actively to the performance. This physicality might come from any number of factors. Literally, from the fact they are standing or sitting on a backless wooden bench, or from their ability to make eye contact with actors and for the actors to read their reactions. Or from external factors: the sun, the rain, a pigeon landing on stage, a helicopter circling above, an eye-catching audience member on the opposite side of the theatre. The architecture creates an environment in which the audience are constantly reminded that they are in a theatre watching a performance of a play. Before the Globe, many audience members were accustomed to dark theatre spaces that work to an extent to deprive the senses and that encourage the audience to experience theatre in their heads. The physical, sensory experience of the Globe required a different kind of response and in the early days of playing in the theatre, actor and audience learnt how to respond to the unique architecture together. Interestingly it was young people, usually without much experience of theatre-going, without knowledge of conventions such as the 'fourth wall', who have made some of the most spontaneous and instructive responses to the Globe space.

Story telling

In the Globe theatre Shakespeare's plays can be viewed simply as stories to be shared between the actor and audience. Directors make interpretative choices about the production as they would in any theatre, but we have learnt that in the Globe these work best when they are choices which serve the story of the play. Mark Rylance observed in early theatre seasons that audiences were 'hungry for the story itself, not a story about the story'.[2] Theatre artists at the Globe have to ask themselves: how does this moment or scene move the story forward or contribute to our understanding of the story? It is a question that has come to permeate Globe Education's teaching and session planning. Activities that explore this question often provide a key way into exploration of text.

Language

In the Globe, in the daylight, with limited set and special effects, the words of the play are the actor's primary tool. The words spoken by the actors are all-important. They play a physical role, as everything actor and audience need to know about the play is contained within the words Shakespeare has written. When we consider Shakespeare's language in the context of the Globe architecture it emerges as a workhorse (albeit a sometimes very beautiful one), the beginning and end of all our explorations about the play. This realization has been central to Globe Education's approach to the teaching of Shakespeare. It also reminds us that the words of the play are not something we should experience solely in our heads, but also physically in our bodies as actors do.

All of the core elements above can exist singly, but in the crucible of the Globe come together to produce performance. In order to understand further how this might impact on teaching approaches to the plays, it is useful to explore some of these interactions in greater detail.

Architecture, audience and social verticality

Research indicates that the original Globe playhouse attracted a diversity of social classes. It was not as prestigious or socially elite as the indoor theatres such as the Blackfriars, but equally was not known as a 'citizen' playhouse such as the Curtain and Fortune, which had a reputation for a 'lower class' of audience. Professor Andrew Gurr has surmised that about 15–20 per cent of all people within walking distance of Shoreditch or Southwark were regular theatre-goers, suggesting a wide range of social classes attended performances at the Globe, not just a social elite.[3] Equally we know that the French ambassador visited the Globe to see *Pericles* in 1608. The diversity of classes at the playhouses was commented on by various people that visited the theatres. John Davies, a law student visiting the theatre in the 1590s, observed:

> For as we see at all the playhouse doors,
> When ended is the play, the dance and song,
> A thousand townsmen, gentlemen and whores,
> Porters and serving men together throng.[4]

The mingling of the social classes was unusual for this time and Davies's further comments record his disapproval.

Swiss tourist Thomas Platter, visiting the theatre in 1599, recorded in his diary:

> The playhouses are so constructed that they play on a raised platform, so that everyone has a good view. There are different galleries and places, however, where the seating is better and more comfortable and therefore more expensive. For whoever cares to stand below only pays one English penny, but if he wishes to sit he enters by another door, and pays another penny, while if he desires to sit in the most comfortable seats which are cushioned, where he not only sees everything well, but can also be seen, then he pays yet another English penny at another door. And during the performance food and drink are carried round the audience, so that for what one cares to pay one may also have refreshment.[5]

Platter describes the different social classes and people at the playhouse by where they sat. The cost of attending a performance varied from 1 penny for groundlings, through to 2p for a gallery, 4p for Gentlemen's boxes and 5p for Lords' rooms. This cost was based on seating position and thus social classes were visible in the theatre. This phenomena has been referred to by Dr Farah Karim-Cooper, Head of Globe Education Higher Education and Research as 'social verticality'. The social verticality of the theatre was also present in part because of sumptuary laws that strictly regulated the materials, colour and style of clothing that people were allowed to purchase and wear, based on social class. Thus from where they sat and what they wore, the social class of early modern Globe theatre-goers was clearly visible to all.

Shakespeare wrote many of his plays for the Globe and his knowledge of the social verticality of the theatre clearly influenced what he wrote and how he wrote it. If we look at the plays with this awareness we can see clearly at moments different layers within the writing. The most obvious example of this is Mark Antony's 'Friends, Romans and Countrymen' in *Julius Caesar* (Act 3 Scene 2 line 74). The 'Friends' here are the social elite, in the Globe audience the Lords' rooms, or possibly the Gentlemen's rooms; 'Countrymen' the senate, in the Globe the galleries; while 'Romans' are the ordinary citizens, in the Globe the groundlings. Other good examples include:

The naming of the dead and prisoners in *Henry V*, which has a constant vertical progression in all the lists, beginning at the top with a prince, and ending at the bottom with mercenaries and the common man.

> *KING What prisoners **of good sort** are taken, uncle?*
> *EXETER Charles, **Duke of Orleans, nephew to the King**; John, **Duke** of Bourbon, and **Lord** Boucicault.*
> *Of other **lords and barons, knights and squires**, Full fifteen hundred, besides **common men*** (4.8.76–80).

Coriolanus's listing of all the people. The character's concern with the differences between the citizens and the upper class which is a core issue throughout the play are exemplified in the way each class must be differentiated from the others, even in how they react.

> *FIRST CITIZEN We are accounted* ***poor citizens****, the* ***patricians good****. What authority surfeits on would relieve us* (1.1.13–14).
> *MENENIUS AGRIPPA* ***Why masters****, my* ***good friends****, mine* ***honest neighbours****, Will you undo youselves?* (1.1.57–58)
> *MENENIUS AGRIPPA* ***The senators of Rome are this good belly, And you the mutinous members:*** *for examine Their counsels and their cares, digest things rightly Touching the weal o'th'common, you shall find No public benefit which you receive But it proceeds or comes from them to you And no way from yourselves. What do you think,*
> ***You, the great toe of this assembly?*** (1.1.143–50)

Hamlet's conversation with Yorick at the grave of Ophelia (5:1) includes references to 'Politicians', 'Courtiers' and 'Lawyer'. Here different classes are referred to but in this instance all are equal in death.

The whole social structure of society was around the actors in the theatre and they would have been able to place or direct their lines accordingly. This understanding informs the way we view status issues within the play. It is also a way of Shakespeare directing the play from within the writing. He is telling the actor what to do, who to play the scene to. He is ensuring that they make different points of contact with the audience, in different parts of the theatre, throughout a speech or scene. This knowledge affects an actor's playing and the audience's engagement and understanding.

Actors working in the modern Globe still look out from the stage and see a socially diverse audience. Their social status will not, however, be so clearly delineated, although ticket prices and corporate hospitality still create a form of the social verticality which would have been so clear in the original Globe. The structure of Shakespeare's audiences and its reflection in his writing has taught modern actors in the Globe the power of directing speeches and lines to different parts of the audience, in order to engage the whole.

Yolanda Vazquez comments that awareness of this as an actor led her to discover that 'Shakespeare seems to work on the power of three', that characters often speak with three questions or make three points. She found it most effective to play each different point to a different section or member of the audience. This is exemplified in Beatrice's soliloquy in Act 3 Scene 1 of *Much Ado about Nothing*, a role which Yolanda played at the Globe in 2004:

> *What fire is in mine ears? Can this be true? Stand I condemn'd for pride and scorn so much?* (107–9)

There are several implications here for the ways in which we understand and teach Shakespeare's plays. First it reminds us that Shakespeare, at the time when he was writing, was not regarded as high art or the domain of the cultural elite. He was for all social classes, popular entertainment, the enjoyment of which provided a shared experience for a cross-section of society. This informs Globe Education's work to make Shakespeare's plays accessible and engaging for all young people. It reminds us that any production of a Shakespeare play (that we take young people to see, or that we create for young people) has to be appealing to a socially diverse audience. It needs to be both accessible and challenging for all.

It is clear that Shakespeare created and uses the language of the plays for a purpose: to direct the actors and to reach different parts of the audience. In the classroom we can use this knowledge as a tool to look at speeches with an active focus. Many of the activities in this book are informed by this approach. Such understanding of audience and social diversity informs the questions we might choose to ask about about any given moment in any play.

The role of the audience

Treat the audience as another actor

This was the advice often given by first Globe Artistic Director, Mark Rylance to companies of actors arriving to play the Globe theatre season. It emphasizes the importance of the connection between the actor and the audience and provides us with a clear way of thinking about its potential role. Yolanda Vazquez comments:

> In a proscenium arch theatre the audience are a fly on the wall listening to a story. At the Globe the audience are part of that story, they need to help us. As an actor the audience are always there to help me in my quest to win the scene.

The audience here are like an extension of the company on stage. They can be addressed, included, questioned, or put into a specific role such as Henry V's army or the people of Rome. This can happen at any point in the play. In *Shakespeare's Globe A Theatrical Experiment* Gordon McMullan reflects on director Tim Carroll's comment about the 'audience's ability to play the role required of it'. Carroll, he observes, seems to view the audience as another actor to direct and speaks 'as if he were directing everyone, not just those on stage'.[6]

The idea of the audience as another actor is a powerful one. It opens up all kinds of possibilities for directors at the Globe and for our interpretation of Shakespeare's plays. How much this idea might be utilized universally, throughout a production, remains an artistic choice for individual directors and actors. There are, however, key times when actors speak directly and only to the audience. This is best seen in asides, prologues, epilogues and most notably in soliloquies.

Actors talk to the audience for a number of reasons, usually to:

- Set the scene. To tell the audience about location, time of day, characters involved and situation. The Prologue in *Romeo and Juliet* is a good example.
- Make the audience part of the play. The Prologue of *Henry V* provides a clear example of this, as does the Epilogue of *A Midsummer Night's Dream.*
- Explicate their character's feelings and establish or emphasize plot points. Any soliloquy in Shakespeare's plays demonstrates this point.
- Clarification. For example *Henry V* 1:2.38, in which the Latin is translated for the audience, or in *Othello,* where Iago runs through his plans in asides to the audience to let them know what his real motivations are.
- Introduce information. The Chorus in *Henry V* 2:0 is a good example, as is Helena's introduction to Parolles' character, before he enters in *All's Well that Ends Well* 1:1.

The audience can also be put into role as a crowd, army or any other large group of people as required. They are like a group of instant extras. For example, in the marketplace in Verona, in *Romeo and Juliet,* at the wrestling match between Orlando and Charles in *As You Like It,* or before the battle at Harfleur in *Henry V*. The following piece of dialogue from *Henry VI pt 2*, 4.2.29–34 provides a typical example of the way the audience can be used in this fashion.

Drum. Enter CADE, Dick Butcher, Smith the Weaver, *and a Sawyer,* ***with infinite numbers***

CADE We, John Cade, so termed of our supposed father –
BUTCHER Or rather of stealing cade of herrings.
CADE For our enemies shall fall before us, inspired with the spirit of putting down kings and princes. Command silence.
BUTCHER Silence!

'Infinite numbers' alludes to the fact that the crowd can never be fully represented by actors and in this instance it is more than likely that the audience represent the crowd and that Cade is speaking to them as such. When a character on stage demands that people be silent it is often a clue that the audience are being used in role as a large group. Whenever large numbers of people feature in a play we need to consider the role of the audience and look for points in the text where the actor might address the audience, in role, directly.

The Globe is a playing space that requires both actor and audience to play a part in the performance. The democratic nature of the Globe and the way in which architecture, audience and play fuse together is encapsulated by Dominic Dromgoole, Artistic Director:

> I don't think I had a full understanding of the importance of theatre architecture until I came to the Globe. The scale of the space, the lit audience, the physical alertness of that audience, all of these factors transform the way in which a play is heard, and thus the way it has to be delivered. You are joining a pre-existing excitement rather than creating one; you are allowing the audience to choose where they put their eye rather than dictating it to them; you are collaborating in an act of imagination rather than forcing one on people; you are inviting their participation rather than disapproving of it.
>
> This is most clear with soliloquy where for centuries in theatres shaped wrongly there had been confusion about what a soliloquy was ... Was it someone talking to themselves? To other imagined characters? To their own past? To a literary tradition? The Globe has made all this clear. It is talking straight, true and sincere to the audience and into their eyes about the things most important to them. It's simple really but it is only fully or properly unlocked by performing in that space.

We have learnt that in the Globe a soliloquy is not spoken in a bubble. In a dark proscenium arch theatre, or on film, the soliloquy is often internalized, presented as the character's private thoughts and reflections. The character is talking to his or herself, thinking things through. In the Globe the bubble is burst. The actor may be alone onstage but s/he stands before c 1500 people that s/he can see clearly. The soliloquy becomes a private moment between the actor/character and the audience. The character is telling the audience something that no other character in the play knows, whether it be their plans, dilemmas, thoughts or (in)decisions.

Giles Block reflects about the role of the soliloquy and the audience in the Globe.

> From soliloquies in the Globe you get the idea of the actor sharing a speech with the audience. Sometimes thoughts can come to an actor, which are necessary for the character, but while they are looking at the audience it is as if the audience is sometimes offering them solutions to their problems.
>
> Soliloquy only makes sense where we're all in the theatre in the same light. I suppose for actors it becomes the delight of playing at the Globe. When a character is unburdening themselves, or wanting the audience to

> help them move themselves on, they can see them, they can look them in the eyes as they speak. That's the extraordinary thing about soliloquies. An actor can be absolutely in character, absolutely in the middle of the situation, and yet at the same time, sharing it with an audience, and learning things from the audience, which may prompt him/her to a particular choice. Sometimes it seems that Shakespeare will write the script using a rather subtle or clever way of speaking about something, and then immediately, he'll translate it into more common language. That is connected with all the different kinds of people who will be in the audience. They will probably be physically in different parts of the theatre too. In Hamlet's 'To be, or not to be' soliloquy when he asks 'For who would bear the whips and scorns of time' it is if he starts this thought in the upper gallery of the theatre and then there follows a whole panoramic list, it's like coming down through the tiers, to those sitting in the middle gallery, and then all the way down to the lower gallery and the groundlings get the final line: 'with a bare bodkin' – some groundlings in Shakespeare's time might actually have a bodkin on them.
>
> The audience frequently become different characters at different times; in *Richard III* within the space of minutes, they become Richard's army, and then Richmond's, and the language reflects the way the audience is prepared and happy to play both roles. In the context of the scene, when an actor is playing with other people, they are speaking to someone else but can spread their speech to the audience as well, as if to include them. The text that we've been left seems to demand that and encourages that. In a darkened theatre, we tend to get caught up in ourselves and not see how these plays really work. That we are all in it together.

Actors in the Globe have generally found that being able to share the soliloquy with the audience helps them to perform it. They can perform part of it to a special person or group within the audience and change their point of focus or the person they are talking to as the speech develops. Sharing the soliloquy with the audience can help actors to find the different rhythms within it, the moments of change, decision and understanding. Mark Rylance describes this process:

> I now like to imagine moving through soliloquies with an audience like you move through a landscape; over hills, round corners, to dead ends, backing up again, realising you have to go through that river, there, then being wet for a few lines because you have gone through a river and you are in a different place. It is the sense of taking an audience in the present through this text that became paramount.[7]

Hamlet's soliloquy in Act 2 Scene 2:

> *Now I am alone. O, what a rogue and peasant slave am I!*

Is it not monstrous that this player here,
But in a fiction, in a dream of passion,
Could force his souls so to his own conceit
That from her working all the visage wanned
Tears in his eyes, distraction in his aspect,
A broke voice, and his whole function suiting
With forms to his conceit – and all for nothing –
For Hecuba? What's Hecuba to him, or he to her,
That he should weep for her? What would he do
Had he the motive and that for passion
That I have? He would drown the stage with tears
And cleave the general ear with horrid speech,
Make mad the guilty and appal the free,
Confound the ignorant and amaze indeed
The very faculties of eyes and ears. Yet I,
A dull and muddy-mettled rascal, peak
Like John-a-dreams, unpregnant of my cause,
And can say nothing. No, not for a king
Upon whose property and most dear life
A damned defeat was made. Am I a coward?
Who calls me villain, breaks my pate across,
Plucks off my beard and blows it in my face,
Tweaks me by the nose, gives me the lie i'th'throat
As deep as to the lungs? Who does me this,
Ha? 'Swounds, I should take it. (484–511)

illustrates how this knowledge of the role of the audience can affect our understanding. The opening question is accurate within the action of the play but in the Globe becomes comic, as Hamlet is not alone but surrounded by hundreds of people. Hamlet asks a series of questions throughout this speech, all of which can be directed to the audience. He also groups his thoughts in clear sections, each of which could be delivered to a different part of the audience. The repetition of 'who' towards the end of the speech again suggests that he is speaking directly to the audience. His language is accusatory in tone, which further suggests this connection.

This understanding of the way soliloquy works in the Globe can be applied to any play. Patrick Spottiswoode, Director, Globe Education comments:

> *Macbeth* is an interesting play in which to explore the role of soliloquy in the Globe.
>
> Duncan does not have soliloquies, because he doesn't need them, he believes in absolute trust. Macbeth murders that trust and uses soliloquies, which brings him into the world of the audience and makes

> them complicit with his actions. Malcolm does not use soliloquies, not because like his father he has absolute trust, but because he cannot even trust the audience. He is one of the only characters in Shakespeare who does not have this trust. It is interesting in this context to ask the question which characters don't have soliloquies, as well as looking at the characters which do. In *Macbeth* after the regicide we have a play where people have to hide: in England and Ireland, behind trees and in Malcolm's case from the audience. In the 'England' scene, Act 4 Scene 3, when Malcolm begins by lying to Macduff, the audience hear the scene in the same way as Macduff. Shakespeare does not give Malcolm a soliloquy at that point, or any other, to explain to the audience what he is about to do. In the Globe during soliloquy there exists a special relationship between actor and audience. It is when the audience becomes complicit with the character and when the character and the actor become most vulnerable. Vulnerability is really interesting. As an audience in the Globe we are drawn to characters who share their vulnerability with us in soliloquies. Macbeth, Richard III, Iago and Hamlet are all good examples. In the Globe, during soliloquy, characters share private thoughts publicly.
>
> It is not just during soliloquies that the audience play a part. In the Globe the audience becomes a character in the play. Ralph Cohen (Founding Executive Director and Director of Mission, American Shakespeare Center) says that you do not sit **at** a play, you sit **in** a play. A Globe audience is part of an event. As an audience member, remembering the play after a performance, you remember an event in which you played a part.
>
> We now have young actors who have been 'brought up' with the Globe. Engaging with the audience is second nature for them. In the 2013 *Playing Shakespeare with Deutsche Bank* production of *Romeo and Juliet*, Will Featherstone, playing Romeo, asked questions to the audience, engaged with their response and used it in his performance. In this production the actors used their phones to film the audience – they were as much a part of the show as the actors on stage.

Awareness of the potential role of the audience in Shakespeare's playhouse enables us to ask different questions and explore text with clear focus and a fresh perspective. Actors playing in the Globe ask themselves questions such as: who is this speech to? Who needs to hear it? On what different levels might the characters on stage and the audience receive this information? What role does the audience play at this moment? Some of the activities in this book work with students in groups, each of them playing the characters in the scene and another one the audience. In this way we are always able to explore how an awareness of audience impacts on on our potential understanding and interpretation of a moment or scene. In some activities students are asked to point to who they are talking to and about on every line they speak. All such activities are derived from the awareness of the audience's role in the Globe.

Language and setting time and place

In the original Globe theatre there would have been little in terms of elaborate set design and props, although stage effects were often used. The back of the stage was painted, as were the heavens and the pillars, but there was no particular set that changed with each play. Shakespeare uses language to set the scene for his audience and to ensure they have all the information they need about what is taking place on stage.

The Prologue of *Henry V* is a direct appeal to the audience to use their imagination and provides them with the information necessary to do so:

> *...Can this cockpit hold*
> *The vasty fields of France? Or may we cram*
> *Within this wooden O the very casques*
> *That did affright the air at Agincourt?*
> *O pardon, since a crooked figure may*
> *Attest in little place a million,*
> ***And let us, ciphers to this great account,***
> ***On your imaginary forces work.***
> *Suppose within the girdle of these walls*
> *Are now confined two mighty monarchies,*
> *Whose high upreared and abutting fronts*
> *The perilous narrow ocean parts asunder.*
> ***Piece out our imperfections with your thoughts.***
> *Into a thousand parts divide one man*
> *And make imaginary puissance.* (11–25)

Often battles or events that cannot easily be staged take place offstage and are described for the audience. Language was Shakespeare's most powerful and cheapest method of constructing a scene. It was also a primary method of compensating for the architecture of the Globe, giving the audience, whose view of an important moment is obstructed, a clear idea of what has just taken place. Act 4 Scene 1 of *Much Ado About Nothing* provides a good example of how this works in practice. Hero is slandered at her marriage to Claudio and, after she is rejected by Claudio and her father, faints. Beatrice's line which follows – 'Why, how now, cousin! Wherefore sink / you down?' (110) – makes little sense in a proscenium arch theatre where all the audience have just watched Hero do this. In many productions the line is cut for this reason. In the Globe theatre, however, it makes perfect sense. Some members of the audience will not have been able to see the actor playing Hero and the only way they know she has fainted is from the reaction of other audience members and crucially because Beatrice has just told them. Shakespeare is directing this scene from within the text, telling the actor playing Hero when to faint and letting all the audience know, wherever they are seated, that this has happened.

Shakespeare often uses dialogue to tell us specific information. The opening scene of *Hamlet* is a clear example:

> ***Barnardo:*** *Who's there?*
> ***Francisco:*** *Nay, answer me. Stand and unfold yourself.*
> ***Barnardo:*** *Long live the King!*
> ***Francisco:*** *Barnardo*
> ***Barnardo:*** *He.*
> ***Francisco:*** *For this relief much thanks. 'Tis bitter cold,*
> *And I am sick at heart.*
> ***Barnardo:*** *Have you had quiet guard?*
> ***Francisco:*** *Not a mouse stirring*
> ***Barnardo:*** *Well, good night.*
> *If you do meet Horatio and Marcellus,*
> *The rivals of my watch, bid them make haste.* (lines 1–11)

Barnardo's opening greeting tells the audience standing in the daylight of the Globe theatre that it is dark. Barnardo has to ask a solider he knows, who he is, because he cannot see him. We are told it is twelve o'clock. The fact that it is night is enforced as Francisco needs to go to bed. The audience are also told about the weather: it is cold. The scene continues with repetition of these core facts so that by the time the main action of the scene takes place the audience are in no doubt about where and when the scene is set.

Shakespeare often uses dialogue to tell the time of day, particularly when it is an unusual hour, when people are not usually awake, or when characters want to recall or predict an event. Sometimes a clock strikes, such as in *Cymbeline, Richard III, Julius Caesar* or *Twelfth Night*. More regularly, characters ask each other the time, or the time is used to give specificity to events. Good examples are *As You Like it* Act 3 Scene 2:

> *I pray you, what is't* ***o'clock****?* (line 291)

Or Act 4 Scene 1:

> *I must attend the Duke at dinner; by two o'clock I will be with thee again.* (lines 168–9)

While in Act 2 Scene 1 of *Macbeth* a range of time locating techniques are in play:

Banquo: *How goes the night, boy?*
Fleance: *The moon is down; I have not heard the clock.*
Banquo: *And she goes down at twelve.*
Fleance: *I take't, 'tis later, sir.*
Banquo: *Hold, take my sword. There's husbandry in heaven;*
Their candles are all out. Take thee that too.
A heavy summons lies like lead upon me,
And yet I would not sleep: merciful powers,
Restrain in me the cursed thoughts that nature
Gives way to in repose!

Enter MACBETH, with a torch
Give me my sword. Who's there? (lines 1–10)

The audience are told it is night, the clock has not been heard and it strikes at twelve. There are references to candles and torches (the presence of light sources is a frequently used indicator of night). As in *Hamlet*, Banquo has to ask 'Who's there?', when it is Macbeth, whom he knows.

Shakespeare determines place in a similar way, by including references to cities, court and people's households. Sometimes this is achieved simply with devices such as 'Here in Verona...' (*Romeo and Juliet* 1:3 71), or sometimes more subtly, such as 'Through Athens I am thought as fair as she' (*A Midsummer Night's Dream* 1:1 227).

Once you begin looking for these references of time, place and setting they are everywhere. Often parts of the text that students find most inaccessible are those that are laden with information the audience need in order to understand and enjoy the play. Discoveries about how these references work when playing Shakespeare in the Globe have provided us with a good tool for exploring text with young people. It helps to look out for these references, to ask why this information is included, and consider how it contributes to our understanding of the play in performance.

CHAPTER THREE

Core approaches to Creative Shakespeare

The activities in this section form the foundation stage of Globe Education's creative approaches to learning. On their own they are most appropriate for students aged 11–16, but could be taught to students of any age. Many of the more advanced activities which follow in later chapters need to be used in combination with the activities here, or rely on the knowledge work of this kind can generate. Some of the activities are developed further in later chapters, with a greater level of complexity. Together they provide ways into the key issues and areas of study that concern all teachers of Shakespeare. Each activity can be used singly, but many can also be grouped together in a single session, or over a series of sessions.

The activities bring together Globe rehearsal room exercises and approaches with existing drama techniques. Ideas for activities might originate with one person but they will be developed by different consultants and practitioners in different ways. Below each activity which follows, different members of our consultant team comment, providing a range of different variations and approaches. Unless otherwise stated, all of the activities can be used with any Shakespeare play.

Cutting text

The activities in this book serve to facilitate insight and understanding into Shakespeare's plays. Most of them feature an exploration of text. Very few of them feature text that has not been cut in some way. Cut text is a foundation stone of Globe Education's creative approaches to Shakespeare. Text that is well cut and suited to its specific purpose can provide us with accessible ways into the play, boost student confidence and maximize learning.

Why cut text?

1. Very few Shakespeare plays make it to stage or film uncut. Presenting students with a cut text to use in an activity mirrors what happens in the rehearsal room. A director might make some cuts to a play before rehearsals begin, others will be made organically throughout the rehearsal process. Sometimes actors might offer up some of their lines to be cut, other times they will fight to keep them. Which lines are cut depends on the artistic objectives of each particular production. No two productions will features lines cut in the same way.
2. Cutting text enables a teacher to get to the heart of the lesson objective quickly. It leaves time for experimentation. There is often very little time to teach a Shakespeare play. Cutting text enables each individual teacher to consider what is important for their group and to plan sessions which move through the play with focus and clarity. Actors at the Globe typically have five weeks of rehearsal. They would find it difficult to cover the play in that time if it was not cut. This gives some perspective on the feat regularly attempted by teachers in schools.
3. Cutting text can make it more manageable and approachable for students. It allows a teacher to focus on what is key to the learning objective of the session. It enables students to experiment with working with the same piece of text in different ways. It can, in some instances, help them to memorize short lines and experience what it is like to have the words in their bodies as actors do, rather on a piece of paper that they need to read.
4. Cutting text can provide a key method of differentiation. Small groups within each class can work on different versions of the same scene, each cut to reflect the needs of the group. There is then also potential to compare the effect of each different cut version on the group's understanding of text.
5. Working with a piece of text, rather than a long unwieldy passage, builds student confidence in their ability to read, speak and interpret the language of the play. As student confidence grows, the length of text given to them can increase. This can happen within one session, or over a series of sessions.
6. Shakespeare's plays are not sacred. There is no single correct interpretation of play or character. Working with cut text helps to underline this ethos and establishes an active, experimental working environment. As students become more confident they can be given a specific objective and asked to cut text for themselves. This gives them ownership of the play and places Shakespeare in the hands of

young people, encouraging their artistic interpretation of a moment or scene.

How to cut text: Key considerations

Generally there are two different circumstances that require cut text. The first is when preparing a piece for performance, the second is for a classroom activity. The demands of each exercise are different. Cutting text for performance is dealt with at greater length in Chapter 6: *Performance*. The focus here is on cutting text for a classroom activity, although some of the same principles apply to both situations.

1. Text should be cut specifically, in response to a particular learning objective and the needs of a group (age, ability, etc.) What we want to achieve through working with a piece of cut text is the key to deciding what to leave in and what to cut.
2. Keep the text that tells the story of the play. When creating cut text for an activity, look for meaning/s and ensure that the cut does not present a one-dimensional view of any character (unless that is what you want to explore in the activity).
3. Wherever possible, preserve the rhythm of the text in the cut. Sometimes this is not possible and other demands, e.g. the length of the cut, or the amount of the scene that needs to be covered in a short number of lines, takes precedence. However, the rhythm is a key tool that we can use to access character and meaning, so it is important to keep it, if viable.
4. Do not be afraid to be brutal or to remove 'famous' or favourite lines. Once the cut has preserved story and rhythm, everything else is luxurious. There may be some fantastic lines or phrasing, but if they do not further the aim of the activity the cut is being created to serve, they can (sometimes regretfully) be lost.
5. Consider the desired length of your final cut. If you have a group that is new to Shakespeare, or finds it challenging, you may want a shorter cut than with a more experienced and confident group. Time will also be a factor. It is possible to achieve the same broad learning objective with cuts of different lengths and detail.
6. When the cut is finished, read it aloud to yourself. Any potential problems with storytelling, character and rhythm become more apparent when we hear the words, rather than read them.

The following example shows three different cuts of Act 2 Scene 2 (lines 1–73) of *Macbeth,* the moment where Macbeth and Lady Macbeth meet immediately after the murder of Duncan. The longest is first (although it is possible to make more lengthy cuts of the scene). The cuts become progressively shorter. All enable students to explore the scene in the same way.

T
Cut 1

LADY MACBETH
Alack, I am afraid they have awaked
And 'tis not done. Had he not resembled
My father as he slept, I had done't.
Enter MACBETH
My husband!

MACBETH
I have done the deed. Didst thou not hear a noise?

LADY MACBETH
I heard the owl scream and the crickets cry.
Did not you speak?

MACBETH
When?

LADY MACBETH
Now.

MACBETH
As I descended?

LADY MACBETH
Ay.

MACBETH
Hark! This is a sorry sight.
Looking on his hands

LADY MACBETH
A foolish thought, to say a sorry sight.

MACBETH
I had most need of blessing, and 'Amen'
Stuck in my throat.

LADY MACBETH
Consider it not so deeply.

Why did you bring these daggers from the place?
They must lie there: go carry them; and smear
The sleepy grooms with blood.

MACBETH

I'll go no more:
I am afraid to think what I have done;

LADY MACBETH
Infirm of purpose! Give me the daggers
Exit. Knocking within

MACBETH
Whence is that knocking?
How is't with me, when every noise appals me?
Re-enter LADY MACBETH

LADY MACBETH
My hands are of your colour; but I shame
To wear a heart so white.
Knocking within
I hear a knocking, retire we to our chamber;
A little water clears us of this deed.
Knocking within
Be not lost so poorly in your thoughts.

MACBETH
To know my deed, 'twere best not know myself.
Knocking within
Wake Duncan with thy knocking! I would thou couldst!
Exeunt

Cut 2

LADY MACBETH
Did not you speak?

MACBETH

When?

LADY MACBETH

Now.

MACBETH

As I descended?

LADY MACBETH
Ay.

MACBETH
This is a sorry sight.

LADY MACBETH
A foolish thought, to say a sorry sight.

MACBETH
I had most need of blessing, and 'Amen' Stuck in my throat.

LADY MACBETH
Why did you bring these daggers from the place?
They must lie there:

MACBETH
I'll go no more:

LADY MACBETH
Infirm of purpose! Give me the daggers
EXITS

MACBETH
Whence is that knocking?

LADY MACBETH
My hands are of your colour; but I shame
To wear a heart so white.

MACBETH
To know my deed, 'twere best not know myself.
Cut 3

MACBETH
I have done the deed. Didst thou not hear a noise?
Did not you speak?

LADY MACBETH
When?

MACBETH
Now.

LADY MACBETH
As I descended?

MACBETH
Ay.
This is a sorry sight. *(Looking on his hands)*

LADY MACBETH
A foolish thought, to say a sorry sight.

LADY MACBETH
They must lie there, go carry them and smear
The sleepy grooms with blood.

MACBETH
I'll go no more
I am afraid to think what I have done;

LADY MACBETH
Infirm of purpose! Give me the daggers

Key rehearsal room questions

Many of the activities in this section provide ways of exploring the key questions that actors often ask themselves during the rehearsal process. It's useful to be aware of these areas of consideration when working with the activities. Yolanda Vazquez shares her list that she applies whenever she rehearses a play, below:

Yolanda's seven important questions

1: Who am I?
What kind of person is the character? What is the character's background, influences, education, experiences, likes and dislikes, relationships? What are their inner and outer characteristics?

2: Where am I?
What kind of place is the character in? Is it familiar or unfamiliar? What does it mean to the character, if anything? How does the character feel about their surroundings?

3: When is it?
What is the time of year, day, or season? Why is the scene set at that moment? What's happened before? Where is the character going to afterwards?

4: What do I want?
This is the character's primary need, their desire. Actors often refer to this as a character's 'objective'.

5: Why do I want it?
The character must have a good reason for wanting it. It justifies their objective.

6: How will I get it?
What does the character need to do to accomplish his/her objective? (E.g. beg, plead, tease, threaten etc.) What tactics does s/he use? These can be both verbal and physical.

7: What must I overcome?
This is the resistance. It's what's stopping the character from obtaining his/her objective. This might be an inner obstacle (coming from the character's own characteristics or physical or mental state of being) or an outer obstacle (coming from the character's situation or relationship). This might also be affected by the objectives of other characters.

Core approaches: Activities

Warm-ups

All sessions begin with some form of warm-up activity. This should always be an activity that prepares students for the work they will do in the session. There are many books full of warm-up activities and for that reason I have not compiled a list here, although there are some more specific warm-up activities in later chapters. Everyone has their favourites and the activity you pick will reflect the session being delivered and the group concerned on that particular day. A group that walks into a session excited and voluble will need a different type of warm-up to a group that lacks energy. A group's ability, or not, to work together can also be a key factor when selecting a warm-up activity.

Crucially, the warm-up activity chosen should start to build the skills needed in the session. For example, if teaching *Archetypes* below, we might start the session with 'triangle, square, circle' in which we ask the whole group together, without talking, to physically make a shape called out by the group leader. These shapes can become more challenging as the group becomes more skilled. Objects such as a computer or clock might also be used. Time limits can add focus to the activity. It always works well to end this activity with a circle, as the students are then ready to start the next exercise. This warm-up would encourage the group to work collaboratively and physically, which would prepare them for embodying the different archetypes.

Wherever possible and appropriate, we try to build the first piece of character work or text into the warm-up. A Globe Education Practitioner favourite warm-up is Augusto Boal's *Stop, Go, Jump, Clap* in which the whole group move around the room responding to an instruction (as the name suggests either, 'stop', 'go', 'jump' or 'clap'). These instructions are then swapped around, e.g. 'when I say 'stop' you 'go', when I say 'go' you 'stop', and so on. If appropriate, students who make the incorrect movement can be 'out' and the game played until only one, or a small number of students, is left. We might finish this exercise by introducing character types, e.g. hero, villain, and asking students to create a physical shape that they feel represents a hero or villain when that name is called. These can then swapped around just as 'stop', 'go' etc., and text added. E.g. if the session is focused on *Macbeth,* instead of the character types hero or villain the teacher could call 'Brave Macbeth' for the hero pose and 'hell hound' for the villain pose. This simply gets students thinking about text and different aspects of character right from the beginning of the session. Whatever warm-up you pick for a session, consider how it will feed into, and inform, the ideas you wish students to explore. Always ask: how does the warm-up facilitate student learning?

Archetypes

This activity uses the idea that there are key character archetypes within Shakespeare's plays, to provide students with a method of exploring and analysing character. The use of character work based on archetypes at the Globe originated with Glynn MacDonald. Glynn started working with actors in rehearsal to explore the key archetypes of Sovereign, Warrior, Carer and Trickster. She encouraged them to explore the movement of each archetype and to find the different archetypes within their character. Glynn based this work on Jung's description of the different archetypes that exist within the human psyche. She found that identifying physically the different archetypal roles that their character played helped actors to understand how their character changes and to communicate this to the audience in the Globe.

Aim

To explore character. To consider the different aspects of a character and the different roles s/he plays. To consider how characters can change within a speech or scene. To provide students with a simple method of analysing character.

Practical considerations

Archetypes is one of the longest activities in this book and requires a space that allows a whole group of students to move around freely. It's worth the investment, though, as it provides students with a focused way of looking at character that helps them begin to construct simple, then detailed textual analysis. After the initial activity it can be built on and referred to in other activities. It provides a collective shorthand for students and teachers when looking at any character in any Shakespeare play.

Activity

Explain to the students that they are going to be working on archetypes – these are the types of character most frequently found in any literature. In this activity they will work physically on four of the most important archetypes that we find in Shakespeare's plays, although there are others. The four archetypes used in this activity are Sovereign, Warrior, Carer and Trickster.

The teacher should describe each archetype in turn to the group, using the Archetype descriptions *below. After each archetype is described the teacher should model the physicality of the archetype. The group should then adopt it and all walk around the room as the archetype, maintaining the physicality for all the time they are walking. (See the pictures on pages 42–5 for the physical position that should be adopted and below for a description of each archetype.) It is usually most beneficial to do this in silence as it helps students to relate to each other physically, e.g. as two kings might behave to each other when passing.*

While students are walking around the room, the teacher should ask the following questions. These are not questions that need to be answered verbally, they are simply things for the students to think about. The same questions should be repeated for each of the four archetypes:

- *Are you walking quickly or slowly?*
- *Are you looking up, down or straight ahead?*
- *Do you want to look at people and be sociable or would you rather be on your own?*
- *What attributes or characteristics does being this type of person suggest to you?*

These questions are most effectively asked individually for the first two archetypes, the Sovereign and the Warrior. For the Carer and the Trickster it works well to ask the students to keep thinking about these questions as the move around the room, but not to ask them individually.

Finally, after each archetype the teacher should ask the students: If you had to describe this character to friend which words would you use? The students should answer this question and share/discuss ideas as a whole group. They need to remember the words or phrases they used for later on in the activity. Sometimes students need encouraging to think about the light and shade of every archetype.

When the students have completed this exercise four times, once for each archetype, bring them back together as a whole group and ask them to think about which archetype they most identify with today – not in life generally, but the archetype that they most connect with at this moment in time. They do not need to share their answer at this point.

Place four pieces of paper in different parts of the room, each labelled with one of the archetypes. Draw a line down the middle of each piece of paper and label one side + and the other side –. Ask the students to stand by the piece of paper for the archetype they most connected with. It does not matter if some archetypes are vastly more popular than others.

Ask one student to be the scribe. Ask all the students to think of the characteristics that they like about this archetype. The scribe should record these on the paper on the + side.

Next ask the group to stand by the piece of paper for the archetype they least connected with. Again one student should scribe. Ask all of the students to think of the characteristics they dislike about this archetype. The scribe should record these on the – side of the paper.

The group have now created a list of positive and negative characteristics for each archetype. These could also be described as the light and shadow of the archetype.

*Explain to the group that they are going to be given a line from a play. (*Macbeth *for this example – see* Macbeth *lines below.) They should adopt the body/physicality of the archetype they are standing at and mingle around the room saying the line. Stress to the group that although they are starting with the archetype they least identify with today, they will move through each archetype in turn; this is just the starting point.*

NB: The group do not need the line written down but should remember it. We have found that it works really well to ask the students to repeat the line three times before they start the movement part of the activity. It is important that all of the group work with the same line each time, even if it does not seem to be an obvious fit with the archetype they are standing at.

The group should then move to the next piece of paper and repeat the above exercise with a new archetype and new line. This exercise should be repeated four times in total, once for each archetype. By the end of this part of the exercise students should have experienced saying four different lines in the body of the four different archetypes.

Bring the whole group back together and explain that you will now go through each line, one by one. This time they should stand by the piece of paper for the archetype they feel is best represented by the line.

After you read each line and the group have chosen their archetype, discuss the reasons for their choice – why that archetype best suits the given line. Each group should choose a speaker to explain their point of view. They should give at least three characteristics to prove their point. It is important to ensure that students link their points to the line. For example, if a group say that 'fail not our feast' is a Sovereign line because it is powerful and regal, they then need to explain what words in the line make this the case, or what is it about the construction of the line that suggests power etc. In this way the group begin the process of detailed textual analysis.

After this process has been repeated for each of the four lines, bring the whole group back into a circle and tell them that each of these lines comes from the same character, in this case Macbeth. Ask the group: What does this tell us about the nature of character in Shakespeare's plays?

This brings the basic archetype exercise to a close. Once the students have experienced physicalizing the archetypes and begun to apply them to their analysis of text, there are any number of variations and extensions that can be used. It becomes a tool for looking at character that can be applied to any piece of text.

The most obvious everyday extension of this activity is to provide students with a piece of cut text and ask them to identify which archetype is dominant at any given point. They can then justify these choices with lines from the text and thus chart how a character or characters change and develop through a speech or scene. If you wish, this process can also be physicalized with students reading the lines and making what they consider to be the most appropriate archetype gesture on each line.

Archetype descriptions

Read these in conjunction with the picture of each archetype.

FIGURE 3 *Sovereign*

FIGURE 4 *Warrior*

Sovereign

Key characteristics: upright and responsible. The sovereign wears a crown, which is formed by placing your hands either side of your head, palms touching the top of your ears and fingers pointing upright. The sovereign wears a cape on which rests all the responsibilities of the kingdom. Imagining they are wearing this helps give students an idea of slowness and gravitas

FIGURE 5 *Carer*

Warrior

Key characteristics: alert and ready for action. The warrior carries a shield which s/he holds in his/her left hand, protecting the heart. The warrior's right hand is raised straight up, vertically at his/her side with fingers pointed upwards, representing a sword.

Carer

Key characteristics: selfless and open. The carer walks around the room and when s/he meets another person flings open his/her arms in a wide gesture. Arms should be stretched as wide as possible, resembling the upper part of a cross. This is usually the most difficult physical archetype for students, for obvious reasons. It sometimes needs more modelling and encouragement than the others.

Trickster

Key characteristic: naughty, a joker, likes to divert attention. The trickster walks around the room, when they see another person they turn or spin around to the left, look at the other person and click their fingers. Think the Fonz in *Happy Days* or Del Boy in *Only Fools and Horses*. Playing this archetype usually produces hysterical laughter from students.

FIGURE 6 *Trickster*

Example

'Macbeth' lines: **Macbeth**

1. *Fail not our feast* (soverign) (3:1.27)
2. *Give me mine armour* (warrior) (5:3.36)
3. *Dearest chuck* (carer) (3:2.45)
4. *Goes Fleance with you?* (trickster) (3:1.35)

This exercise can be applied to any play. Further examples:

'A Midsummer Night's Dream' lines: **Puck**

1. *Lord what fools these mortals be* (sovereign) (3:2.115)
2. *Here villain drawn and ready* (warrior) (3:2.402)
3. *Pretty soul* (carer) (2:2.75)
4. *I'll put a girdle round the earth in forty minutes* (trickster) (2:2.175)

'Romeo and Juliet' lines: **Romeo**

1. *Gentle Mercutio put thy rapier up* (sovereign) (line 83)
2. *...fire-eyed fury be my conduct now* (warrior) (line 126)
3. *I...love thee better than thou canst devise* (carer) (line 68)
4. *Courage, man. The hurt cannot be much.* (trickster) (line 97)

NB: All of Romeo's lines are taken from Act 3 Scene 1, which is a really useful way of looking at character change/progression within one scene.

Tips

Adam: Archetypes are a brilliant way of enabling students to engage with character, first physically, then textually. I love looking at possible shadows of the archetypes, e.g. king to tyrant, warrior to aggressor, carer to manipulator and trickster to psychopath. It's a great way to begin to analyse character.

Bill: Archetypes are a brilliant way of introducing the idea of playing a different character. After I have worked through the first part of the exercise and played around with the archetypes a bit, I often ask the group to think of figures in the media that correspond to different archetypes, maybe who walks in a certain way or who has qualities of the archetype. This encourages the group to start to use their imaginations and can help them to connect with the way the characters behave in the play. Then I give them some lines!

Chris: The teacher modelling part of this activity is really important. It has to be really clear and committed. I find the trickster quite difficult so I have to be aware of this when I model it for students. I find this a really useful story-telling activity and often use it as a way into a play or as a way of introducing character. I also like to complete the activity by asking students to mark up a piece of text – looking at the different archetypes a character plays within a scene, but also at how this affects the archetypes played by the other characters in the scene. Often I find that the archetypes characters play change in direct relationship to each other.

Colin: I find this useful for exploring all the possibilities in a speech or scene. It can challenge students' preconceptions. Characters we think of as warriors can have carer lines within the same speech. I find the trickster the most difficult. It's fine to have little variations on the movement if this helps students feel comfortable and commit to the physicality of the archetype.

Glynn: I always think that the simpler you can keep this exercise, the better. It can work well to think about the archetypes at different ages and the light and shade of each archetype. It is important to recognize the difference between a warrior and a soldier. The warrior fights for all s/he loves, but for a soldier it is a professional occupation. The carer is particularly effective when thinking about performance at the Globe and engaging with the audience. I ask actors to imagine they are opening their hearts to the great heart of the Globe.

Patricia: I like to think of character types as well as archetypes and introduce different character types, depending on the play – e.g. if I was working on *Romeo and Juliet* I might have a teenager and a parent. I find this gives me a greater degree of freedom with the exercise.

Yolanda: This is a good opportunity for students to consider the inner and outer qualities of a single character. There are times when a character might play one archetype outwardly while displaying privately the feelings of another. I find *Archetypes* really useful when creating a performance with young people as well as when exploring text in a workshop. I ask performers to make sure they have the physicality of the archetype in their body, but then let it go, keeping the essence in their final performance.

Tactics

These activities use the idea that characters always speak and act to achieve what they want. In order to get what they want characters employ a range of different tactics, just as we all do in everyday life. The idea for *Hook/Probe* came from Colin Hurley, who wanted to find a way of bringing his rehearsal preoccupation with identifying and exploring his character's objective/super objective or wants into his work with young people. *Yes/No* was developed by Adam Coleman, who wanted to find a way to make clear to students the distinction between tone of voice, body language and words. By separating them in stages of the activity, then putting them back together, the students could consider the role played by each and their collective effect on the way a piece of text is understood.

Practical considerations

This is an activity that can be carried out in a classroom with desks. It is probably best if students stand for the exercise, as it gives them a greater range of movement, but this could be in the space by their desk. The activity could be carried out with students seated at their desks, if required. *Hook, Probe, Deflect* is an activity for any scene. It works very successfully on duologue as a pair activity. *Yes/No* is a pair activity for duologues. We usually use *Hook, Probe, Deflect* as the second or third activity in a session, possibly after an activity like *Pointing on the Pronoun*. *Yes/No* can be used at the beginning of a session, or at any point.

Aim

In these exercises students work to identify the tactics characters use. They consider how our understanding of these helps us to interpret what motivates a character at any given moment in the play. Working on tactics helps students to focus on language and to identify how the words a character speaks work to produce their desired outcome.

Hook, probe, deflect

Activity

Give the students an edit of the text to be explored. Long and short edits both work well, whichever is more appropriate for the group. The description below assumes the students are working on a duologue, in pairs, but the exercise can be adapted for scenes with more characters.

Explain that the students are going to read the scene but will need to do so using one of three tactics: Hook, Probe *or* Deflect. *Model the physical gesture for each tactic (see description and picture below). The group should repeat and practise each gesture after it is modelled.*

Tactics gestures: Hook

A hooked finger on one hand, starting at arm's length and moving toward the body. This can be repeated any number of times.

FIGURE 7 *Hook*

FIGURE 8 *Probe*

Objectives:
Super
objectives.

Probe

An outstretched arm with the index finger on one hand pointing forwards. The finger should be moved around and forward as if it is digging into something, rummaging around.

Deflect

An outstretched arm with the palm of one hand facing upwards, as if pushing something away. A 'talk to the hand' type gesture.

The students should read the edit, making the tactics gesture they feel is most appropriate on each line. If they feel a character changes tactics within a line they can make two different gestures.

If it is useful to stimulate discussion, one or two pairs can be asked to run through the edit, using their chosen gestures, for the rest of the group to watch. If it is more appropriate for the group, move on to a discussion without this step. Key questions include: Which gesture did you use most in this scene? What might that tell us about the character or the situation s/he is in? What tactics gesture did you choose for each line? (It can work well to go through the edit line by line.) What words in the line made you think that the tactics gesture you chose was the most appropriate? Do the

FIGURE 9 *Deflect*

tactics the characters use change throughout the scene? If so, at what point do they change? What does this tell us about a) character, and b) the way the scene is structured?

Next ask the students if there was any tactic they felt was missing. What kind of tactics did they wish they had when working through the activity? Choose one or two tactics from the group's suggestions and create a gesture for them. The group should then add these to hook, probe and deflect and repeat the exercise. What does the use of these new tactics tell us about the character at that moment in the play? How does it add to our understanding?

T

***Othello* Act 3 Scene 4 lines 51–91**

OTHELLO
I have a salt and sorry rheum offends me;
Lend me thy handkerchief.

DESDEMONA
Here, my lord.

OTHELLO
That which I gave you.

DESDEMONA
I have it not about me.

OTHELLO
Not?

DESDEMONA
No, faith, my lord.

OTHELLO
That is a fault. That handkerchief
Did an Egyptian to my mother give;
To lose't or give't away were such perdition
As nothing else could match.

DESDEMONA
Is't possible?

OTHELLO
'Tis true: there's magic in the web of it.

DESDEMONA
Then would to God that I had never seen't!

OTHELLO
Ha! wherefore?

DESDEMONA
Why do you speak so startingly and rash?

OTHELLO
Is't lost? is't gone? speak, is it out o' the way?

DESDEMONA
Heaven bless us!

OTHELLO
Say you?

DESDEMONA
It is not lost; but what an if it were?

OTHELLO
How!

DESDEMONA
I say, it is not lost.

OTHELLO
Fetch't, let me see't.

DESDEMONA
Why, so I can, sir, but I will not now.
This is a trick to put me from my suit.
Pray you, let Cassio be received again.

OTHELLO
Fetch me the handkerchief: my mind misgives.

DESDEMONA
Come, come; You'll never meet a more sufficient man.

OTHELLO
The handkerchief!

DESDEMONA
I pray, talk me of Cassio.

OTHELLO
The handkerchief!

DESDEMONA
A man that all his time
Hath founded his good fortunes on your love,
Shared dangers with you,–

OTHELLO
The handkerchief!

DESDEMONA
I'faith, you are to blame.

OTHELLO
Zounds

This exercise works well for most duologues, particularly ones with conflict or where a character needs something from another character. Other examples of scenes that work well with this exercise are:

Macbeth: Act 1 Scene 7

Much Ado About Nothing: Act 1 Scene 1 (see below)

Romeo and Juliet: Act 2 Scene 2

A Midsummer Night's Dream: Act 2 Scene 2 (Hermia and Lysander)

Yes/No

Activity

Ask the group to get into pairs and label themselves A and B. Explain that they are going to do a short improvisation to begin this activity.

Give A and B the following instructions:
A: You want your partner to come to your way of thinking and to do as you wish. You can only use one word to convince them to do this and win your argument. That word is 'yes'.

B: You do not want to do what A is asking you to do. In fact you want A to come to your way of thinking and do as you wish. You can only use one word to convince them to do this and win your argument. That word is 'no'.

Ask each pair to stand opposite each other but explain they will have to do the improvisation without using physical gesture at all. They should stand with their legs together and hands behind their backs. They can only use the words to win the argument.

The group should then improvise for about 2–3 mins max. Afterwards discuss their findings. Key questions could be around whether it was easy or hard to win the argument without using the body and why this should be the case. It's important for students to come to understand at this point that communication comes from movement or action as well as words. A play is created to be played for an audience, so when we are looking at Shakespeare's words, as well as the words themselves we need to think about what action might be taking place at the same time and how this also helps us to interpret and understand the plays.

A and B should now repeat the exercise, still trying to both get the other to do what they want. This time, however, they cannot speak. They can move and use physical gesture (without touching) but no words.

Choose one pair to show the group what they were doing. Ask the group to suggest the verbs they would use to describe what the pair were doing. Common suggestions here might be begging, pleading etc. Ask a second pair to show the whole group the work they were doing and afterwards ask for more verbs.

Explain to the group that the verbs they have suggested are what actors often refer to as tactics. We all use tactics in everyday life to get what we want. The tactics we chose to use depends on what we want, who we want it from and how we are feeling at that moment. This is what characters in a play do. A character has an objective and then uses a tactic to achieve that objective. Explain that the group are now going to look at how that works in practice in a piece of text.

Example

An edit from *A Midsummer Night's Dream* Act 2 Scene 1 – a scene between Helena and Demetrius is being used for the purposes of this example. This activity works on any piece of text that features two characters who are in some kind of conflict or competition. A list of possible plays and scenes is given below. Edits for use in the activity can be of any length depending on the needs of the group. We usually use an edit of at least 8–20 lines.

T
A Midsummer Night's Dream: Act 2 Scene 1 Lines 188–229

DEMETRIUS
I love thee not, therefore pursue me not.

HELENA
You draw me, you hard-hearted adamant;

DEMETRIUS
Do I entice you? do I speak you fair?
Or, rather, do I not in plainest truth
Tell you, I do not, nor I cannot love you?

HELENA
And even for that do I love you the more.

DEMETRIUS
Tempt not too much the hatred of my spirit;
For I am sick when I do look on thee.

HELENA
And I am sick when I look not on you.

DEMETRIUS
I'll run from thee and hide me in the brakes,
And leave thee to the mercy of wild beasts.

HELENA
The wildest hath not such a heart as you.

In pairs, ask the group to read through the edit. It can be helpful to use an exercise like Pointing on the Pronoun *(see pages 57–63) to do this. If the group are quite confident with text this may not be necessary.*

After the group have read the edit in their pairs discuss: a) What Demetrius wants (students often make suggestions such as, to be as far away as possible from Helena or for Helena to leave him alone); b) What tactics Demetrius uses to achieve his aim, e.g. to get Helena to leave him alone. Students will make suggestions such as, 'he insults her'. For each suggestion ask the students to come up with the line or words from the edit that led them to that conclusion. In this way the group are very quickly able to analyse text.

Repeat this exercise for the other character in the scene – in this example, by asking the group what Helena wants and the tactics she uses to achieve her aim.

The pairs should now read the edit again, but this time with an awareness of the objectives and tactics of their character. They should think particularly about the words and lines that the characters use to achieve their particular aim. Remind the students to think about how they might express themselves physically, as well the particular way in which they might speak the lines.

Discuss the students' findings from this repeat reading. What did they find out about the character's thoughts, feelings and desires in the scene? Did they feel the character underwent any changes in the scene?

At this point the students can be given a longer edit or the whole scene, whatever is most appropriate. A logical conclusion of this exercise is to log a character's objectives, tactics and the lines that demonstrate how they achieve them, throughout a scene and to consider how a character might develop as the scene progresses. It is also helpful for the students to consider what has happened to the character before this moment (with textual references where appropriate) and to discuss how this might affect him or her in the scene they are analysing. These observations can then be put together to produce an analysis of each character in the scene.

Tips

Adam: *Yes/No* is a brilliant way for students to engage with desire and action. It also helps them to understand that in drama what is said is only part of the picture; how it is said is equally important. A quest to decide how something is said can lead students to detailed analysis of context and the construction of a scene. I sometime use the sentence 'I never stole your money' to illustrate the importance of context. I work through the sentence, stressing a different word each time. The sentence means something different according to which word is stressed. *Tactics* is a great way to reveal the psyche of a character. The tactics s/he uses tells us a lot, it helps students understand subtext.

Bill: *Hook, Probe, Deflect* is a great way of starting to move a scene. It can help students to explore their responses to other characters and how they might move, or position themselves in relationship to the other character as a result of what s/he is saying.

Chris: It works well if the students continue to repeat the tactic gesture throughout their line. This can create a dance-like movement. When students have experienced this they can then take away the gesture but say the line incorporating any discoveries they made through this physical work.

Colin: I now insert a sequence that I've called 'Approach, Retreat, Manoeuvre' before *Hook, Probe, Deflect.* Students should read the speech and for each line should either approach (step forward), retreat (step back) or manoeuvre (move in some way to the side). Any speech can usefully be explored in this fashion. It can feel a bit like a game of chess. Eye contact activities can also work well. Play the whole speech with one character giving eye contact and the other refusing, then swap the characters round and discuss what we learn by doing this about status in the scene. I also find *Yes/No* very useful. I like to add in 'please/sorry' as well, depending on the scene.

Patricia: The physicality of the tactics exercise is all-important for me. It is essential to remember when you work on these exercises that you are bringing a text to life in your body. There needs to be emotion informing movement. When I work with *Yes/No* I like to ask students to experiment with saying 'yes' but meaning 'no' and saying 'no' but meaning 'yes' (asking them to shake hands with each other while they do this works well). It is important to remember that what a character says doesn't always reflect what is going on internally. Lady Macbeth's welcome to Duncan in Act 1 Scene 4 of *Macbeth* is a good example of this behaviour. These activities can help students to understand interpretation – that there is more than one way to play a character.

Yolanda: I ask students to be aware of the difference between physical and psychological tactics in these exercises. Exploring the difference can lead to really rich discoveries.

Pointing on the Pronoun, word before, interrupting

This sequence of activities provides a simple way of looking at a piece of text from lots of different perspectives and establishing character, situation and relationships. It was used in the Globe rehearsal room during the first week of rehearsals for *Much Ado About Nothing* in 2007. Director Tamara Harvey spent the first week of rehearsals going through each of these activities for the whole play. By the end of the week the actors understood who their character was taking to and what they wanted to achieve through their speech and actions at any given moment. Each actor also had a list of all the words that were most important to their character throughout the play. These lists were put on the rehearsal room walls. Yolanda Vazquez, who played Beatrice in this production, immediately saw the potential of these activities for her work with young people and developed them into the form that follows below.

Aims

This activity encourages familiarity with a single piece of text and enables students to consider it from lots of different angles. By the end of the sequence they should have a clear idea about who a character is talking to and about. They should also understand their focus and key motivations in that scene and be able to identify and comment on the key language a character uses and for what purpose. *Pointing on the Pronoun* particularly is a good way to introduce students to a piece of text. It takes them straight to the core of what is happening in a very simple way.

Practical considerations

These activities can all be done at a desk if desired. It works well for pairs to work through them standing (no large space required) but really in this instance it makes little difference whether the students are standing or sitting at their desks. This is a sequence of activities made up of six different distinct parts. They can all be used singly if desired. We most commonly do this with *Pointing on the Pronoun* as it is a quick way into text that can be fitted into many other activities. It takes away the focus from reading to pointing and this is liberating for less confident students on any first reading. If used together, we have found they are best carried out in the order given below, as they build familiarity and knowledge as the sequence progresses. Do experiment, though, if you feel a different order would best serve a particular group. Each activity should be used on the same piece of text. For the purposes of this explanation it is assumed that this sequence is being used as a pair activity, but it can be used with larger student groups, as the scene concerned requires.

Activity

Pointing on the Pronoun

Give the students a cut piece of text. Ask them to read through it in pairs. Each time they encounter a pronoun they should point to the person in the scene that the pronoun refers to. If the pronoun refers to a character or place outside of the scene they should point to a place on the wall of the room, a different point for each different character or place.

Afterwards ask the students: Who they were talking about? Was the person they were talking about with them or somewhere else? What does this tell us about the characters and their preoccupation at this moment in the play?

The following example of dialogue between Beatrice and Benedick in Act 1 Scene 1 of Much Ado About Nothing *shows us how this exercise can work in practice. The pronouns show us that Beatrice and Benedick are totally absorbed with each other and are only aware of others outside the scene as they might relate to, or comment on, them.*

T

MUCH ADO ABOUT NOTHING Act 1 Scene 1 lines 107–39

BENEDICK
If Signior Leonato be her father, she would not have his head on her shoulders for all Messina, as like him as she is.

BEATRICE
I wonder that you will still be talking, Signior Benedick, nobody marks you.

BENEDICK
What, my dear Lady Disdain! are you yet living?

BEATRICE
Is it possible disdain should die, while she hath such meet food to feed it, as Signior Benedick? Courtesy itself must convert to disdain, if you come in her presence.

BENEDICK
Then is courtesy a turncoat. But it is certain I am loved of all ladies, only you excepted: and I would I could find in my heart that I had not a hard heart, for truly I love none.

BEATRICE
A dear happiness to women, they would else have been troubled with a pernicious suitor. I thank God and my cold blood, I am of your humour for that: I had rather hear my dog bark at a crow than a man swear he loves me.

BENEDICK
God keep your ladyship still in that mind! so some gentleman or other shall 'scape a predestinate scratched face.

BEATRICE
Scratching could not make it worse, an 'twere such a face as yours were.

BENEDICK
Well, you are a rare parrot-teacher.

BEATRICE
A bird of my tongue is better than a beast of yours.

BENEDICK
I would my horse had the speed of your tongue, and so good a continuer.
But keep your way, a God's name. I have done.

BEATRICE
You always end with a jade's trick: I know you of old.

Act 2 Scene 2 of Macbeth *between Lady Macbeth and Macbeth after the murder of Duncan is another good example. (See the end of the* Cutting Text *section on pages 35–6 for edits of this scene.) Here the pronouns reveal the state of mind of each character and their relationship with one another. When students work through* Pointing on the Pronoun *on this piece of text they discover that Macbeth is pointing continually at himself, while Lady Macbeth is continually pointing at him. Nobody outside of the scene features. This example also particularly illustrates what the physicality of pointing can tell us about a character's attitude or state of mind.*

Word before

Ask the students to read through the scene. They should focus very carefully on what the character they are speaking to is saying to them. From each line that comes before their own they should choose the word that stands out to them more than any other. The students should let that word affect them, then repeat the word they have chosen after the character speaking before them has finished their line. They should then start their own line. (See the example below.) It is important that the students do not prepare for this exercise by going through the text and marking it before they read. They should choose the word when they hear it, as it strikes them in that moment. There are no right or wrong words to choose. The choice of word can be revealing and enables students to focus on the key words in the scene and their dramatic impact.

The following segment of text provides an example of how this activity might run. The words chosen to be 'the word before' are simply examples, any word at all can be chosen.

T
BENEDICK
If Signior Leonato be her father, she would not have his head on her shoulders for all Messina, as like him as she is.
Beatrice: 'head'

BEATRICE
I wonder that you will still be talking, Signior Benedick, nobody marks you.
Benedick: 'nobody'

BENEDICK
What, my dear Lady Disdain! are you yet living?
Beatrice: 'Disdain'
And so on...

Key questions to ask students after this activity are: What is the character hearing in this scene? What is the connection between the characters? What are the operative words in this scene?

This exercise helps students to think about structure, the way in which the scene is written. It mirrors conversations in everyday life; we listen to someone and respond. We do not hear everything. We respond to the words we hear that motivate us or engage us emotionally. It's useful to think of the iambic pentameter as Shakespeare's way of writing in the length of speech that people are most likely to hear before losing focus – the original sound bite.

Interrupting

Ask the students to read through the scene. This time they should interrupt the person speaking before them by starting their line one or two words before their partner has finished speaking.

This exercise helps students to get an idea of the tempo of the scene. In some exchanges it feels very natural, in other instances it seems to work against what a character is saying. Discussing the effect of interrupting on the scene will help students to think about how it is constructed and how the characters in the scene are relating to each other. If working with students on a performance, this particular exercise can help them to come in on cue and think about the pace of the scene.

The 5 second pause

This is the anthesis of the Interrupting *exercise. Ask the students to read through the scene. This time they should pause for 5 seconds before starting each of their lines. Students should think during the pause about why their character is taking that pause. They can move around if they wish.*

After this exercise, discuss the effect of pausing as with Interrupting above. Explore whether Interrupting *or* The 5 Second Pause *works best for the scene.*

From here

This exercise asks students to start to think about the physical or spatial relationships between characters and begins the process of considering staging and the role of the audience.

This time, before reading their line students should think about where they want to stand in relationship to their partner/s when they are speaking. They should then move to that place in the room and speak their first line.

The person with the next line should then consider where s/he wishes to stand to deliver his/her line. S/he should move to that place, state 'From here', then speak the line.

This process should then be repeated for every line in the scene.

Question the students. Why did you move to that particular space at that point? What word/s was it in the line that suggested that particular movement or spatial relationship between characters?

Final run through

The students have now explored who they are speaking to, why they are speaking to them, the tempo of the scene and the spatial relationship between characters.

To conclude this activity, they should read the speech again, putting everything they have discovered into interpretative choices. These should shape the way they speak and emphasize lines and their reactions to the other character. This can be developed into a performance if desired. The Yes/No *exercise can also be added into this sequence so that students can incorporate a choice of tactics into their final reading.*

If appropriate, ask some of the group to share the final readings/performances and discuss their different interpretations of the scene. Students should justify their choices with words/lines from the text.

Tips

Adam: I tend to use this sequence with groups when I feel they are quite confident with the language. I really like using it to get deeper into language, although it does work well with less advanced groups.

Bill: I find this exercise is particularly brilliant for exploring prose, because it can be harder to find the stresses of a speech in prose and to find a character's through line in the speech.

Chris: I like to ask students to look for any patterns in the 'pointing' exercise and to consider what these might tell us about the two characters. Sometimes I morph the 'word before' and 'interrupting' together, which can be quite chaotic but can provide a real insight into the rhythm of the scene. If a student cannot find a suitable 'word before' in their line it might indicate that their character is not listening to the other character in the scene. Sometimes I also add 'speaking the character's thoughts' into this sequence. Students say the line, then immediately afterwards speak in their own words what s/he believes the character is thinking. This is a good way for a teacher to gauge understanding of the scene and for students to look at the difference between inner thoughts and outer actions.

Colin: This sequence is very good for taking the abstract and making it concrete. The *Pointing on the Pronoun* part of the exercise is particularly effective at making the relationship between characters very clear and solid.

Patricia: This sequence is a really good way of helping the text to become dramatic. Working through the activities helps the lines to become more than words but a moment between two people. It helps us to discover the relationship between two characters and the emotions in the scene.

Yolanda: Make sure the pointing is really clear, 'large' and theatrical.

Status

Status exercises are a common feature of drama classes and rehearsal rooms. They are useful when looking at Shakespeare, but also any drama. Plays are full of examples of characters who are motivated by either, gaining or maintaining status for themselves, or affecting (in either a positive or negative way) the status of others. The status dynamic often drives a scene, or even a whole play. It is the driving feature of the relationships between many of Shakespeare's characters. In other plays status may play a more subtle part, but it is always a factor. When looking at a scene or moment in Shakespeare, it is always useful to ask: What role is status playing here? How does it affect the dynamic of this action? The status exercises used by Globe Education derive largely from the work of Max Stafford-Clark with his company Joint Stock in the mid-1970s. Stafford-Clark used rehearsal approaches in which he believed 'The actor's sole objective becomes to make their status as clear as possible'.[1] The most well-known of these is his work using playing cards to develop status games. Globe Education Practitioners have adopted these activities, and where appropriate developed them to meet our particular learning objectives.

Aims

To understand what status is and how it can affect the motivation and actions of a character in any given play or moment. To be able to play with status and understand how changing status can affect the dynamic of a play or scene. Students should gain another tool that can be used to analyse character, or Shakespeare's construction of a scene.

Practical considerations

The initial status exercises in this sequence are most easily carried out in a space in which students can move around freely, although it is possible to do them in a classroom without moving the desks, if required. Later exercises can be done standing or sitting by desks. Some of these exercises require a pack of playing cards. When first exploring status with a group, it can be useful to use two packs of cards and simply use the extremes of the pack, i.e. ace, 1, 2 and 3 signifying low status and 8, 9, 10 signifying high status. This can produce some very clear results for students and lead to interesting discussions. For more able or experienced groups, use one deck with all of the cards so they can explore the subtleties of status, i.e. the difference between playing the status of a 6 or a 7. We usually remove the picture cards for this exercise. Ace is always lowest.

Activity

Status line-up

Ask the whole group (ideally standing in a circle) 'what does status mean to you?'. Discuss student responses. Explain that status can mean different things to different people and that in different cultures status can be signified in a variety of different ways. Try to find examples that are relevant to the particular group, or to you as a teacher.

Explain that you will walk around the circle with a playing card held to your forehead. If it is a high number you are a person of high status, if a low number (ace is lowest in this exercise) you are a person of low status. Ask the group to react to you as you walk around, according to your status. Do this first with a high number such as a 10, then with a low number, such as an ace.

Groups usually react very differently to each extreme status. Ask the group what you were doing differently to provoke such different reactions? The answer, of course, is nothing! Other than hold a different numbered playing card to your forehead.

Ask the group what happens if a King or Queen walks onto the stage and nobody reacts to them as a King or Queen? It is in part the way that characters react to one another that gives status. Broadly, status in drama is created by a character's social position, the way s/he behaves and the way other characters behave to him/her. This is a complex and quite subtle issue and can be discussed here in a way which is most useful and appropriate for the group.

Give each member of the group a playing card, from a range of different numbered cards in the pack. Tell them not to look at it, but to hold it face outwards on their forehead. Ask the group to walk around the room, reacting to each other according to the status on their card. They should do this in silence.

Still without looking at their card, ask the group to line up according to what status they think they are playing: 10s at one end of the line, aces at the other. It may be easier to call up each group – 10, 9, etc. to ace – one at a time. This exercise is easier for students with cards at each end of the scale. The middle numbers often find it harder to place themselves and this can often be a source of rich discussion. When the line-up is complete, let students look at their card and discuss their findings from this process.

Structured improvisation

This improvisation is set in a football ground. The group should get into pairs. A is a premier league footballer who has had a bad season and is not scoring goals. He is a good player but is fearful he may be sacked. B is the manager of the club. S/he is unhappy with A's performance.

A and B should then improvise the conversation that takes place. Throughout the improvisation A, the player, should play the status of a 2. B, the manager, should play the status of a 10. This stage of the improvisation should last for no more than 2 minutes.

Stop the group and explain that you want them to continue improvising and that B should continue to play a 10. However this time, each time you clap, A should change status according to the number that you call out. Begin the improvisation again. Break it at intervals by clapping and introduce new levels of status. The levels we most commonly use are 2, 6, 10, then back to 2 again. At the end of the sequence, ask the students what they have experienced in this improvisation and discuss findings.

Ask the students who were playing the managers how they changed their behaviour when the player became a 10. Students will typically report that they began to try to convince the player or that they tried to squash him or her. From this discussion it is useful to draw two points (although naturally there will be more): that status and a character's desire to assert status leads to the use of tactics (see activities on pages 47–57), and that status is not fixed – it changes depending on a character's situation and who they are with.

NB: Status activities can be productively used with the tactics activities on pages 46–56. The improvisation used can be about anything as long as it fits the status situation. Choose a subject or area that will connect with your students.

Text

In pairs, give the students a cut piece of text. An example is given below. This text is the exchange between Ariel and Prospero in Act 1 Scene 2 of The Tempest, *but it could be any exchange in which the role of status is clear or interesting.*

If the group are not confident with text, ask them to do the Pointing on the Pronoun *exercise (see pages 57–63) at this point to familiarize themselves with the words and rhythms. If the group are confident, this stage can be omitted. Ask the group to think about everything that they have discovered about status and apply it when they read the scene.*

After the exercise, ask the group what they can find out about the characters by focusing on the way they play/use their status in this scene. Key questions to ask here are: What does Prospero do? What does Ariel do? How does their status change in the scene? How would you describe the power play between them in the scene?

T

Ariel and Prospero: THE TEMPEST Act 1 Scene 2 lines 189–257

ARIEL
All hail, great master, grave sir, hail!

PROSPERO
Hast thou, spirit, perform'd to point the tempest
That I bade thee?

ARIEL
To every article.

PROSPERO
My brave spirit! Thy charge
Exactly is perform'd; but there's more work.

ARIEL
Let me remember thee what thou hast promised,
Which is not yet performed me.

PROSPERO
How now? moody? What is't thou canst demand?

ARIEL
My liberty.

PROSPERO
Before the time be out? no more!

ARIEL
I prithee,
Remember I have done thee worthy service

PROSPERO
Dost thou forget
From what a torment I did free thee?

ARIEL
No.

PROSPERO
Thou liest, malignant thing! Hast thou forgot?

ARIEL
No, sir.

Changing status

It is possible to go straight from the *Status Line-up* activity into work with text, omitting the *Structured Improvisation*. The following exercise works well with the Ariel and Prospero scene above or the Cleopatra and Messenger example from *Antony and Cleopatra* given below. It can be adapted for any exchange in which status plays a predominant role. In this exercise the text and characters perform the same function as A and B in the *Structured Improvisation* above.

In pairs, give the group your chosen piece of text. Antony and Cleopatra *is used for this example. Ask Cleopatra to start as a 10 and the Messenger to start as a 2. The pairs should read the scene.*

Immediately repeat this exercise, this time with the Messenger playing a 10 and Cleopatra playing a 2.

Discuss the differences between each reading. What does the change in status do to each character and an audience's perception of them?

Ask the group, in their pairs, to read through the scene again. This time they should judge for themselves where the change in power is throughout the scene. If it is helpful, they can mark each line with a number from the status cards (ace to 10), indicating the status of each character at any given moment. It is important they reference the text to justify their decisions about a character's status. The whole group can then compare the status number they have attributed to each character and discuss similarities and differences.

Thus through this status game it is possible to analyse language and what is happening in the scene.

T
Cleopatra and Messenger: ANTONY AND CLEOPATRA Act 2 Scene 5

Messenger
Will't please you hear me?
CLEOPATRA
I have a mind to strike thee ere thou speak'st:
Yet if thou say Antony lives, is well,
Messenger
Madam, he's well.
CLEOPATRA
Well said.
Messenger
But yet, madam,–
CLEOPATRA
I do not like 'But yet,' it does allay
The good precedence;
Messenger
He's bound unto Octavia.
CLEOPATRA
For what good turn?

Messenger
For the best turn i' the bed.
CLEOPATRA
I am pale, Charmian.
Messenger
Madam, he's married to Octavia.
CLEOPATRA
The most infectious pestilence upon thee!
Strikes him down

Messenger
Good madam, patience.
CLEOPATRA
What say you? Hence,
Strikes him again

Horrible villain! or I'll spurn thine eyes
Like balls before me; I'll unhair thy head:
She hales him up and down

Messenger
Gracious madam,
I that do bring the news made not the match.
CLEOPATRA
Say 'tis not so, a province I will give thee,
And make thy fortunes proud:
Messenger
He's married, madam.
CLEOPATRA
Rogue, thou hast lived too long.
Draws a knife

Messenger
Nay, then I'll run.
Exit

Status partners

This activity can be done directly after the *Status Line-up*. It requires two packs of playing cards so that you have two of each number, ace to 10.

Give each student a card. This time they can look at the number, and should not show their card to anyone else. The aim of this activity is for them to find their status partner, the member of the group that has the same number card as they have.

Give each member of the group the same line. This line should be taken from the scene you are using later in the exercise. For this example the line is Caliban's 'He is not valiant' from Act 3 Scene 2 line 23 of The Tempest. *See below for the full scene. Ask the group to move around the room saying this line, and greeting others playing their given status. When they think they have found their status partner they should sit down.*

Discuss the group's findings. This exercise highlights how characters give themselves status and the dramatic effect it produces. It works well for scenes in which characters of similar status vie for status/position among each other.

Give the group the edited scene from which the line was taken. (See example below.) In groups (of three in this case) ask them to read the scene. At each point or line in the scene each member of the group should decide on their status at that moment and indicate it by either standing, sitting or kneeling as they say their line. This exercise works best when students decide as they go, rather than working it out beforehand and then reading the scene. However only one person can be standing, sitting or kneeling at any one time. This means that if one person stands, anyone who was standing before has to sit or kneel.

This exercise highlights the power play in a scene and what a character really wants in terms of status. Discuss the group's findings and compare decisions, justifying choices with evidence from the text. How does status change in this scene? What power games are being played? What does each character want to achieve?

T

Stephano, Caliban and Trinculo: THE TEMPEST Act 3 Scene 2 lines 17–39

STEPHANO
We'll not run, Monsieur Monster.

TRINCULO Nor go neither – but you'll lie like dogs, and yet say nothing neither.

STEPHANO Moon-calf, speak once in thy life, if thou beest a good moon-calf.

CALIBAN (*Very drunk*) How does thy honour? Let me lick thy shoe. I'll not serve *him*. He is not valiant.

TRINCULO Thou liest, most ignorant monster!

CALIBAN Lo, how he mocks me! Wilt thou let him, my lord?

TRINCULO 'Lord,' quoth he? That a monster should be such a natural!

CALIBAN Lo, lo, again! Bite him to death, I prithee.

STEPHANO Trinculo, keep a good tongue in your head. If you prove a mutineer – the next tree! The poor monster's my subject, and he shall not suffer indignity.

CALIBAN I thank my noble lord. Wilt thou be pleased to hearken once again to the suit I made to thee?

STEPHANO Marry, will I. Kneel and repeat it. I will stand, and so shall Trinculo.

Tips

Adam: These exercises are really useful but I find it very important to make sure that I do not spend too long on different status games but move fairly rapidly into applying knowledge acquired in the game to a piece of text.

Bill: The *Status Line-up* is a really good way of enabling students to talk about the story of the play and to begin to make more detailed analysis. Once I have worked through the activity with playing cards I give the students a card with a name of a character from the play, ensuring all characters are covered. I then repeat the activity and discuss the results, asking students to justify their choices/responses and the place they are standing in the line-up. This can provide an excellent stimulus for discussion.

Colin: Eye contact games are a great way of getting into status work. I do this in the same way I would for the *Tactics* exercises. It is good to challenge possible preconceptions about status, e.g. a character who says a lot in a scene might not be the most powerful.

Patricia: If I could only work with one sequence of exercises, I would choose *Status*. These exercises can be used to explore everything. You can look at how status affects a character's position externally and sense of self internally. I particularly like the exercise where students have to find their status partner. It is a wonderful method of bringing drama into the body to help students to begin to explore physical methods of communication. It is important to remember that ideas of status can change within different societies. What we understand as being high or low status can change within different cultural situations.

Soliloquy

The soliloquy can be one of the most intimidating elements of studying Shakespeare for young people. This sequence of activities provides an easy way of accessing any Shakespeare soliloquy. It is structured to take students on a journey of discovery about the soliloquy as the sequence progresses. It begins by encouraging students to play with words from the soliloquy in a fun, accessible manner and builds to facilitate analysis of the whole speech. It is a combination of various approaches encountered and developed by Globe Education Practitioners, to try to take the pressure off analysing a soliloquy and to get students into it by focusing on the words, rather than worrying about the whole speech. The sequence also draws on rehearsal room voice exercises that work to help actors get at the sounds and feel of a speech.

Aims

To facilitate students in the analysis of any soliloquy. To provide accessible ways into the text that promote connection and understanding. To provide a structured way of exploring structure, character and the imagery of any soliloquy.

Practical considerations

This sequence is an introduction to a soliloquy and works best if the students do not already know it, or have not analysed the text in detail. It works well if the students stand in a circle, but it can also work well in a classroom with desks, as long as students have space to stand at their desks and can break into small groups to work for short periods. It requires a print-out of a soliloquy with each line on a separate strip of paper. It can also help to number each line so it is easy to put the speech back in order when the strips of paper have been given out to students. If there are more lines in the soliloquy than students in the group, cut the soliloquy so it has the right number of lines. Alternatively you can give some students more than one line to work with (but not from the same part of the speech). There are no text examples given for this activity as it works with any soliloquy you are studying.

Activity

Four word soliloquy

Give the group a line each from a soliloquy, in the order it occurs in the text. It is important that each student knows who in the group has the line before them and after them as they will need to put the lines back in order later in the activity.

Ask the group to imagine they can only communicate using four words from their line. They must pick the four words that they feel best encapsulate the line and will communicate and make themselves understood. They must pick the four words from their line that they think really convey what it is about.

Work round the group in the order of lines in the soliloquy, with each student trying to communicate their line with the four chosen words. Discuss what came through about the scene. What seemed to be important in this first reading? Were the words chosen similar throughout or did they change at any point?

Students should then choose the one word from their original four that they think is most important – the operative word. Go through the soliloquy again. This time the students should just say their one word.

Repeat this exercise adding a gesture for the chosen word. What kinds of words and gestures have been chosen? What kind of feel does this give to the soliloquy? What kinds of images are evoked?

Still working with the same word and gesture, students should one by one make eye contact with someone across the room and 'throw' their word and gesture to them. The person who receives it should pick someone else in the room and do the same with their word and gesture, and so on, until everyone has had a turn. When students are used to doing this, the exercise should move very quickly. Some words/gestures may be repeated. Encourage students to play with the words and use their gesture to help them convey what they feel is the meaning of the word.

A development of this activity is to ask each student who receives a word/gesture to react physically to it, according to the type of word or gesture they are receiving, and repeat it, before throwing their own line and gesture across the circle – a bit like a tennis player reacts to the ball they receive, or someone in battle would react to the blow they have been dealt before sending their own attack. This helps students become familiar with the sounds and impact of the words as well as highlighting the imagery within the speech.

Small group story

Ask the group to line up or stand in a circle in the order of their lines. Divide them into small groups of about five, so the first group contains the students with the first five lines of the soliloquy, and so on.

Each group should make a moving story that represents their five lines. The only word each student can use is the one they chose as their most important word earlier in the sequence. They can repeat this word as many times and in as many different ways as they like. Only give a short time frame for this: c 3 minutes.

Arrange each group of five in order around the room. Ask them to show their story, one after the other. Discuss what the group have discovered about the speech through this activity. The character's emotional journey through the soliloquy invariably becomes very clear. The imagery of the speech also comes through in the stories and this provides a useful starting point for discussing it and the effect of Shakespeare's use of language on our response as an audience to the drama.

The soliloquy

Bring the group back together in order of their lines. Now they are going to read the whole soliloquy. In order, they should each say their whole line and make their original gesture, using it now for the whole line instead of just one word. They should remember all their discoveries from their work so far and use them to help with the delivery of the line.

Discuss what is happening in the speech. Key questions could be: what changes are there in the speech and where do they occur? Where is the speech lighter and where darker in mood or content? At what points do the character's thoughts progress? What are the words that tell us about these changes or ideas? All of these questions facilitate discussions about structure, character and language.

You may wish to repeat the group reading of the soliloquy after various stages of discussion. It can also work well to ask questions such as 'who thinks they have the line where Macbeth is least likely to kill the King?', or 'in what part of this speech do you think Juliet is most fearful?'. The students can then justify their opinion through the words of the line, or if there is more than one contender they can each debate the relative strengths of their line.

Additions

Usually we would end the sequence at this point. However this activity can be developed further depending on the needs of the group. The activity below is an example of what is possible.

Ask the group to identify what different types or categories of words reoccur in the scene, e.g. words that are dark/light or about power, love/

hate, decisive/indecisive, hope/despair, etc. The types of words will depend on the soliloquy and would usually have naturally arisen out of discussions earlier in the exercise. Agree a list. Divide the group into small groups and give each group one of the categories on the list. Each group should go through the soliloquy and identify all the words that are in their category. The teacher or a member of the group should then read the soliloquy. When the students hear one of the words they have identified spoken in the speech, they should repeat it.

This process highlights what types of language occurs most frequently in the speech and how this might change as the scene progresses. It leads well into writing activities that ask students to track how a speech is structured or how a character's thoughts develop as a soliloquy progresses.

The activities in this sequence are the first stage of working with a soliloquy. They do not deal with the effect and role of staging or audience. For extension activities focusing on staging and audience see Chapter 5: *Actor, Stage and Audience*. Similarly, more detailed work on language can be found in Chapter 4: *Language: Inside, Out*

Tips

Adam: I like to use a conscience alley framework to explore soliloquy. Students take one line each and speak or whisper it as group members take it in turns to walk down the middle of the student lines. (See *Walk of Fame, Walk of Shame* later in this chapter for a fuller description of the conscience alley technique.) I sometimes also do a version of this just using one chosen word from each line. This works particularly well for Juliet's 'God knows when we shall meet again' soliloquy in *Romeo and Juliet* 4:3 14–58.

Bill: I use the *Whispering* activity (see Chapter 4) to begin to explore soliloquy because I think you can learn so much about a character from the sounds s/he creates. Even for actors, looking at a big piece of text can be intimidating, and if a group whisper it together it takes away much of the nervousness. I then ask students to feed back on the sounds they hear. I believe that Shakespeare was very conscious about the sounds he was creating with a speech.

Chris: I find it useful to ask students to find the questions in the soliloquies. When each student says their line of the soliloquy, the rest of the group can question him or her, using the line as appropriate – e.g. in *Macbeth* Act 1 Scene 7 line 32 'if it were done, when 'tis done…' might be questioned by the group: 'when what is done?'.

Patricia: Soliloquies for me are all about finding clues to the emotional state of the character. I use many of the rhythm exercises in Chapter 4 to do this. They work well combined with the exercises above.

Yolanda: It works best for me if students stay in the circle when they do the *Small Group Story* part of this exercise, as this enables the students to see clearly exactly how the speech develops. Reflection on the images made by the groups observing is a key part of this exercise.

Telling the story

More often than not it works well to plunge straight into a moment in the play, or engage students with a character's situation or dilemma, without prior knowledge of the story. Students respond well to discovering the story from the inside, engaging with the characters and drama as it unfolds, experiencing the story of the play as it is revealed bit by bit. For this reason Globe Education rarely begins a session by telling the whole story of the play. Connecting with characters, plot etc. and developing a desire to know what happens next is what keeps our attention as audience and reader. Sometimes, however, we need to tell students the story of whole or part of a play quickly. This might be because it is important to study a part of the play in a limited time frame and telling the story up to that point is an effective method of covering the necessary scenes. There are many reasons and occasions when this might be the best route for a group. If this is the case, the activities below provide ways of covering the whole story, a part of the story, or encouraging students to engage with specific situations they encounter in each story.

Aims

To tell the story of the play, or to engage quickly with key moments and developments in the play.

Practical considerations

These activities work well in a drama room; some require students to be able to stand in a circle. Most, however, work equally well in a classroom, although a space where the whole group can look at a still picture is required for some activities – this could be in a corner of the room. *Story Pictures* and *Story Circle* require preparation of play segments and instructions for small groups and individuals.

Activity

Story pictures

Divide each act of the play into three parts. For each part, write a short paragraph that tells the story of that part. When you have finished this you should have three paragraphs, telling the story for each act of the play – 15 paragraphs in total.

Choose some text that best encapsulates the story of each paragraph and write it under the three paragraphs. See the example from A Midsummer Night's Dream *below.*

Divide the group into five. Give each group an act of the play and a piece of paper containing the paragraphs and text for their act.

Each small group should create three still images or frozen pictures, one depicting each paragraph. These pictures should be shown to the whole group, one by one, act by act. The whole group should discuss what they see in the pictures and what they can tell about the story of the act. What are the key elements, characters, plot developments, etc? How do these seem to evolve as the story progresses?

When this process has been completed for the whole play, ask each small group to put their still images together, performing them one after another. Each group should speak the text they were given at the bottom of each paragraph as they perform their images, adding the text where they feel it is most appropriate.

After each act has been seen, discuss the key words that emerged. How do they add to our understanding of the story and confirm or change the ideas that came out of viewing the images alone?

By the end of this exercise the group should have a clear idea of the whole story of the play and have discussed key lines of text.

It is important to be aware that when we tell the story in this way, we are telling our version of the story. In preparing paragraphs and pieces of text, we become editors of the play. Upon exploring the text for themselves, students may not agree with our choices. This can lead to a good activity, of course. What paragraphs would they create for the scene and what text would they pick to best encapsulate it? Giving full reasons for these answers can provide the beginning of a piece of writing about the scene or moment.

Example

Story pictures: A Midsummer Night's Dream *Act 1*

1. Duke Theseus of Athens and his fiancée Hippolyta are discussing their wedding day when Egeus, a nobleman, disrupts them. Egeus wants his daughter Hermia to marry Demitrius but she is in love with Lysander and refuses to marry. The punishment for disobeying a father is death.

Theseus:

Either to die the death or to abjure

Forever the society of men. (1:1.65)

2. Lysander and Hermia decide to run away rather than obey. They tell Helena, who is Hermia's close friend. Helena is in love with Demitrius. Left alone, Helena reflects on the blindness of love. She decides to tell Demitrius of Hermia's plan to run away and maybe then he'll like her again.

Helena: *I will go tell him of fair Hermia's flight* (1:1.246)

3. Six labourers (a tailor, a carpenter, a joiner, a bellows mender, a tinker and a weaver) meet in the woods to rehearse a play for the Duke's wedding. Nick Bottom, the weaver, wants to play all the parts and demonstrates how good he would be.

Bottom: *If I do it, let the audience look to their eyes; I will move storms* (1:2.22–3)

Act 2

1. Puck, an impish fairy and follower of the king fairy Oberon, meets one of Queen Titania's fairies in the woods. They reveal that their rulers have been fighting because Oberon wants a little Indian boy that Titania will not part with. Titania and Oberon arrive and quarrel. When Titania leaves, Oberon remembers a flower that is a love potion. The juice of this flower will make anyone fall in love with the first thing they see. He sends Puck to fetch it. He will use it on Titania.

Oberon:

I'll watch Titania when she is asleep,

And drop the liquor of it in her eyes. (2:1.177–8)

2. Demitrius is in the woods looking for Hermia; Helena is following him and he doesn't like it. He is cruel to her. When Puck returns, Oberon orders him to place the juice on Demitrius, making sure it is Helena he first sees.

Oberon:

Thou shalt know the man

By the Athenian garments he hath on (2:1.263–4)

3. In another part of the forest, Titania is being sung to sleep by her fairies. Oberon pours the juice in her eyes when she's asleep. Meanwhile Puck has found Lysander and Hermia asleep on the ground. Thinking Lysander is Demitrius, he pours juice in his eyes. Helena, walking in the woods, comes across Lysander and tries to wake him. Lysander, seeing Helena, falls in love with her instantly.

Lysander: *Not Hermia but Helena I love* (2:2.112)

Act 3

1. The labourers are rehearsing in the woods when Puck comes across them and transforms Bottom the weaver. He places an ass's head on him as he enters to speak his lines. The rest of the group, petrified, run away. Titania wakes up and, seeing Bottom, falls madly in love with him.

Titania: *Oh how I love thee, how I dote on thee* (4:1.44)

2. Oberon, realizing that Puck has charmed the wrong Athenian, puts some juice on Demitrius' eyes. Helena, running away from Lysander, trips over Demitrius, who on waking up immediately falls madly in love with her. Helena thinks they are making fun of her. Hermia arrives and is very angry with Helena; she thinks Helena is a boyfriend thief.

Hermia:

You thief of love! What, have you come by night

And stolen my love's heart from him? (3:2.283–4)

3. Oberon orders Puck to sort everything out. Puck leads the lovers into the woods, making them chase each other until they are exhausted. As they sleep he un-charms Lysander.

Puck:

Jack shall have Jill;

Nought shall go ill (3:2.461–2)

Act 4

1. Oberon, having obtained the little Indian boy from Titania, decides to un-charm her. When she awakes Titania is horrified to think she has been in love with a donkey. The king and queen are reunited and all are happy in fairyland.

Titania: *Methought I was enamoured of an ass.* (4:1.76)

2. While out hunting, the Duke and Hippolyta stumble upon all four young lovers on the ground. They awake and Demitrius finds that he loves Helena, not Hermia. The four lovers are reunited and all are happy. None will be punished.

Demitrius:

My love to Hermia melted as the snow

The object and the pleasure of mine eye,

Is only Helena (4:1.164–70)

3. Bottom the weaver awakes to find he is alone in the woods; he thinks he has had a marvellous dream that should be turned into a play. He goes to tell his friends, who are thrilled to see him well.

Quince: *Bottom! O most courageous day! O most happy hour!* (4:2.26)

Act 5

1. Theseus chooses 'Pyramus and Thisbe', the labourers' play, for his wedding. The labourers are thrilled.

Bottom:

And, most dear actors, eat no onions nor garlic, for we are to utter sweet breath (4:1.39–41)

2. The play is performed in front of the Duke, Hippolyta, the lovers and everyone at court. It is the story of Pyramus and Thisbe, two lovers, who decide to meet by a tomb. Thisbe gets there first and is frightened off by a lion, leaving her bloody scarf on the ground. Pyramus arrives and, seeing the scarf, thinks Thisbe has been killed and so kills himself. Thisbe arrives and, seeing Pyramus dead, kills herself.

Thisbe:

And, farewell, friends;

Thus Thisbe ends:

Adieu, adieu, adieu. (5:1.32–5)

3. The fairies arrive to bless the house and all the couples. They dance around as Puck tells us we may all have been dreaming.

Puck:

And this weak and idle theme,

No more yielding but a dream, (5:1.413–14)

Story circle

The act breakdowns and pieces of text created for *Story Pictures* can be used for this activity if desired. Alternatively a specific version of the story and text segments can be created for this exercise.

Explain that in a moment you are going to tell the story of the play act by act. Before you can do this, however, you need to give different groups and individuals specific and secret instructions.

Split the group into small groups – one per act works well. Give each group member specific instructions on how to react when they hear a key word. The instructions can be verbal or given on a piece of paper (which is quicker and adds to the sense of secrecy) – for example: 'When you hear the character name Hippolyta, *step forward and make a warrior pose', or 'When you hear the word* death, *speak Theseus's lines* Either to die the death or to abjure /Forever the society of men'. *There can also be instructions for small groups or the whole group, e.g. 'When you hear the word marry, make a gesture that you associate with marriage'. Instructions can obviously be differentiated to suit individual students and the group. You can also ask students to represent a place, such as Athens. It can help to work clearly act by act. Where appropriate, students can be told their their key word reaction should only be given in their designated act.*

With the whole group standing in a circle, the teacher then tells the story of the play, act by act. When the students hear their key word they should step forward and carry out their given instructions.

This is a simple exercise that involves the whole group in telling the story. The student interactions/responses can be as complicated or straightforward as you wish.

Silent movie

Divide the group into small groups. Each group should be given a different section of text of approximately 8–10 lines. The size and number of the groups will depend on the amount of text you wish to cover. This example uses three different pieces of text that provide different insights into Caliban's character in The Tempest. *Other examples are given below. For this activity you can choose text from different places in the play or cut a speech or scene from the play into segments. The text you choose and how you cut it will depend on your particular learning objective. It is important that the text chosen demonstrates progression or change in plot or character. This exercise works well when there is backstory to cover, such as the example from* Twelfth Night *at the end of this exercise, where the events of the shipwreck, the situation of Orsino and Olivia and Viola's plans to disguise herself are covered in one scene.*

T
THE TEMPEST Act 3 Scene 2

1: Caliban: lines 87–97
Why, as I told thee, 'tis a custom with him
I'th'afternoon to sleep. There thou may'st brain him,
Having first seized his books – or with a log
Batter his skull, or paunch him with a stake,
Or cut his wezand with thy knife. Remember
First to possess his books – for without them
He's but a sot, as I am, nor hath not
One spirit to command. They all do hate him
As rootedly as I. Burn but his books.
He has brave utensils – for so he calls them –
Which, when he has a house, he'll deck withal.

2: Caliban: lines 98–103
And that most deeply to consider is
The beauty of his daughter. He himself
Calls her a nonpareil. I never saw a woman
But only Sycorax my dam and she –
But she as far surpasseth Sycorax
As great'st does least.

3: Caliban: lines 135–43
Be not afeared. The isle is full of noises,
Sounds and sweet airs, that give delight, and hurt not.
Sometimes a thousand twangling instruments
Will hum about mine ears – and sometime voices,
That, if I then had waked after long sleep,
Will make me sleep again. And then, in dreaming,
The clouds methought would open, and show riches
Ready to drop upon me – that, when I waked,
I cried to dream again.

The group should first create a still image that depicts what they feel their segment of text is about. These images should be shown briefly to the rest of the group and comments invited – e.g. What does this scene appear to be about? What key words or ideas are suggested by the picture? When all images have been viewed, ask what are the similarities or differences between them?

Each group should then look at their piece of text again. Their next task is to turn their image into a silent movie. They must decide what genre they think their movie should be – e.g. love story, comedy, horror etc. – and play their silent movie in the style of their chosen genre. Each group should keep their chosen genre a secret from the other groups until they show them their silent movie.

Each group should perform their silent movie in the order their text segment appears in the play. Afterwards the whole group should try to guess the chosen genre for the movie. Each group should explain/justify their choice to the other groups.

The group should pick out the key words of the text that suggested the movie genre they chose – the operative words of the scene. They should play their movie again for the whole group, but this time adding their key words (which they can repeat any number of times they wish) and any other sounds that they feel suggest the emotion or content of the scene. The whole group should discuss and question each group's choices.

Afterwards the whole group should discuss whether there could be other possible genres to use and identify the key words for these alternatives.

Key points for consideration and discussion:
What different genres/moods are there in the chosen speech or scene/s?
How do these change as the speech or play progresses?
Why is this and what does it tell us about the dramatic arc of the story or character?

T
Twelfth Night: Act 1 Scene 2 lines 7–58

1: *Viola and Captain*

Captain
True, madam: and, to comfort you with chance,
Assure yourself, after our ship did split,
When you and those poor number saved with you
Hung on our driving boat, I saw your brother,
Most provident in peril, bind himself,
Courage and hope both teaching him the practise,
To a strong mast that lived upon the sea;
Where, like Arion on the dolphin's back,
I saw him hold acquaintance with the waves
So long as I could see.

2: *Viola and Captain*

Viola
Who governs here?

Captain
A noble duke, in nature as in name.

Viola
What is the name?

Captain
Orsino.

Viola
Orsino! I have heard my father name him:
He was a bachelor then.

Captain
And so is now, or was so very late;
For but a month ago I went from hence,

And then 'twas fresh in murmur, – as, you know,
What great ones do the less will prattle of, –
That he did seek the love of fair Olivia.

Viola
What's she?

Captain
A virtuous maid, the daughter of a count
That died some twelvemonth since, then leaving her
In the protection of his son, her brother,
Who shortly also died: for whose dear love,
They say, she hath abjured the company
And sight of men.

3 Viola and Captain

Viola
There is a fair behavior in thee, captain;
I will believe thou hast a mind that suits
With this thy fair and outward character.
I prithee, and I'll pay thee bounteously,
Conceal me what I am, and be my aid
For such disguise as haply shall become
The form of my intent. I'll serve this duke:
Thou shall present me as an eunuch to him:
It may be worth thy pains; for I can sing
And speak to him in many sorts of music
That will allow me very worth his service.
What else may hap to time I will commit;
Only shape thou thy silence to my wit.

This exercise is very versatile and works well to tell any segment/s of story. It also works well with any prologue or chorus speech.

Structured improvisation

Structured improvisation is used elsewhere in the *Status* section of this chapter. It's worth including here, though, as it is a really useful and versatile tool that brings students to the heart of a story and can be used in combination with most of the activities in this chapter. It works particularly well before the *Yes/No* activity in *Tactics*. *Structured improvisation* encourages students to engage with a key part of a story. It can also bring them straight into a character's situation and help them to connect with his/her dilemmas or decisions.When creating a structured improvisation the aim is always to choose a scenario for improvisation that a) mirrors a situation in the story and b) connects with the interests of the group. Usually the group should always explore text that mirrors the situation played out in the improvisation, immediately afterwards. When planning a structured improvisation, begin by considering what is the core situation in the text you wish to explore. Also think about the language that is used and the status of the characters. Then identify a contemporary situation that allows you to explore these situations/issues in away that will be relevant to your students.

The following example works with *Macbeth* Act 3 Scene 1 (lines 73–139), Macbeth's meeting with the murderers.

In pairs the group should label themselves A and B.

Secretly (away from Bs) A should be given the following brief: A, you are a well-respected student in your school. You do not want to do your homework tonight but want to employ B to do it for you so you can pass it off as your own. B is known for providing this service, at a price. You must ask B to do this for you this evening. However you cannot mention the word 'homework' or refer directly to what you would like B to do.

Secretly (away from As) B should be given the following brief: B, you are well known for providing homework for other students at a fee. You have been called to see A about a job. You want the job because A is a well-regarded older student and you need the money. You must find out about the job but you must not mention the word 'homework' or refer directly to the kind of service you provide. You must, however, find out exactly what A requires you to do.

The pairs should improvise this situation for c 3 mins. Afterwards discuss findings. Did A and B manage to do the deal and be clear about what each other wanted? What tactics and methods did they have to utilize to achieve this? Why do they think neither might have mentioned homework directly (apart from being given a instruction not to do so!)?

Give the pairs the following edit. Ask them to remember their improvisation and read it to each other. A should take the role of Macbeth and B the role of Murderer. NB: for the purposes of this edit the roles of First Murderer and Second Murderer are conflated into a single Murderer.

T

Macbeth

Was it not yesterday we spoke together?

Murderer
It was, so please your highness.

Macbeth
Well then, now
Have you consider'd of my speeches? Know
That it was he in the times past which held you
So under fortune,

Murderer
You made it known to us.

Macbeth
I did so, and went further, which is now
Our point of second meeting. Do you find
Your patience so predominant in your nature
That you can let this go?

Murderer
We are men, my liege.

Macbeth
Ay, in the catalogue ye go for men;
Now, if you have a station in the file,
Not i' the worst rank of manhood, say 't;
And I will put that business in your bosoms,
Whose execution takes your enemy off,
Grapples you to the heart and love of us,
Who wear our health but sickly in his life,
Which in his death were perfect.

Murderer
I am one, my liege,
Whom am reckless what I do to spite the world.

Macbeth
You know Banquo was your enemy.

Murderer
True, my lord.

Macbeth
So is he mine; and in such bloody distance,
That every minute of his being thrusts

Against my near'st of life: and though I could
With barefaced power sweep him from my sight
And bid my will avouch it, yet I must not,
For certain friends that are both his and mine,
Whose loves I may not drop, but wail his fall
Who I myself struck down; and thence it is,
That I to your assistance do make love,

Murderer
We shall, my lord,
Perform what you command us.

Macbeth
Your spirits shine through you. Within this hour at most
I will advise you where to plant yourselves;
Acquaint you with the perfect spy o' the time,
The moment on't; for't must be done to-night,

Murderer
We are resolved, my lord.

Macbeth
I'll call upon you straight: abide within.

Afterwards, discuss the similarities and differences between the improvisation and the scene. Possible areas for discussion include: Why is murder not mentioned directly? What might this tell us about Macbeth at this point in the play? What tactics does Macbeth use to get what he wants? What does he say is his reason for using the murderers? Does this ring true? (NB: some directors choose to have Macbeth play the third murderer in the murder scene itself, while others do not.)

Tips

Adam: I like to play a game called *Story Quiz*. Create ten cards (more if you wish), each describing a key moment of the story. The moments can be obvious or more obscure, depending on the group. After any of the activities outlined above, lay the cards out and ask the students to put them in the correct order. This works well with small groups and can be a race to see which group finishes first, if desired. Compare the order of the cards for each group, discuss differences and give the correct story sequences. I also use a DVD pause activity where I ask students to create two frozen images, each from a moment in the story a few scenes apart. After students have shown me their first frozen picture, I tell them what happens between that and the next image they have prepared and ask them to imagine they are a DVD on fast forward and silently create all the action I have described until they reach the moment of their next frozen image.

Bill: I like to tell the story of a play using c 10 lines or alternatively one line for every member of the group. The lines should represent the whole arc of the story. I usually pick these, but it could be a good exercise to ask a group to choose their lines. I then put together a short performance. This is a really fun, free way of telling the story. (See *Endgame* Chapter 6 for a possible method of putting together this type of performance.)

Chris: While looking at the story can provide an overview, I try to avoid it if I possibly can. I like to go on a journey of discovery with students. Telling them the whole story at once can limit the potential for discoveries.

Colin: I like to tell the story by taking the cast list and choosing the most appropriate line for each character from the play – e.g. Caliban from *The Tempest* would say 'This island's mine'. This can be anything you like that you feel sums up the character. Assign each member of the group a character. More than one student can play each character. Teach each character their line. Read a version of the story of the play. Each time their character's name is mentioned, students should step forward and say their line. I don't tend to do *Structured Improvisation*. I do use a Meisner activity in which I give pairs of students one line each from the same exchange and ask them to continually challenge each other with that line, over and over, and to see where that takes them with the scene. I find I can discover a surprising amount from this exercise and it is so simple.

Yolanda: Before embarking upon *Structured Improvisation* be very clear about what you want the group to explore. This sounds obvious, but unless the situation is set up very clearly and precisely it might not offer the insights into text that you desire.

Opposites

This group of activities all explore the way that opposites work in a play, speech or scene. This is a useful tool for breaking down a character's journey over the whole or part of the play and for looking at the way language is used to create tension and opposition.

Positive and Negative line was created by Adam Coleman on a training day for Globe Education Practitioners. He wanted to find a really straight-forward way to chart how a speech or dialogue unfolds – a tool that can be applied to any speech that helps students focus on the way language is used by different characters to achieve their goals. *Walk of Fame, Walk of Shame* is the creation of Colin Hurley, originally used with *Macbeth*, hence the name, but applicable to most plays (see different examples below). Colin took the well-known drama technique *conscience alley* and adapted it to look at a character's journey throughout a play. This is a good activity to do at the beginning of the study of a play as it gives the idea of the scope of the play, the arc of the drama, and creates an interest in finding out what happens in the play to bring about the change. It also helps students to engage directly with the situation of a central character.

Where on the line? is another simple method of charting how a character's situation changes throughout a play. It's a really good exercise to return to quickly again and again. Often students who may find it difficult to answer questions about character development or plot progression find physicalizing their response to the questions easier – they can then think about the justification for their response.

Aims

To provide simple ways of looking at character progression and use of language in a play, scene or speech.

Practical considerations

These activities ideally need some space. *Walk of Fame, Walk of Shame* certainly needs a space where the whole group can stand apart in a long line. The other activities are best carried out physically, but we have done these in classrooms with desks, with students lining up at the front or sides as necessary. *Where on the line* works well on a drawn line on paper, although it helps if the students have experience of the activity physically first.

Activity

Positive and Negative Walls

Look through your chosen text for this exercise and make a list of the positive and negative words. This example uses the scene between Richard and Anne in Act 3 Scene 2 of Richard III. *This edit is fairly short, but longer edits can work well in this exercise, if it is more appropriate for the group.*

Example word lists:

Positive	**Negative**
Charity	Curses

Blessing	Beast
Truth	Devils
Angels	Infection
Patient	Slave
Pity	Slew

Label one wall of the room the + wall and the opposite wall the –. Call out the words on the positive and negative lists (mixed up). For each word students should run to either the + or – wall, whichever they feel is appropriate. Afterwards discuss the language that is used in the scene.

Group the students in pairs and give them the edit. They should read the edit. However, each time they hear their partner say a positive word or phrase to them, they should move towards the positive wall. Each time their partner uses a negative word or phrase to them, they should move towards the negative wall. The aim of the exercise is for each student to move their partner as far as possible towards the wall that corresponds with the comments they are making. Sometimes this works clearly in one direction, other times characters move back and forth between the walls. The exercise reveals physically how language is used in the speech to manipulate or persuade. Students experience the tension between characters, their dilemmas and the pull of opposites.

It is possible to change the names of the walls to reflect the themes of the play e.g. loveand hate, inaction and revenge, etc.

T
Richard III ***Act 1 Scene 2 lines 68–91***

RICHARD Lady, you know no rules of charity,
Which renders good for bad, blessing for curses.
ANNE Villain, thou knowest nor law of God nor man!
No beast so fierce but knows some touch of pity.
RICHARD But I know none, and therefore am no beast.
ANNE O wonderful, when devils tell the truth!
RICHARD More wonderful when angels are so angry… divine
perfection of a woman,
ANNE diffused infection of a man,
RICHARD Fairer than tongue can name thee, let me have
Some patient leisure to excuse myself.
ANNE Fouler than heart can think thee, thou canst make
No excuse current but to hang thyself.
RICHARD Say that I slew them not?
ANNE Then say they were not slain.
But dead they are, and, devilish slave, by thee!

Positive and Negative Walls: Soliloquy/speech line

This is a simpler variation of the above activity, which works well with soliloquies or longer speeches.

Ask the group to make one long vertical line in the middle of the room. Label the wall to their left the + wall and the wall to their right the – wall. Give each member of the group an edit of the same soliloquy or speech, or the whole of it, if appropriate for the group. Speeches where a character has a dilemma, or is trying to reach a decision, work well.

The group should now, altogether, read through the speech. Each time they read a positive line they should move to the positive wall while reading. Each time they read a negative line they should move to the negative wall.

This exercise demonstrates physically a character's thought process during a speech. Afterwards, possible areas for discussion include: how often the character moves, where are the most positives and negatives? Are there points where the character goes back and forth a lot or others where s/he remains on one side or in the middle? In this way it is possible to chart the character's journey through the soliloquy and to pinpoint key moments of change or decision. Focus on particular words and seek to pinpoint the pivotal language in the soliloquy.

As with the previous exercise, the walls can be renamed as appropriate for the soliloquy – e.g. murder Duncan/do not murder Duncan for 'if it were done…' soliloquy in Act 1 Scene 7 of Macbeth. Positive and Negative Walls *works well with speeches and duologues where there is some form of debate or argument – where a character is trying to reach adecision. However it can also work well to point up moments of indecision; the 'To be, or not to be' soliloquy in* Hamlet *is a good example.*

Walk of fame, walk of shame

This activity is a quick method of charting a character's journey through a play. It works best where the journey is quite clear. This example uses *Macbeth.*

Make a list of all the positive comments that are made about the character. These should always be direct quotations from the text. Then make a list of all the negative comments that are made about the character. See the list below for Macbeth.

Ask the group to make two vertical lines down the room. Each student should be facing another. There should be enough room between the two lines for two students to walk comfortably.

Verbally give each student one of the lines from the positive list. They should repeat their line two or three times to themselves in order to remember it. It may be useful to discuss what the language suggests about the character at this point.

The two students opposite each other at the top of the line should assume the role of Macbeth. They should walk down the centre of the line of students. As they pass, each of the other students should say their line. Once Macbeth has gone past, the students should continue saying their line to Macbeth, over and over, until Macbeth reaches the end of the line. Encourage all the students to really think about what they are saying and to try to affect Macbeth with their line.

Ask the students who played Macbeth what effect the words had on them and discuss with the whole group. Ask those students to join the end of the line and for the whole line to move up a little. There should now be two new students at the top of the line.

It is now the turn of the rest of the group to do this exercise. Ask the next two students at the top of the line to assume the role of Macbeth and walk down the line as before. When they reach the bottom they should join the end of the line. Immediately they have reached the end of the line, send the next two students down as Macbeth. Repeat this process until all the students have had a turn.

When students have had their turn as Macbeth and rejoined the line, they should resume saying their given positive words as the next Macbeth goes by. This process requires some 'shuffling up' to the top as more and more students reach the end of the line. By the end of the process everyone should be back to the position from which they started at the beginning of the activity.

Discuss the effect of the language with the whole group.

Repeat this process, this time using the negative words.

It is possible to play with the volume of the words and to ask students to think of gestures to go with them. You can build a mini-performance this way. If you are not familiar with the conscience alley drama technique it may be worth looking at some of the videos and explanations that are online. A google search brings up many descriptions and examples.

Discussion points afterwards can focus around Macbeth's change in character. What might have brought this about? This activity could be combined with some of the story-telling activities on pages 76–89 to provide a quick way into the play. When used with some plays it can follow on successfully from work on *Archetypes* (see pages 38–46)

It is possible to change the focus of the activity to suit the play and character. For example, it works well for Romeo in *Romeo and Juliet*, this time with a list of lover words and villain words, or for King Lear with a list of King words and outcast words, or Benedick in *Much Ado About Nothing* with a list of bachelor words or 'married man' words, and so on and so on...

FIGURE 10 *Walk of Fame, Walk of Shame*

Where on the line?

This activity can be carried out at any point in a play. It is best used frequently, as you study a play, act by act or even scene by scene. It then gives a clear sense of character progression or of the development of a central theme in the play. It can also be used to chart how language changes within a part of the play.

Ask the students to imagine there is a line drawn down the centre of the room. One end of the line represents 'strongly agree', the other end 'strongly disagree'. In the middle is 'neither agree nor disagree'.

Make a statement about the play at your chosen moment and ask the students to stand at the relevant point on the line to indicate their level of agreement/disagreement. Question students about the reason for their response, encourage debate. Ask them to find parts of the text, where appropriate, to justify where they are standing. E.g. if you are tracing Romeo's attitude to love at the beginning of Romeo and Juliet*:*

Statements:
Romeo is really in love with Rosalind.
When Romeo sees Juliet it is love at first sight.
The language Romeo uses when he is with Juliet at the Capulets' ball is more romantic than Juliet's.
Juliet is more practical than Romeo.

The statements can be anything at all that serves the learning objective of the session and can be easily differentiated. This activity can be varied and the ends of the lines renamed to suit the play. The same statement can be used a regular points throughout a play, or questions used instead. E.g. for *Macbeth:* rename the ends of the line 'warrior' and 'murderer' and ask at the end of each act: Is Macbeth a warrior or a murderer?

Tips

Adam: *Positive and Negative Walls* are a great way of engaging students with the moral and ethical dilemmas of the character. It's also a good method of encouraging them to think about their own decision-making process.

Bill: Juliet's speech 'O serpent heart hid with a flowering face!' (*Romeo and Juliet* Act 3 Scene 2 line 73) works brilliantly for *Positive and Negative Walls*. It is also possible to change the names of the walls depending on each particular speech and/or play – e.g. light and shade or hope and despair.

Chris: The organization of *Walk of Fame, Walk of Shame* is key to its success. Sometimes I walk the first few students through the activity as a trial run before it starts – this can then speed the whole process up. When the students are saying their word while people walk down, ask them to think of different levels of sound and to try experimenting with saying their word in different ways. This activity is a really good way of introducing story as it can allow you to look at the arc of a play.

Colin: I like to experiment doing *Walk of Fame, Walk of Shame* in slow motion. It is a great way of focusing in on character reactions to particular words or phrases and exploring the physicality of the language.

Patricia: When using *Walk of Fame, Walk of Shame* I often ask the students calling out the words to create a character for themselves to play when they say the line. This does not have to be a character from the play, but should be related to it – e.g. a soldier whose life Macbeth saved in battle for the Walk of Fame. This helps to create a frame for the activity and can distance students personally from the comments made. This is particularly helpful when the lines being shouted are negative.

Yolanda: I often develop *Walk of Fame, Walk of Shame* so that after the activity I ask one side of the group to create a still image of how Macbeth, for example, is feeling and the other side to depict how the people of Scotland, for example, might be feeling. This enables the students to comment on the whole – in this case, on how Macbeth's actions affect not only himself but those around him.

CHAPTER FOUR

Language: Inside out

Introduction

While earlier chapters have explored methods of analysing language, they have largely done so by looking at external features: understanding of character, situation, motivation, etc. In this chapter we move inside the lines to look at their structure and rhythm, exploring what they can tell us about meaning. It is a forensic approach. Analysing verse structure enables us to recognize patterns, detect anomalies, look for clues. We can use these clues to construct our own hypotheses about all aspects of a play.

There many different ways of approaching Shakespeare's text and many different theories about what is the best approach. There are few set rules. Understanding and analysis of verse structure enables an actor to explore possible meanings from the starting point of Shakespeare's writing. Ultimately, though, everything is a matter of interpretation. This chapter explores the approaches to verse commonly used by Globe Education. Giles Block shares his philosophy and approach to text, while Yolanda Vazquez shares the approach to verse structure she has honed over her career playing many of Shakespeare's leading women, at the Globe, RSC and around the world. By exploring these ideas students can approach the text as actors do and learn a methodology for examining text that can provide the cornerstone of more advanced study of any play.

The activities in this chapter provide ways into verse and facilitate the type of exploration and analysis used by Giles and Yolanda. Simply, analysing verse structure enables us to examine forensically the best evidence of Shakespeare's intentions for the playing of his drama that we have today. Like actors in the rehearsal room, students can then go on to develop their own ideas, imaginings and interpretations. It is important to recognize, however, that these are the approaches used at the Globe. Other theatres, verse experts, actors and scholars may have other approaches. They are simply how we work to create theatre and to explore text with young people.

Text edits should not be used (unless an absolute necessity for the group) with the activities in this chapter, as the aim of this work is to look at verse structure. Most of the activities in this chapter would benefit from being combined with one or more of the activities in *Core Approaches to Creative Shakespeare*, as most appropriate. Many of these activities we would tend not to use with less experienced groups. Some activities are particularly advanced and these are marked with the letter **A.**

Learning from verse

Giles Block: Globe Associate – Text

Why does Shakespeare write in verse? I think it is because, to our surprise, verse replicates real speech more than any of us imagine. When we first look at verse on the page, it can look so intimidating. I find it helpful to begin by thinking about the fundamental qualities of verse. The first is the underlying rhythm that runs through it. It is the most simple of rhythms, it is the rhythm of our heartbeat. I don't think we should try to be over-aware of this rhythm – in fact, I like to think of it as a secret rhythm. In a very real sense, when we are confronted with this rhythm it reminds us subliminally of our humanity. The rhythm makes us feel that someone is speaking emotionally and that, on a very simple level, they mean what they say. It is the sound of sincerity. But it is only the *sound* of sincerity, for we know that there are many ghastly characters in Shakespeare's plays who are able to sound very sincere. Iago is probably the best example. He sounds like a good friend and advisor to Othello, when he is clearly not.

Verse is thought shot through with the underlying emotion of whatever is being said. I believe that the verse line is the length it is, 10 beats, because there is a connection between the length of the line and the breath: how long we can typically speak for before needing to take a breath. I am aware this can be viewed as contentious, but if you try this with some of the most famous lines of Shakespeare,

To be, or not to be – that is the question;
Whether 'tis nobler in the mind to suffer
The slings and arrows of outrageous fortune (Hamlet 3:1.55–7)

you find, I think, that you need to take a breath after 'question' before you can continue to the next line.

Some people think that actors should not breathe in the middle of a line of Shakespeare. I don't think there needs to be a hard and fast rule about this; if breathing in the middle of a line serves an actor's interpretation of a role then s/he should do so. It is important, though, to be aware of the possibility that the line structure represents the duration of a breath and for actors to explore what this might tell them about the role they are playing, at that particular moment.

Verse can be clearly distinguished from prose, as prose does not have a regular rhythm – although, of course, verse has variations of rhythm which an actor needs to seek out, develop an awareness of and question. There is a difference between verse, this sound of sincerity, and prose, which is anarchic. With prose we do not know where the stresses are going to fall. In performance, prose runs faster than verse. In almost all passages of prose there are many more unstressed syllables than stressed. Prose is not connected with our breath and our pulse or heartbeat, it is connected with a cerebral activity: the firings of the human imagination, wit and cleverness. Prose is always used for a different purpose to verse. A shorthand way of describing one of the key characteristics of prose is to say that when characters use prose something is always being hidden, concealed, not shared. One of the best examples of this is Hamlet, who speaks verse in his soliloquies when he is sharing his thoughts with the audience, or in speeches with his 'friends' (the number of which obviously diminish as the play progresses), but when he is concealing something – as with Rosencrantz and Guildenstern, or with Polonius and the Players – he speaks in prose.

I find it helps actors enormously to divide any speech up into distinct thought units, to identify where each separate thought begins and ends. Some thought units might be very short, a line or two lines, others could be six lines or more. Immediately an actor breaks a speech up in this way they find they have accessed the variety of the speech. An actor working through the speech might move from a two-line thought, to a six-line thought, to a one-line thought, to a ten-line thought, and so on. The particular language or phrases used within each thought become clear. When working through this process I'm often struck by the simplicity of much of Shakespeare's language. Again 'To be, or not to be – that is the question' is a very good example. Phrases such as 'Do not touch my lord', 'I set him there', 'I am the cause', 'I will be gone', 'I'll steal away', 'And were that all', 'what was he like?' are in our everyday language. If I walk outside the Globe theatre at any time I will be able to hear many of them uttered by passers-by. Often I just ask actors to say the phrases – to read a phrase like 'were that all' and to imagine that they are talking to someone and to feel the phrase emotionally. Then I ask them to put two phrases together to make a thought and to really try to communicate that thought to me. (NB: an activity based on work with thought units can be found in Chapter 5 *Actor, stage and audience* pages 145–8.)

Some of the most challenging lines for an actor, and interesting lines for those studying verse, is where the thought continues from one line to the next. What happens here is that the thought carries on, but for some reason the speaker has expressed that thought in two (or more) parts. We shouldn't find this surprising because if you listen carefully to the way people speak, speaking like this is very common. In fact, someone saying that last phrase, 'Speaking like this – is very common', might well express that (as that dash indicates) in two parts. We do this partly to give our thought clarity – and so does Shakespeare. Another reason why we speak like this is when we are emotional – our emotion interrupts our run of words. There is always a reason why a line of verse ends where it does. Shakespeare is writing as he hears things said in the world around him. The job of the actor is to consider why Shakespeare wrote each particular piece of verse as he did.

The extraordinary thing about verse is that it can capture how someone spoke (in Shakespeare's imagination) 400 years ago and it is so much better than if we had a recording of Shakespeare and his fellow actors that we could listen to today. When we read or hear contemporary verse we are very aware if it mirrors everyday speech, because it reflects our everyday reality. I believe that Shakespeare's verse reflects his everyday reality. He simply used the language he heard all around him. In a lecture to Harvard University in 1950 T. S. Eliot argued that '...[t]he verse rhythm should have an effect on the hearer without them being conscious of it'. In the theatre we should not be aware that verse is verse. I believe this was the case for Shakespeare's audience. It provides an excellent note for a contemporary actor. Verse in Shakespeare's plays is simply speech. Generally our speech is far more eloquent than we often believe.

Shakespeare goes out of his way in his writing to preserve the iambic rhythm. That is his secret power, unless he wants to change it – for example, with a deliberate trochee. Usually Shakespeare would have ten syllables, sometimes eleven in a line. If a line breaks the rhythm of the iambic pentameter it is a clue for the actor to look at what is happening at that moment. Sometimes lines have twelve or more syllables. These are called over-packed lines. A good example of an over-packed line is Isabella's speech in Act 2 Scene 4 of *Measure for Measure:*

> *Sign me a present pardon for my brother*
> ***Or with an outstretch'd throat I'll tell the world aloud***
> *What man thou art* (lines 151–3)

Overpacked lines are fairly rare. To summarize, I'm fairly certain now that the iambic pentameter is connected to the amount we can say in one breath; that does not mean than an actor might not need to breathe in some lines, but it is a really good starting point, a place to work from for an actor preparing to play a role in a Shakespeare play.

Going through the iambic pentameter for each line, looking at where it is regular and where irregular, will release the thought of the line. Shakespeare has done the work for you. Actors have to be careful, however, of not getting stuck in an 'iambic wash', where they speak the rhythm of the iambic pentameter without interpretation. It is important to examine each line on its own merits. Often the iambic rhythm, or the variation in it, tells an actor how to say the line. Sometimes, however, an actor will need to make his or her own interpretation, which might not reflect the written rhythm. There are no set rules to follow. Interpretation is key. What is crucial is that the actor listens to the rhythm Shakespeare has written and uses his or her knowledge of how that rhythm is written to inform his or her interpretation of a speech.

Everything in the end comes back to the thought. An actor needs to be clear about each section of thought, each phrase. Looking at rhythm, the structure of verse is a key tool for an actor as s/he seeks to understand and interpret a character's thoughts for the audience.[1]

Exploring the iambic pentameter for performance: An actor's approach

Yolanda Vazquez

When I'm rehearsing a role, how the speech or scene is written is of paramount importance to me. Actors have many different approaches but for me, increasingly, the rhythm of the verse provides me with a blueprint for how to perform a scene. It is a starting point from which to explore the text and to create my interpretation of a character.

We do not speak in prose. The iambic pentameter is the closest we have to the form in which we speak English in everyday life. When we talk, we do not do so without pausing. We tend to stop, to take breath and to think about what we want to say next. Different people have different views about how Shakespeare should be spoken. To me, Shakespeare has written in these rhythms and it seems perverse to ignore them or work against them when performing his plays. My primary source of information is the use of iambs and trochees in the verse, because as an actor they say something to me. The iambs tell me how to speak and where the stresses are. The trochees tell me where the stresses have changed. Wherever a stress has changed I look to see why and what is happening there. What happens next is subjective, as I use the knowledge I gain through the exploration of verse structure to construct my own ideas, imaginings and finally interpretation of the role. In some ways my approach might seem prescriptive, as it focuses on deconstructing verse structure. But I find it liberating, as it provides me with a powerful tool to explore the play and can lead to fascinating discoveries that inspire me imaginatively and creatively. I feel as if Shakespeare is directing me through the rhythm. Exploring rhythm simply deepens my understanding of the text and enables me to question, explore, imagine and interpret my role in a play for the audience.

What follows is a description of the verse features that I look for and examples of what they might tell me. This is subjective. Other actors might focus on different areas and make different deductions. They provide me with my way into verse. When I start working on a role I begin by looking for irregularities or differences in the rhythms of Shakespeare's verse. I do this by referring always to the iambic pentameter. I read the text in the rhythmic beat once I have gone through it for story and character facts. Using the 'Sha-Boom' rhythm of the iambs (see pages 116–17 for this exercise) while reading will reveal where the trochees, the feminine endings, the shared lines, the pauses or the overlaps exist. I then investigate what they might offer me imaginatively and directionally.

Feminine endings

A regular irregularity. An eleven-syllable line. Found frequently more likely than not in any scene of a Shakespeare play. The line ends on the soft unstressed beat rather the hard downward stressed beat of the regular iambic pentameter.

This type of line suggests some kind of inner commotion to me. I try to understand why this inner commotion might have occurred and use that to inform my playing of the line.

For example, Beatrice's line from *Much Ado About Nothing* Act 3 Scene 2 line 111:

'And **Be**ne**dick** love **on** I **will** re**quite** thee'

After four lines of regular verse there is this line with a feminine ending. It is the first time that Beatrice is speaking of allowing herself to love Benedick back. I have a purely personal rule (that helps me explore what might be happening to a character) that regular verse lines represent a regular heartbeat and feminine endings denote a flutter or skipped heartbeat. Using this rule I can ask myself: what is it about this sentiment that startles Beatrice? My answer would be: she is allowing herself to realize that she likes Benedick and is speaking publicly to the audience about it. It's daring and exciting. It's that moment of 'oh my goodness, I want to go out with him and I'm telling you about it – how exciting!'.

Another good example is Gertrude in *Hamlet* Act 4 Scene 7. When she is speaking to Laertes of his sister's death, in the middle of her lyrical speech she says:

Un**to** that **el**e**ment.** But **long** it **could** not **be**
Till **that** her **gar**ments, **hea**vy **with** their **drink,**
Pulled the poor **wretch** from **her** me**lo**dious **lay**
To **mud**dy **death**' (178–81)

The first line seems to have twelve syllables. Gertrude, I think, is trying to calm Laertes and give him an exact, though romantic, view of his sister's death. No one wants to know that a death is prolonged and painful. She has come to the moment when Ophelia is in the water and she is in a rush to tell him that it didn't take long. She startles herself in the urgency needed to reassure Laertes of this. I would think of the pentameter for this line and say it so that it fits into the beat of five (while observing the stresses). It means that 'element' and 'but' are slightly squished or faster. To me this suggests she is at pains to reassure and clarify.

Trochee

A stressed syllable followed by an unstressed syllable. For me, as an actor, a trochee is a bit like a skipped heartbeat. It tells me something is 'up'. I need to look at the speech and explore what is happening to the character that is unusual, exciting or disturbing.

A good example of a trochee is later in the Gertrude speech discussed above. There is a trochee in the third line with 'Pulled'. It would be odd to say 'pulled **the** poor **wretch**'. The first iamb is reversed but the rest remain the same. This is the crunch of the story: the water submerged Ophelia. To me it suggests that Gertrude is inferring that Ophelia died in a terrible accident, not a suicide. The river enveloped her and pulled her down. It's an official version of the facts. The trochee gives us the shock factor. She was pulled. She has drowned.

In *Richard III* Act 1 Scene 3, Queen Margaret, in her speech berating Queen Elizabeth and the rest of the courtiers, says:

> *Long **die** thy **hap**py **days** be**fore** thy **death***
> *And **af**ter **ma**ny **length**ened **hours** of **grief**,*
> *Die **nei**ther **mo**ther, **wife**, nor **Eng**land's **queen**!*
> ***Ri**vers and **Dor**set, **you** were **stan**ders-**by**,*
> *And **so** wast **thou**, Lord **Has**tings, **when** my **son***
> *Was **stabbed** with **bloo**dy **dag**gers: **God**, I **pray** him* (206–11)

After the first three lines, which are all directed at Elizabeth, Margaret turns on Rivers and Dorset. This trochee takes me out of the rhythm for a second and makes me take notice. I always imagine the two men enjoying the berating of Elizabeth and then being shocked into the realization that it's now their turn. She is startling them into taking notice. Also in this little section, the word 'son' at the end of the fifth line is very particularly placed – to me it suggests that this is a very painful memory for Margaret and she needs a breath before she can continue with what she has to say.

The same thing happens with Beatrice in her small soliloquy in Act 3 Scene 1 of *Much Ado About Nothing*:

> *For others* ***say*** *thou* ***dost deserve*** *and* ***I***
> ***Believe*** *it* ***better than*** *reportingly* (115–16)

The 'I' at the end of the line gives Beatrice the time to realize she really does love Benedick, no one needs to convince her. She realizes in the moment. I need to observe the end of the line or the breath at the beginning of the line to get the benefit of this moment. Although the thought continues and there is enjambment, the landing on this last word of the line and slight hiatus/breath before the next line gives it more importance.

As an actor I discover that she has just found this out – this is what I need to communicate to the audience.

Shared lines

A line where two characters complete the iambic rhythm. As an actor, when lines are shared it suggests a speed of response. I need to come in immediately. I'm waiting for the other character. There is a speed in the conversation, with no pauses. This often gives us a sense of urgency and can create the atmosphere of a scene.

> For example *Hamlet* Act 3 Scene 4 lines 12–13
> ***QUEEN GERTRUDE*** *Why,* ***how*** *now,* ***Hamlet!***
> ***HAMLET What's*** *the* ***matter now?***

Hamlet is being rude to his mother, he is coming in straight away, not considering what she says. There are ten syllables and five stresses and they share them. It's like one singular line.

Sometimes the shared lines seem either too long (too many syllables) or not to flow iambically, but if I follow the thought that the aim is always to have ten or eleven syllables to a line, then I work out what I need to do to make those lines fit this thought, and in some cases it may be that they need to overlap – although obviously there are other possibilities.

> For example:
> ***QUEEN GERTRUDE*** *Have* ***you*** *forgot* ***me?***
> ***HAMLET***
> *No,* ***by*** *the* ***rood,*** *not* ***so*** (line 13)
> ***HAMLET*** *Over the* ***nasty sty***
> ***QUEEN GERTRUDE*** *O,* ***speak*** *to* ***me*** *no* ***more*** (line 92)

The underlined words are the ones that could be spoken together. Another good example is the exchange between Macbeth and Lady Macbeth directly after the murder of Duncan. This is discussed later in this chapter (see pages 124–5).

Pauses

A pause can be indicated when a line that has less than ten syllables is followed by a line of ten syllables. As an actor, this tells me to look for what is happening in that missing beat for which there is no syllable or word. A good example is *The Merchant of Venice* Act 4 Scene 1 lines 251–5

> *PORTIA*
> *It is so. Are there balance here to weigh*
> ***The flesh?***
>
> *JEW*
> ***I have them ready.***
>
> *PORTIA Have by some surgeon, Shylock, on your charge,*
> *To stop his wounds, lest he do bleed to death.*

Even if we regard 'The flesh/I have them ready' as a shared line, it is still a line of only seven syllables; there are three syllables, or beats, missing. As an actor, I have a choice of what I do here, but I know that Portia has to wait until Shylock physically has the scales. The pause gives him time to get the scales and place them.

Another good example of a pause written into the rhythm of the verse is in *Antony and Cleopatra* Act 2 Scene 5 lines 60–7.

> ***Messenger***
> *Madam, he's married to Octavia.*
>
> *CLEOPATRA*
> *The most infectious pestilence upon thee!*
> *[Strikes him down]*
>
> ***Messenger***
> ***Good madam, patience.***
> ***CLEOPATRA***
> ***What say you? Hence,***
> *[Strikes him again]*
>
> *Horrible villain! or I'll spurn thine eyes*
> *Like balls before me; I'll unhair thy head:*

[She hales him up and down]
Thou shalt be whipp'd with wire, and stew'd in brine,
Smarting in lingering pickle.

Messenger
Gracious madam, I that do bring the news made not the match.

If we regard the line 'Good madam, patience./What say you? Hence.' As a shared line, it is still only nine syllables. The rhythm suggests that there is a beat for Cleopatra to strike the messenger. This is most obviously between 'you' and 'hence', but this is a matter of interpretation for each actor.

Headless lines

A nine-syllable line where the syllable missing from the iambic pentameter is at the beginning. As with a pause, the missing syllable leads me to question what is happening in the missing beat – although practically I tend not to pay too much attention to headless lines and am far more interested in pauses and shared lines. A good example of a headless line is Lady Macbeth in *Macbeth* Act 2 Scene 2 lines 1–2.

LADY MACBETH
That which hath made them drunk hath made me bold;
What hath quench'd them hath given me fire. – Hark! – Peace!

If I try to put the middle line (in bold) into the iambic rhythm it is odd, so I have to ask myself how might I make this fit? If I start the line with a trochee, it sounds a little less odd, but still does not seem to quite work for me. But if I try leaving the first syllable out (so that the second syllable 'what' is a stressed syllable) then the line seems to work rhythmically. I then need to ask what Lady Macbeth might do with this beat. For me it is almost like room for an extra breath before going on with the line, although other actors might interpret this differently.

Tetrameter

A line of four metric feet. A tetrameter in Shakespeare can either be iambic or trochaic but is normally trochaic. Tetrameter is used in Shakespeare for non-human characters such as the witches in *Macbeth* or the fairies in *A Midsummer Night's Dream*. Tetrameter is fairly straightforward, as its purpose is to denote or create 'other-worldliness'.

I use all of these tools when I approach a role. They are the foundation to my approach to any character in Shakespeare.

Activities

The activities which follow explore the approaches and ideas discussed by Giles and Yolanda. They provide ways into the iambic pentameter, followed by methods of applying knowledge of this rhythm to an exploration of verse. The iambic pentameter is the default setting for verse and it is important that students assimilate this rhythm. Once the rhythm is felt physically, it can be understood and utilized intellectually. Many of the activities which follow require students to apply knowledge of the regular iambic pentameter to a speech and to make deductions based on regular or irregular verse structures. It is therefore important to ensure that basic knowledge of the iambic pentameter is secure before moving forward. There are several different methods of doing this given below. Try all of them, or choose the method to work with that is most appropriate for your group.

Warm-ups for familiarization with a speech

It is helpful if students are familiar with a speech before they begin to look at verse structure. Many of the activities in Chapter 3: *Core approaches to Creative Shakespeare* would fulfil this aim. Two other options follow:

Whispering the speech

This is a very simple exercise that is an effective way into a soliloquy or long speech. Ideally in a circle, but at desks if necessary, ask the group to whisper softly together the speech. Whispering is very easy and no single voice can be heard, therefore it is a very 'safe' way to approach a soliloquy for less confident students.

What sounds come out of the speech? Are any letters and letter sounds dominant? For example, if this exercise is used with 'Now is the winter of our discontent...' (Richard III *Act 1 Scene 1), 's' comes through clearly, creating a hissing sound. Whatever sounds come to the fore, question students about what this might tell us about the character or situation.*

If you wish, go through the speech or part of the speech again, this time only whispering the vowel sounds. What do these sounds suggest about the speech and/or play? Repeat for the consonants.

Words as weapons

This type of activity has been used across Globe Education's work for many years as it's a great way of encouraging students to focus on language and the effects of words used. This particular version was developed by Bill Buckhurst when working on his 2008 production of *Romeo and Juliet.*

Aim

This is a good exercise for thinking about the effect of language, particularly in moments of conflict. It encourages students to think about individual words and how they work in context.

Practical considerations

This activity requires a space where students can stand facing one another. It works best in a space without chairs but can be easily adapted if necessary for a classroom with desks.

Activity

Ask the students in pairs to label themselves A and B and make two lines down the centre of the room with As on one side and Bs on the other. Ask them to think of their imaginary weapon of choice and, without moving towards their partner, hurl it at them. The pairs should have a battle in this manner back and forth for no more than 1 min. Normally students begin to react physically to the imaginary hits. Pause the action and ask them to think about how they do this and how they would make clear the nature and severity of the hit to an audience.

Students should now think of a sound that goes with their imaginary weapon. As they use the weapon, they should make their sound.

Introduce text at this point – any scene where there is conflict between two characters. Scenes that work well with this exercise are:

- Romeo and Juliet *Act 3 Scene 4 Juliet and Lord Capulet, or Act 3 Scene 1, the brawl*
- Much Ado about Nothing *Act 4 Scene 1, Hero and Claudio*
- Othello *Act 3 Scene 4, Othello and Desdemona*
- Hamlet *Act 3 Scene 4, Hamlet and Gertrude.*

Focus on one character first, normally the character who is most vocal in the conflict. Compile an edit just of their lines and give one line to each student (work down the student lines, giving a line to A then B, so that the lines are given out in the order they appear in the play).

Ask the students to choose the word in their line that they believe to be most hurtful or damaging. Repeat the earlier exercise, but this time the word becomes the weapon. Students should throw this at their partner and create an accompanying gesture that complements their word. Which word, of the pair, was the most effective weapon and why?

The words can now be passed down the entire line. The first A should send his or her word to B. The whole group as well as B should react, according to how damaging they think the word is. Encourage the group to think of different levels for their response – e.g. what would be a level 1 reaction and what a level 5? Repeat this for every line. The whole process should move quite quickly. At the end, discuss which words were the most effective weapons and why? Do they appear in one part of the scene? Does the intensity of the weapons build or are they more disparate?

*Repeat the activity for the other character in the scene. This is often a subtler exercise. Encourage students to think about how a word might be received as hurtful even if this is not the intention of the sender. For example, in Juliet's line 'Not proud you have, but thankful that you have' (*Romeo and Juliet *Act 3 Scene 5, line 146), 'Not proud' or 'thankful' could be quite harmful weapon words. Similarly Desdemona's mention of 'Cassio' in* Othello *(Act 3 Scene 4) is a powerful weapon word to Othello. Encourage students to think about context as well as the word itself. Sometimes the most powerful weapon words are not obviously violent.*

An optional, but useful, conclusion to this exercise is to ask the students to identify the vowels in their word and go down the lines as before, but just with the vowel sounds. Repeat with the consonants. Which are strongest in the words and when do we hear more vowels and consonants? What does this tell us about the characters' attitude to each other? How do the sounds of the language contribute to the atmosphere and drama at this moment in the play?

Warm-ups for familiarization with rhythm: Playing with the beats

To get the most out of the language work in this section students need to engage with rhythms physically as well as intellectually. It helps them if they can move beyond thinking about language in their heads and experience the beats or rhythm of the lines physically in their bodies. In this section the focus moves from the words in the line to the beats in the line. These warm-up activities can help students to make this shift. They are examples only. Most rhythm-based warm-up activities would work well.

Atama, Abacku, Laborenna

This is a call and response clapping activity.

Atama: Clap
Abacku: Clap Clap ClapClap
Laborenna: Clap Clap ClapClap Clap ClapClap Clap ClapClap

Teach the students each word and accompanying rhythm pattern. (It looks more daunting written down than when spoken aloud.) When they are secure with the clapping rhythms, call the words in any order or combination you wish. All students should respond together with the appropriate clapping rhythm. Play around and have fun with this until the students get over any initial awkwardness and get into responding to the rhythm. Encourage movement and playfulness. The students can make up words to fit the rhythm themselves, if they wish. They can also take turns at being the caller.

Think of a Brazilian drumbeat when learning the clapping rhythms. You can make up your own words and add character names from any play. The important thing is that the words work with the given clapping rhythm.

Yolanda Vazquez developed this exercise after working with Clean Break Theatre Company, who used an exercise derived from Indian rhythms for company warm-ups. She invented the words here. The beats do not correspond to the iambic pentameter in any way. The exercise works simply to encourage students to work rhythmically.

1 to 10

Standing in a circle, ask the students to count together from 1 to 10, keeping the same speed. When you are happy the students can do this, move onto the next stage.

Repeat this exercise. This time the students should also clap on the number 1 and the number 10. This can be harder than it might seem. Repeat this exercise several times until the students can do this together.

Ask the students to continue repeating the exercise. Now, however, they should stop counting out loud, but count in their heads. They should continue clapping on 1 and 10. Repeat until they are comfortable doing this together.

Now it is time to introduce movement. Ask the students to continue the exercise, counting in their heads and clapping. This time, however, they should move around the room (in different directions, not in a circle) at the same time. This may take practice. When the students are fairly confident, start to vary the tempo of the counting. As they are walking, call 'fast, slow', etc. The speed of their counting should remain constant and should not reflect the speed at which they are moving.

It is important to keep the rhythm going, whatever the speed or tempo of the movement. When you are ready to end the exercise, ask the students to come back into the circle, still counting and clapping.

This exercise was created by actor and director Kathryn Hunter. It introduces students to working to the rhythm of 10 – the rhythm of the iambic pentameter. It requires them to work together and teaches the difference between rhythm and tempo. In this exercise the rhythm (counting 1–10) always stays the same but the tempo of the rhythm varies throughout: fast, slow, medium, etc.

The exercise is also a useful diagnostic tool with a new group. It requires students to symbiotically reach a group consensus for any given tempo. It can also help students to think about the ways in which people speak and the occasions on which the rhythm and tempo of conversations may work harmoniously or discordantly.

Getting inside verse structure: Mastering the iambic pentameter

Some different methods for learning the iambic rhythm follow. We find it usually most effective to start with the Hakka, then learn some of the other methods for easy and quick use.

Hakka

As the name suggests, this exercise is based on a Hakka. Globe Education Practitioner Michael Gould began using a traditional Hakka as a warm-up activity in his work. Yolanda could see that this worked really well and was a good way of learning rhythms. The rhythm in the Hakka was, however, not the rhythm of the iambic pentameter. She wanted to capture the energy of the Hakka and to make it work as a method of teaching the iambic pentameter physically, so created the version below.

This Hakka has 10 beats. There are six different movements to learn. Each movement (apart from the last) is accompanied by the spoken word Hutta (pronounced 'who ta' rather than 'hut ta'). **Hutta** consists of two syllables. Like the regular iambic pentameter, the first is unstressed, the second is stressed. The stressed syllable is indicated in bold. The first five movements of the sequence represent the rhythm of the iambic pentameter. The sixth word in the sequence is 'Ha' – this enables the breath an actor takes at the end of one line and the beginning of the next.

Stomp with the right foot: Hu **tta**
Stomp with the left foot: Hu **tta**
Hit the right shoulder with the left fist: Hu **tta**
Hit the left shoulder with the right fist: Hu **tta**
Cross hands at the level of the belly and wiggle: Hu **tta**
Stretch both hands out in front: Ha

Teach the students the sequence one movement and at a time. Stomp, stomp, hit, hit, wiggle, Ha. When they are confident with the movements you can ask them to count with the movements: 1, 2, 3, 4, 5, Ha. Do this about four times.

Next introduce Hutta, to be spoken with each movement. Repeat the whole Hakka until the students have the rhythm in their bodies and they feel comfortable.

The students have now mastered a physical representation of the iambic pentameter.

There is often some awkwardness and always some hilarity at the beginning of this exercise. It is worth persisting, as once students have the Hakka rhythm they can use it to look at the structure of an iambic pentameter. We usually do not mention iambic pentameter until the end of the exercise. Some students can find the idea daunting. The Hakka can easily be achieved by all students. Once they have mastered it they have mastered the structure, rhythm and principle of the iambic pentameter and it is usually at this point that we tell them this!

We usually follow the Hakka with a simple explanation of an iambic pentameter. How and when you wish to do this will obviously depend on your students. Core information we usually give at this point is:

- Pentameter describes a rhythm of 5 beats.
- An iamb is 2 syllables: 1 stressed, the other unstressed. Easy examples are words such as un**like**, dis**like**, to**night**, hu**tta**.

- There are 5 beats in a line of Shakespeare's verse and 2 syllables per beat.
- This means that there are 10 syllables per regular line of Shakespeare's verse.
- Irregular lines have 11 beats. This is described as a 'feminine ending'.

The Ha in the Hakka is not part of the iambic pentameter. We explain to students that we have included it because to keep the rhythm going actors need to breathe at the beginning of the line, not in the middle or two-thirds of the way through. If we say Ha at the end of each Hutta sequence, it forces us to then take a breath in before speaking again. Interestingly, breathing in is a reflex (which is prompted by the Ha), while breathing out is not. The breath we are forced to take in is the breath we need before beginning the next line.

FIGURE 11 *Hakka*

Applying the Hakka to lines from a play

Once the students have the rhythm of the Hakka in their bodies and understand the idea of stressed and unstressed syllables, they can start to apply this to the play they are studying. This example uses *Romeo and Juliet.*

> *Romeo and Juliet:* Act 2 Scene 5
> *The clock struck nine when I did send the Nurse.*

In half an hour she promised to return.
Perchance she cannot meet him. That's not so. (1–3)

Any lines will work for this part of the exercise as long as they are regular 10 syllable iambic pentameters. Irregular lines are dealt with later.

Teach the students the first line and ask them to speak it with the movements of the Hakka – basically replacing Hutta with the words. Keep Ha at the end of the sequence. Repeat this for all three lines.

Ask the students to speak all three lines together with the Hakka movements. Repeat this exercise until they feel comfortable with it and you feel that the rhythm is in their bodies – at least four times.

Explain to the students that they are effectively using their bodies and the Hakka as a metronome, to keep the rhythm of the speech.

Now that they have the rhythm physically, they can learn to clap it. This can be very useful when space is limited and is a technique students can use seated at any time.

Clapping the iambic pentameter

Teach the students the following clapping sequence:

Two claps on knees
Two claps
Two clicks
Two claps on knees
Two claps
It can help if they count on each clap. This reinforces the 10-beat rhythm.

Try using the line 'We Stress The Words We Want the World To Hear'. Teach it to the students. Ask them to apply it to the clapping rhythm and repeat until comfortable. This line is a really useful aide memoire.

Next add the lines used earlier. Each clap corresponds with a syllable in the line. Repeat this until the students have the rhythm and feel comfortable. It works well to try this at different speeds. Finish this exercise by asking students to clap the rhythm and the line quickly.

Ask them if the sound of this fast rendition reminds them of anything. Normally someone will say 'horses'. This is a way into the next part of the activity.

Galloping: Finding the heartbeat

This part of the activity can be omitted if you feel it will not work with your students or you do not have the space. However it is worth doing, as it is memorable and helps to reinforce ideas about rhythm.

Ask the students to gallop around the room. This is something that Glynn Macdonald, Globe Associate – Movement does with actors in rehearsal at the Globe. She even makes them name their horses!

Immediately they have finished galloping, ask the students to feel their heartbeat or pulse and clap out the rhythm they hear. Alternatively you can ask them to clap the rhythm of galloping. Either way, the rhythm they are hearing is the rhythm of the iambic pentameter.

Giles Block talks about the iambic pentameter echoing the sound of our heartbeat (see above). He believes that when Shakespeare's characters speak in verse it is 'the sound of sincerity' – their speech is heartfelt. When they speak in prose they are speaking from the head, the brain. This does not mean that verse is not logical or that prose cannot be heartfelt. This theory provides a useful tool for an actor when rehearsing a play. If a character changes from verse to prose in a scene s/he knows to investigate what has happened to bring about the change.

NB: Prose in Shakespeare has long been associated with more lowly characters, while verse has been regarded as the domain of more noble characters. As with all constructed 'norms', this is not necessarily the case. Some characters of a lower social status do speak in prose, but it may be their situation that brings about this speech rather than social position. Shakespeare plays constantly with the way verse and prose are used. *As You Like It* provides a good example. In the court characters speak largely in prose, while in the Forest of Arden shepherds speak in verse.

Creating iambic pentameter

At the beginning of this chapter Giles Block likens Shakespeare's verse structure to the structure of everyday speech. He believes the structure of the iambic pentameter is more similar to our everyday speech than we realize.

Before the session, ask students to take five minutes in which they record the speech of those around them. This can be done by recording a conversation, or by taking notes (if written verbatim). The conversation can take place in any setting. It is important that the people they are listening to are not aware that their speech is being observed or recorded. This is a good homework activity. Obviously care needs to be taken to observe with sensitivity! Any unscripted conversation on television can provide a good alternative. Any recorded conversations (or a short section of them) should be transcribed verbatim.

Explain that we believe that iambic pentameter became a popular form of writing because it mirrors the way English is spoken in everyday life.

Ask students to share their observed speech. Are there any examples of iambic pentameter within the speech? Generally there are usually several 'perfect' examples ('I'll put the kettle on and make some tea' is common), with lots of other phrases of around that length. Discuss at this point also Giles's idea that the length of the iambic pentameter might be the amount we can typically say before taking a breath. Does there seem to be evidence for this theory in the group's own observations?

In pairs, the students are now going to experiment with creating their own lines of iambic pentameter. They should come up with suggested lines and test to see if they are iambic pentameters, either using the Hakka or clapping rhythm to do so.

It can be helpful to experiment creating some lines together before beginning the pairwork. Examples of iambic pentameters could be 'Oh would you like to have a cup of tea', or 'I like to sing and dance all night and day', or 'My birthday is the twentieth of March'.

When the students have created some of their own iambic pentameters, come back as a group to share them. Reassure students if their lines do not quite fit the iambic pentameter and, as a group, try to find ways for them to work.

Trochee

This can be a good point to introduce trochee. A trochee is the opposite of an iamb: a stressed syllable followed by an unstressed syllable. When making up their own iambic pentameter it is likely that at least one of the group will create a line with a trochee. It's a good opportunity to be able to tell the students that, while the line is not an iambic pentameter, Shakespeare used this verse form as well.

Encourage the group to work out why it is not an iambic pentameter by applying the Hakka or clapping rhythm to the line.

An example might be 'the sausages are good from the butcher'. This line has iambs until the word *butcher*, which is a trochee. In speech we say **butch**er, not butch**er**.

Shakespeare uses trochees a lot. When this happens, when anything breaks the regular rhythm of the iambic pentameter, we have to ask ourselves why?

ShaBoom / BoomSha

This is a quick and useful method of identifying iambs and trochees in a line of verse.

Sha**Boom** – represents the iambic, regular rhythm. An unstressed syllable, followed by a stressed syllable. 'Love **looks** not **with** the **eyes,** but **with** the **mind**' (Helena, *A Midsummer Night's Dream* Act 1 Scene 1 line 234)

BoomSha – represents a trochee, an irregular rhythm. A stressed syllable followed by an unstressed syllable. '**Ne**ver, **ne**ver, **ne**ver, **ne**ver, **ne**ver' (King Lear, *King Lear* Act 5 Scene 3 line 307)

Teach the students each word and provide them with examples of each. Go through some lines together, checking to see if each group of two syllables is a ShaBoom or a BoomSha. This will tell the students whether it is an iamb or a trochee.

Tips

Adam: I find galloping works well as it helps students to connect with the rhythm. Thinking of iambic pentameter as the rhythm of the heartbeat can really help students to connect and gives them an easy reference point for thinking about iambic pentameter.

Chris: It is really important that students are clear about the rhythm of the iambic pentameter before they go on to do anything else. It is important that they feel the rhythm of the language in their bodies; once they have done this they are more likely to have ownership of it and have something they can refer to every time they look at a line of verse.

Patricia: Of this sequence, galloping is my favourite approach. I ask students to gallop for quite a while, until they are 'puffed out'. Then it is so easy for them to feel their heartbeat and the rhythm of the iambic pentameter becomes tangible. They can then start to tap out the rhythm on the floor or a table. This provides a clear route into the *Cardiogram* work.

Yolanda: Remind students to breathe while doing the *Whispering* activity. Often the intensity of speaking like this can make them tend to go on without taking the breath they would naturally take in everyday speech. After galloping around the room I like to ask students to vocalize the rhythm they hear in their heartbeat. They discover for themselves that this is the rhythm of the iambic pentameter.

Using knowledge of the iambic pentameter diagnostically

We can use our knowledge of the verse structure to look at the verse diagnostically.

When looking at each line students should ask:

Is the line a regular iambic pentameter?
If it is not, how does it vary?
What might this variation tell us about the character or specific moment in the play?

It's useful to think of the iambic pentameter as Shakespeare's default setting for verse. If a speech is all in iambic pentameter, we need to think about why this should be so. Equally, if the default setting is changed, we need to think about why this should be the case. This is a diagnostic process. When we have made a diagnosis we then need to think imaginatively, as actors do, looking at what is happening in the play and what the verse structure might tell us about that given moment.

Little is known for certain about early modern rehearsal practice but it is likely that there were not a great many rehearsals and that the role of director did not exist in the form we know it today. In this context, the verse structure could be viewed as an instruction manual. Shakespeare used it to provide actors with the information they needed to play their role.

For actors, a change in the verse structure can be like an alarm going off. It can tell them that something significant is happening, about a character's state of mind or simply how Shakespeare wants them to speak the verse. How an actor speaks the verse can change how it is received by the audience and consequently our understanding of any given moment in a play.

Applying knowledge of verse structure

The following activities provide some practical methods for applying knowledge of verse structure to a speech or scene and capturing findings.

Cardiogram

This exercise was created by Patricia Kerrigan. She wanted to find a way to make looking at verse structure manageable and tangible for students. It's a really useful tool for looking at a speech. Students test the verse structure and plot their findings on a chart. By the end of the exercise students have a graph resembling a heart trace print-out for the speech. They can then use the cardiogram to look at plot and character development throughout the speech.

Aims

To help students to look at the structure of a speech line by line and to plot how verse structure varies throughout a speech. By the end of the exercise students should be able to trace character development through a speech purely by looking at the structure of the verse.

Practical considerations

This exercise can be done at a desk. Students can make cardiograms individually, but it works best – especially for the first time – if they work in pairs or small groups. This takes the pressure off 'getting the rhythm right' and much learning can take place when students discuss the lines together.

A cardiogram is simply three horizontal lines, with spaces between them, drawn one below the other across a page. The top line should be labelled with a + and the bottom line with a –. See the example below:

+ ______________________________

____

– ______________________________

Activity

Give the students a speech or section of a speech. If you wish, you can share a long speech around the whole group, giving each small group a section of lines. It is advisable not to cut the text for this activity as students need to look at the varying verse structure of each line.

Ask the students to look at each line. If the line is regular and has 10 syllables they should make a dot on the middle line. If the line has more than 10 syllables they should make a dot on the + line. If the line has less than 10 syllables they should make a dot on the – line. The students should use the Hakka or clapping rhythm to help them do this. When they have made a dot for every line in the speech they should join them up – like a graph.

Students should look at what is happening on the finished cardiogram in order to make a structural diagnosis. Is the cardiogram constant or do the lines go up and down a lot? What is the character saying or what is happening on each line? Is there a pattern of any kind? Where are the most marked changes or constants? Why might this be the case?

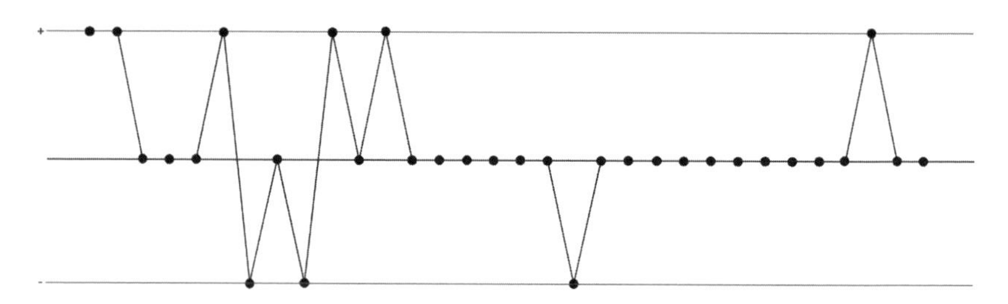

FIGURE 12 *Cardiogram*

Students should focus on the lines that deviate from the iambic pentameter. They should go back to the text to see what is happening at those moments and question what the change in rhythm might tell us about the character at that moment in the play.

Each group should discuss their findings and make a case for their particular interpretation of the verse structure and its implications for our understanding of the speech or scene.

The cardiogram above is Macbeth's 'Is this a dagger, which I see before me' soliloquy in Act 2 Scene 1 (lines 33–64) of Macbeth. *If we look at the lines with more or less than 10 syllables, we can see that they are all lines that refer to something unsettling for Macbeth. The most notable shift in the speech comes with the lines:*

> I see thee yet, in form as palpable **10**
> As this which now I draw. **6**
> Thou marshall'st me the way that I was going; **11**

The beats of the iambic pentameter need to be counted for every line, whether there are words for them or not. In the line 'As this which now I draw' we have 4 beats not covered by words. In this instance, an actor needs to ask himself what is happening in these 4 beats? What has Shakespeare left them for? There are various possibilities. It could be that the 4 beats give the actor time to speak, then draw his dagger, or that they provide time for the actor to take in the audience and see the dagger moving, which he then refers to in the following line, 'Thou marshall'st me the way that I was going'. Alternatively the beats could give time for the actor to recognize that he is going to go through with the murder of Duncan. There is no right answer; it is up to each individual actor to decide and interpret this line. But the verse structure does tell us that the moment is significant and indicates that this line is pivotal to the speech.

First and last stressed syllables

This activity can build on work in the cardiogram or can stand alone. This works for any speech and any character. If you wish, you can divide a long speech between different groups, as with the cardiogram activity.

Either individually or in small groups, ask students to work their way through a speech. They should identify the first and last stressed syllable of every line and compile these in a chronological list.

When the list is complete, look at the words that have been identified. What do they tell us about the character or action of the play at that moment in time? Is there a progression in type of words chosen, a pattern? Or do they change at a particular point?

Usually the words listed provide a fairly accurate picture of character and action. Thus, through the verse structure, Shakespeare is telling us what is important in this speech. If desired, these lists and the cardiogram can be used as a starting point for a written analysis of this speech. Cardiograms can also be a useful tool for comparison of characters in the same or different play at key moments or of the structure of a scene.

Metric feet: Walk the line

This exercise provides another way of looking diagnostically at verse structure and provides a similar result to the *Cardiogram*. It was devised by Colin Hurley, who wanted to find a physical method for students to explore Shakespeare's use of the iambic pentameter.

For the purposes of this exercise, students should know that a metric foot has two syllables with a beat, i.e. the first two syllables of the line with the second syllable marked verbally to provide the beat. A standard iambic pentameter is five metric feet. The exercise is really walking these feet, so do not worry if not all students are confident with this idea at the beginning of the exercise.

The whole group are now going to walk some lines from Shakespeare. On each unstressed syllable of the line they should raise their foot up; on each stressed syllable they should put their foot down (the complete action is like taking a step).

Start the exercise with a regular line, e.g. 'The clock struck nine when I did send the nurse' Romeo and Juliet *Act 2 Scene 5 line 1*

U D U D U D U D U D
U = foot up, D = foot down.

This produces a complete (if exaggerated) walking action. Next try the line:

'To be or not to be, that is the point'
U D U D U D U D U D

Again this produces a complete walk. Ask the students how this feels – they will normally offer words like 'good' and 'confident'. Someone is also likely to point out that this is not the correct line from Hamlet, *it is changed at the end.*

Give the group the correct line:

'To be or not to be, that is the question' Hamlet *Act 3 Scene 1 line 55*
U D U D U D U D U D U

The students should end this line with a foot raised, as it is an irregular eleven-syllable line. They will be balancing. Ask them how this feels and they usually offer words such as 'unsure', 'up in the air'. The irregular line indicates an uncertain or unusual situation, something that is unsettling for the character.

Other good examples are Macbeth's 'Is this a dagger, which I see before me', (Act 2 Scene 1), indicating his unsettled state of mind, his shock at the state of a phantom dagger, etc.; or Beatrice's 'So Benedick love on I will requite thee' (*Much Ado about Nothing* Act 3 Scene 2), suggesting her surprise or recognition of the fact she does love Benedick.

As with the *Cardiogram* exercise, you can apply this approach to any speech you are studying. Students should walk through it line by line recording whether their foot ends on the ground or up in the air at the end of the line. This works well in pairs, with one student walking and the other recording. At the end of the speech they should look at which lines were irregular and make the suggestions about why this might be the case and what this tells us about the character at that moment. By end of the process they should be able to write an analysis about what is revealed by the verse structure about the speech or scene.

As with the *Cardiogram* exercise, you can compare speeches from different characters in comparable situations, such as Macbeth and Othello before they murder Duncan and Desdemona.

A

Shared lines and pauses

Before beginning this kind of work, students should be familiar with the scene chosen for the exercise and understand the objectives of each character. We would usually cover *Pointing on the Pronoun* (pages 57–63) and *Tactics* (pages 47–57) exercises before progressing to explore the verse structure of a scene.

Identifying shared lines

This simple exercise is a useful way of identifying shared lines. It requires students to work in pairs, or for one pair to do the exercise while the rest of the group watch and advise.

Take ten pieces of paper and lay them out, an easy stride apart, across the room. Newspaper works well for this as two students can easily stand on the same piece of paper if required. This activity can be carried out using chairs to sit on, instead of paper to stand on, if preferred.

Each character in the scene should go to one end of the paper, so they are standing looking across the paper to their partner on the opposite side of the room.

Each piece of paper represents a syllable in the line. Each time their character speaks the student should move forward, stepping on one piece of paper for each syllable, like stepping stones.

If we look at the exchange between Puck and Oberon in *A Midsummer Night's Dream* Act 2 Scene 1:

> Puck: Ay, there it is.
> Oberon: I pray thee give it me. (line 248)

It is clear this is a shared line. The students playing Puck and Oberon will end the activity facing each other on their piece of paper in the middle of the room.

This activity can be applied to any line of text. It is also a good way of identifying eleven or more syllable lines in any speech and can help identify instances where characters might overlap within a speech.

An interesting scene to explore with this activity is *Hamlet* Act 3 Scene 1 lines 91–115, in which Ophelia and Hamlet move from fairly regular verse, to shared lines, to Hamlet starting to speak in prose while Ophelia continues in verse. Clearly this provides a focus through which to examine what is happening to their relationship in these moments.

Similarly *Othello* Act 3 Scene 4 lines 52–100, in which Othello asks Desdemona for the handkerchief he gave her, is a good scene to explore in this manner.

A

Applying knowledge of shared lines and identifying pauses

This example uses *Macbeth* Act 2 Scene 2 lines 14–30. In pairs ask the students to read through the scene. They should look at each line and see whether or not it is a regular iambic pentameter. Each pair should report back their findings to the whole group. NB: at this point, once the group have mastered the rhythm of the iambic pentameter, the easiest way to count the beats might be on fingers (usefully there are 10!). This is what many experienced actors do in rehearsals. However if it is more helpful to continue to clap or use the Hakka movements, students should do so.

In this example students will usually notice straight away that some lines between Lady Macbeth and Macbeth are shared, in other words each character has part of the 10 beats, and that if both their lines are put together they make an iambic pentameter. Having discussed initial findings, students should go through the scene again, identifying which lines are shared. They should remember these general principles:

- The iambic pentameter is Shakespeare's default setting for verse. We should assume he wants to keep it going, either as whole lines or shared lines. If he breaks the rhythm he has a purpose for doing so.
- Not all short lines are going to be shared lines. The maths has to work for 2 lines to be shared. If there is a 10-syllable line followed by a 3-syllable line followed by a 9-syllable line, these lines are not shared. Something else is happening in the missing syllables. This might be a pause.
- Shakespeare writes time for pauses and stage business into the lines. In this way he not only tells the actors how to play a moment but creates his desired atmosphere from within the verse structure.

It may be helpful at this point for students to annotate what they think is a shared line or what might be a pause, or other piece of action. Groups should then come back together and compare findings and ideas. The whole group can debate key lines and the purpose of the verse structure for those lines. See annotated example below.

MACBETH I have done the deed. Didst thou not hear a noise? **11**
LADY MACBETH I heard the owl scream and the crickets cry. **10**
Did not you speak? **4 – shared line 1**
MACBETH When? **1 – shared line 1**

LADY MACBETH
Now. **1 – shared line 1**
MACBETH As I descended? **4/5**
LADY MACBETH Ay. **1**
MACBETH Hark! **1**
Who lies i' the second chamber? **7/8 (depending on how the 'i' is read) – shared line 2**
LADY MACBETH Donalbain. **3 – shared line 2**
MACBETH This is a sorry sight. **6 (There are 4 syllables missing – beats for Macbeth to look at his hands? At the beginning or the end of the line?)**
[Looking on his hand]s
LADY MACBETH A foolish thought, to say a sorry sight. **10**
MACBETH There's one did laugh in's sleep, and one cried **10**
'Murder!' **1**
That they did wake each other: I stood and heard them: **12**
But they did say their prayers, and address'd them **10**
Again to sleep. **4 – shared line 3**
LADY MACBETH There are two lodged together. **7 – shared line 3**
MACBETH One cried 'God bless us!' and 'Amen' the other; **11**
As they had seen me with these hangman's hands. **10**
Listening their fear, I could not say 'Amen,' **10/11**
When they did say 'God bless us!' 7
LADY MACBETH Consider it not so deeply. **8**

This is one possible annotation of this speech only, there are different possibilities. Groups should compare their annotations and ideas. The rhythms here direct the actor. S/he can use them to consider how to play the scene. Using this approach, each pair should attempt a performance, speaking as directed by their annotated version, keeping the beat together of their shared lines, and pausing where lines do not have 10 syllables.What does this do to our performance and understanding of the scene?

Argue syllable counts – some may be subjective, i.e. Macbeth's line 'As I descended' is a 5-syllable line but could be said as a 4. The latter keeps the iambic pentameter. Is this an instruction to the actor about how to speak the line? If 'descended' is condensed it definitely adds to the sense of urgency in the scene. The final two lines of this extract both have less than 10 syllables but are not shared lines. What should an actor do with the extra beats? Lady Macbeth tells Macbeth to 'Consider it not so deeply' but might this 8-beat line suggest that she is spending 2 beats possibly doing just that? Or is she speaking over Macbeth, interrupting him? It is these kinds of questions that we hope students will explore through this exercise, using their knowledge of the verse structure to make a forensic examination of the text.

Tips

Adam: I personally find it hard to use the cardiogram. But I love watching colleagues, it works well for them! I'm more likely to use *Metric Feet: Walk the Line,* I like more physical activities.

Bill: I'm a big fan of the cardiogram. It can make verse seem less intimidating. It's a great way to start thinking about the way the beat of the iambic pentameter runs through the plays. When I talk about verse I refer frequently to the idea of 'riffing'. It is as if Shakespeare is writing a piece of jazz with the rhythm of a heartbeat running through it. The beat changes, it goes up and down and then it comes back to the original tune. Just as the rhythms can change in this way in a speech, so can the images and ideas, 'riffing' around a particular issue or concern for the character at that moment. Often the changes in images relate to changes in rhythm and it is good to look at a speech to see if, how or when this happens. The rhythm of verse is nothing to be afraid of, it's just there, giving structure to the piece. You can see this tangibly with the cardiogram.

Chris: I like to make a human cardiogram. Exactly the same as the paper version but using students to physically represent each dot on the cardiogram, standing on the relevant place on one of three lines. If you wish, wool can be stretched from student to student so that it is possible to look physically at how the dots join up. It works well to ask students to read their line (in order). This forms a really good basis for discussion, as it is immediately apparent which lines deviate from the iambic rhythm and it is easy to analyse instantly why this should be the case.

Colin: I'm interested most of all in where the rhythm changes in verse. In life we usually try not to cry, not to lose our temper etc. I believe that when characters are speaking verse they are trying not to lose their rhythm. When the regular rhythm of the iambic breaks, Shakespeare is directing the actor to the significance of that moment. The actor then needs to decide why that break has occurred.

Patricia: The most important part of the *Cardiogram* activity for me is deciding why syllables are added or missing. This takes students into debate about choice and interpretation. It makes verse structure tangible. It is a powerful form of story telling.

Yolanda: It can take a bit of practice with the *Metric Feet: Walking the line* activity to get students to end an 11-syllable line with a foot in the air. It is simply human nature to put your foot down, so it is worth doing a few trial runs.

Focus on language features

By utilizing some of the approaches outlined above, students will have a understanding of verse structure and some tools and a methodology through which to interrogate it. The remaining activities in this chapter focus on particular aspects of language – on the way it is punctuated, the use of sound and on the words themselves. They can be used in conjunction with the activities focusing on verse structure above, on their own, or with a combination of most of the activities in Chapter 3: *Core approaches to Creative Shakespeare*

Walking the punctuation

Aims

This exercise was devised by RSC director of voice, Cecily Berry. Globe Education use it as a method of furthering students' exploration of line structure. It gives them another way of looking at what is happening in a scene or at a character's journey within a speech or scene.

Practical considerations

Shakespeare's plays were not published until after his death. The punctuation we see in a play text today is mostly the work of the editor of the play. The punctuation of Shakespeare plays will vary from edition to edition. It is important that students understand the subjective nature of punctuation when doing this exercise. *Walking the Punctuation* is still an incredibly useful activity as it provides a physical way of looking at a speech and thinking about change and focus within a speech or scene.

This activity needs to be carried out in a space in which students can move around and frequently change direction without hitting one another.

Activity

Give the students a speech, or part of a speech or scene. Ask them to walk around the room reading it. Each time they get to a piece of punctuation they should change direction.

Discuss findings. Did the students change direction often or infrequently? What might this indicate about the character or scene?

Repeat the exercise but this time only changing direction on the full stops. It can be useful to think of the full stops as indicating a character's thoughts.

Afterwards discuss. What do we find out from this exercise? What does it tell us about the character at this moment in the play?

Finally, give the students a copy of the speech with all of the punctuation removed apart from the full stops. Ask them to become editors of the play and to put in the punctuation they feel is most appropriate for the speech. They should remember that in doing so, they are potentially providing an actor with their version of a character at that moment. Students can try walking the punctuation of their version of the speech as they are creating it, or when the process is complete.

If appropriate, students can create a written commentary to accompany their punctuated script, explaining why they have chosen to punctuate in a particular manner at a particular moment. If desired, this could be presented as instructions to the actor or an explanation to the general editor of a Shakespeare edition.

A

Heckling

Often when we are teaching Shakespeare's plays to younger students we might tell them they do not need to understand every word in the line to understand what is happening at that moment. This is true. It is a useful approach. However as students get older, particularly when they are studying Shakespeare post-16, this is no longer necessarily the case. This exercise is a method of ensuring that students engage with every single word in a line and understand it. All the words are important to an in-depth understanding of a speech or scene; none can be ignored or dismissed as unnecessary.

Aims

To encourage students to really examine what each character is saying. To identify difficult or challenging words in a speech. To ensure complete understanding of a speech.

Practical considerations

This exercise works for any moment in any play and can be done easily at a desk or in a bigger space. This example uses small groups of c 4 but it can equally be done with the whole group divided into two or with pairs. The students will require some means of looking up words they identify as complex or do not understand. This would work with a dictionary. David Crystal and Ben Crystal's *Shakespeare's Word: A Glossary and Language Companion* (Penguin 2004) is a useful reference book at for this activity.

Activity

Each group should assign characters. Each person playing a character should have a heckling partner, e.g. if the scene has three characters the exercise works best with a group of six, although group members can double up if necessary. Ask each group to begin to read the speech or scene. If a heckling partner hears their character say a word or phrase they do not understand they should heckle, by repeating the word. The character should then read the line from the beginning trying to make the meaning of the word clear from their reading. If they succeed, their heckling partner should say nothing. If the word is still not clear they should heckle again. If after a few heckles the word is still unclear, it should be noted. The character should then move on with the speech.

At the end of the speech or scene, each group should make a list of the words that were repeated. They should discuss which of those words they feel they do have a collective understanding of and which they do not understand or feel unsure about. What were the words that were repeatedly 'heckled'?

The group should then come back together as a whole and each small group should share their list of words and key areas of their small group discussion, compare lists and discuss meaning. At this stage, if there are words that are unknown or about which there is uncertainty and debate, look them up. By the end of this process the whole group should have a clear understanding of every word in the speech or scene.

Back in their small groups, the students should now repeat their reading of the scene. Each character's partner should still repeat or heckle the character with the words they do not understand, but hopefully by this stage in the activity most words should be understood. Each small group should discuss what they have found out about the character or scene from focusing on the words. Why is particular language chosen for a particular moment? Which do they feel are the most effective words in the speech or scene and why? Feed each small group discussion back to the whole group.

A

Thematic heckling

This exercise is a variation on the above activity that focuses on identifying the thematic nature of words and imagery. It helps students to highlight different types of language and how it is used in a speech or scene. This example uses Othello's speech at the beginning of Act 5 Scene 2. However, this exercise is useful for any key speech or scene.

Identify the key types of thematic language in the speech or scene and compile a list. This can be done prior to the session by the teacher, or by the group if more appropriate. A list for Othello's speech below might read: nature, light, blood, death, the cosmos.

T
Othello: Act 5 Scene 2

OTHELLO
It is the cause, it is the cause, my soul!
Let me not name it to you, you chaste stars,
It is the cause. Yet I'll not shed her blood;
Nor scar that whiter skin of hers than snow,
And smooth as monumental alabaster.
Yet she must die, else she'll betray more men.
Put out the light, and then put out the light:
If I quench thee, thou flaming minister,
I can again thy former light restore,
Should I repent me. But once put out thy light,
Thou cunning'st pattern of excelling nature,
I know not where is that Promethean heat
That can thy light relume: when I have pluck'd the rose,
I cannot give it vital growth again. It must needs wither:
I'll smell it on the tree.
[Kissing her]

Ah balmy breath, that dost almost persuade
Justice to break her sword! Once more, once more:
Be thus when thou art dead and I will kill thee,
And love thee after. Once more, and that's the last.
So sweet was ne'er so fatal. I must weep,
But they are cruel tears. This sorrow's heavenly;
It strikes where it doth love. She wakes (lines 1–22)

Divide the group into small groups, one for each category on the list. Give each group a category. Ask a student/s to read the speech. Each time a group hears a word that falls into their category, they should heckle and echo it back.

As a whole group, discuss findings. Did each group heckle separately or were there places in the speech where several groups were heckling at one time? Which groups were these? Why does this imagery come together? Do some words or phrases fall into more than one category? What does the use of different types of language tell us about what is key to the scene and the character's state of mind at that moment?

Vowels and consonants

Aim

This activity focuses on what we can learn from the sounds of the words Shakespeare has chosen.

Practical considerations

Vowels and Consonants can be used as a stand-alone activity or can follow on from *Heckling* or many of the activities in Chapter 3: *Core approaches to Creative Shakespeare*. It is useful to begin this exercise with a vowel and constant warm-up (repeating different vowel sounds together as a group), although this is not essential to the activity.

Activity

In pairs, ask the students to have an argument with their partner only using vowel sounds. They should then repeat this exercise only using constants. What was the difference? When were vowels most effective and when constants?

Repeat the exercise, but this time the partners should try to woo one another with the vowels and consonants.

Both vowels and consonants are important in both scenarios, but perform different functions and might predominate in a scene according to the situation and intent of the characters.

In pairs, students should now work through a speech or scene only making the vowel sounds in the words. They should run the vowels together so it sounds as if they are speaking a foreign language. What do they hear? If they heard only the vowel sounds alone, what would they think about the characters? What dramatic situation would they imagine the character to be in? Repeat this exercise for the consonants.

As a whole group, discuss how both vowels and consonants featured in the scene. What does this tell us?

Sometimes the results from this activity and Heckling can be surprising. For example, if we looked at the first scene between Theseus and Hippolyta in A Midsummer Night's Dream *Act 1 Scene 1 and maybe tried some* Tactics *activities we might conclude that, because of their history (as enemies at war) and what they say to each other, Theseus and Hippolyta do not want to be together. However, if we look at the thematic imagery of their speeches and at their use of vowels and consonants, we see images of desire, love and marriage and sounds where long vowels, 'oohs' and 'aahs' predominate. Their language suggests that, whatever their history, these characters are attracted to one another.*

A

Caesura

Aim

This is a simple exercise for identifying if or where caesura occurs in a line.

Practical considerations

The exercise works for any speech, but initially it is advisable to pick a speech where caesura is quite strong. The Prologue, Act 1 Scene 1 of *Romeo and Juliet* is a good and easy example to use for the first stage of the exercise. Ideally the group will need room to stand in pairs with space around them, although there is an option to work this activity at a desk – see below. The punctuation should be removed from the speech for this exercise.

Activity

Ask the group to read the speech, one line per person, around the circle or the room. Repeat this exercise, but instead of reading one line per person students should read to where they think the natural break in the line occurs, the caesura, then pass to the next person. Stress that some lines will not have a break, others may have two.

Discuss where the breaks came in the reading. Do all the group agree with the choices made? Are there other possibilities for breaking the lines? If appropriate, try different readings of the speech.

Take a speech from the part of the play the group is currently studying. It is helpful to put the speech on the whiteboard for this part of the activity. Students should stand opposite each other, holding hands, and lean back, so that they are balancing one another. Students should practice a seesaw-type action.

Starting on a neutral position, one of the pair should start reading the speech. When their partner feels there is a break in the line s/he should pull their partner towards them while speaking the line. This seesaw action should be repeated by both partners as they read through the speech, pulling their partner towards them when they feel there is a break in the line and that the reader should change. This activity can also be carried out at a desk with arms in an arm wrestling-type action, back and forth.

As a group, discuss where the breaks came in this exercise. What was the effect of the caesura on the part of the line which followed? What does the placing of caesura in the speech and/or line tell us about the speech, character or situation? In what way does the use of caesura contribute to the atmosphere of the scene?

The exercise also works well as a method of breaking down and exploring complex sections of prose. Dromio's speech in Act 2 Scene 1 of The Comedy of Errors *is a good starting example, if using the exercise for this purpose.*

A

Finding the rhythm in prose

Aim

This activity uses principles explored above in *Walking the Punctuation* and *Vowels and Consonants*. It provides a way into large sections of prose that seem very dense and difficult to break down.

Practical considerations

This activity works with any piece of prose. Hortensio's speech in Act 1 Scene 1 of *The Taming of the Shrew* is used in the example below. It can easily be carried out sitting at desks.

Activity

T

HORTENSIO
Faith, as you say, there's small choice in rotten apples. But come; since this bar in law makes us friends, it shall be so far forth friendly maintained til by helping Baptista's eldest daughter to a husband we set his youngest free for a husband and then have to't a fresh. Sweet Bianca! Happy man be his dole! He that runs fastest gets the ring. How say you, Signior Gremio?

Ask the group to read through the speech, aloud but individually. Each time they get to a punctuation mark, students should tap their desk. This process begins to convey a sense of the rhythm of the speech. Tapping on the desk is a bit like a drum beat.

The group should read the speech again, tapping on the desk as before. This time, however, they should also try to emphasize the vowels and the constants as well.

For the next part of the activity, students should work in pairs A and B. A should read a section of the speech again to B. S/he should incorporate the rhythm and sounds s/he discovered from the first two readings. B should then turn A's reading into gibberish, keeping the rhythm and sounds and sense s/he heard in A's reading.

A should read the piece again, taking the sense and musicality B gave in his/her gibberish reading and incorporating it into the reading.

Through this process the group will begin to get a sense of the rhythm of the character's speech.

Repeat the reading. However this time A should speak the section of speech as musically as s/he can. B should dance the speech, reflecting the musicality of A's speaking. This can be danced with hands only, if students prefer.

Discuss what these readings might tell us about the character and his or her emotional state at that moment. Looking at prose in this way can provide insights into character and situation. As with verse, if these rhythms change, actors ask themselves why. The rhythm in which a character speaks can tell about the situation they are in and their emotional state at that moment.

It can be useful to compare two different characters in this way. If the section of prose taken from the Nurse in Act 2 Scene 4 of Romeo and Juliet *is compared with Hortensio, we can clearly see differences between the two characters, simply by looking at the rhythm of their prose:*

T

Nurse

Now, afore God, I am so vexed, that every part about me quivers. Scurvy knave! Pray you, sir, a word; and, as I told you, my young lady bid me enquire you out. What she bid me say, I will keep to myself. But first let me tell ye, if ye should lead her into a fool's paradise,as they say, it were a very gross kind of behaviour, as they say, for the gentlewoman is young and therefore, if you should deal double with her, truly it were a nill thing to be offered to any gentlewoman, and very weak dealing. (155–64)

Tips

Bill: Any activity that makes the participant work harder when they say the words is useful. Asking students to hit the paper on words that strike them as important, or that should be stressed, is a good example. It can make words that we might not hear when reading the speech normally jump out at you. It can also help to reveal the rhythm of a speech.

Colin: I like to do the *Whispering* activity and the *Vowels and Consonants* together.

Patricia: *Vowels and Consonants* is a favourite activity. Giles Block introduced me to it when I was playing Goneril in *King Lear* at the Globe. I spent the first part of the play largely unhappy, spitting consonants in my speeches. When I fell in love with Edmund my language changed and vowel sounds predominated. It was a revelation I wanted to share with students. This activity can reveal a character's emotional state at any given point in a play.

Yolanda: When working on *Vowels and Consonants* make sure the vowel sounds flow into each other and are not separated in a robot-like way.

CHAPTER FIVE

Actor, stage and audience

In this chapter we focus on how the work and interpretations of the actor interface with and serve playing space and audience. This work is often shaped by what is known of early modern theatre practice. Knowledge of this practice can inform work in the rehearsal room and classroom and can provide students with a framework from which to develop ideas for contemporary interpretations of Shakespeare's plays.

The activities in this chapter all focus on the interaction between actor, stage and audience. They draw on and explore many of the ideas and issues discussed in Chapter 2: *Context: Learning from the Globe*. It is important for students to be aware of these before focusing on the activities in this chapter. While some of the activities stand alone, many of them require combination with activities in Chapter 3: *Core approaches to Creative Shakespeare*. The work explored in this chapter often forms the last part of a workshop structure. It needs foundations on which to rest. This mirrors the rehearsal process in which performance is the last stop in a company's exploration of a play.

Early modern theatre practice

The following notes provide useful background materials for students exploring the activities in this chapter. This knowledge is not essential, but provides a context for the activities. The activity *Cue Scripts* relies on this knowledge of early modern theatre practice.

Rehearsal

We know surprisingly little about early modern rehearsal practices. There is very little solid evidence. Early Modern scholars have been able to make some deductions, however, based on evidence of the working practice of theatre companies. We do know that some form of rehearsal took place, due to a contract found among Philip Henslowe's (founder of the Rose Theatre) papers. These committed actor Robert Dawes to 'attend all such rehearsal which shall the night before the rehearsal be given publicly out'. This paper also established the penalties for lateness, drunkenness at rehearsal and removing costumes from the playhouse.[1] The document, dated 7th April 1614, confirms with certainty that there was some form of rehearsal process, but it provides no information about what exactly those rehearsals entailed. In his book *Renaissance drama in action: An introduction to aspects of theatre practice and performance*, Martin White suggests that the insistence on punctuality and curb on drinking during rehearsals shows that 'such unprofessional behaviour would not be tolerated – there was too little time'.[2] Henslowe also indicates that rehearsal periods were generally short – probably closer to days rather than the weeks (at the Globe generally five weeks) that actors have to rehearse today. Martin White considers it is fair to assume that companies were required 'to work rapidly and in a disciplined way'.[3]

Early modern actors worked in a high-pressure time-focused environment, where in order to attract crowds and collect revenue, they had to provide both variety and originality to their audiences. This was achieved by presenting numerous different plays (no play was performed on successive days before the 1630s) and acquiring new plays.[4] Martin White provides an example of the sort of schedule that players worked with:

> At the Rose in April 1597, the Admiral's Men performed on twenty-five days of the month, during which time they presented thirteen different plays of which certainly three, and possibly four, were new, and another was a revival of a play they had not performed for two years.[5]

Any rehearsal process which facilitated this volume of material must have been efficient and impressive. It also could not have been protracted or focused for any length of time on a single play.

It has been suggested that 95 per cent of Shakespeare's lines are spoken by the fourteen principal actors of a company ('principal' being defined as any man or boy who had more than ten lines). This meant that the principals could work together first, with the supporting actors entering the rehearsal process towards the end. A leading actor like Edward Alleyn would have learned perhaps ten new roles in each season, while keeping perhaps twenty old ones fresh in his memory. A supporting actor playing a number of parts in each play 'might need to have as many as a hundred parts committed to memory'.[6]

The role of the director

There is no record of the role of the director, as we understand it today, in early modern theatre practice, and little clear information about what may have taken place. The first record of a director in the contemporary sense is Georg II, Duke of Saxe-Meiningen (1866–1914), over 200 years after Shakespeare was writing and performing his plays.

A number of references, however, throughout the early modern period point to an individual adopting a function which seems close to directing. Two months before his death in 1566, Richard Edwards was referred to as being in Oxford preparing a lavish production of his (lost) play, *Palamon and Arcite*. Playwright and publisher Francis Kirkman praised actor and theatre manager William Beeston as 'the happiest interpreter and judge of our English stage-plays', whose 'instruction, judgement and fancy' had befitted the 'poets and actors of these times'.[7] Johannes Rheanus, who translated *Lingua* by Thomas Tomkins into German, wrote in the preface to this work in 1613:

> So far as actors are concerned they, as I noticed in England, are daily instructed, as it were in school, so that even the most eminent actors have to allow themselves to be taught their places by the Dramatists, which arrangement gives life and ornament to a well-written play, so that it is no wonder that the English players (I speak of skilled ones) surpass and have advantage of others.[8]

Virtually all extant plays that dramatize the act of staging a performance indicate that one person, rather than the group at large, was charged with the responsibility of 'guiding' the production. A good example of this is Hamlet and 'The Mousetrap' and Peter Quince in *A Midsummer Night's Dream*. Although these representations of play production within plays are frequently of amateur or private performances, they are written by professionals, and it seems probable that something similar was the customary practice in public playhouses.[9]

Scripts

Shakespeare's plays were not printed in his lifetime in any form that we would recognize today. We believe that individual actors were not in possession of a copy of the whole play, but only their individual part or lines. They also had the few lines that preceded their speech. These actor's parts have often become referred to as 'cue scripts'. Tiffany Stern, in her book *Documents of Performance in Early Modern England* provides a more detailed exploration of this area.

Whole manuscripts of some Early Modern plays survive, although none of Shakespeare's. Their existence indicates that they were written down currently with actor's parts. There is a variety of ways play texts were written down. How this was done depended on the individual authors, and whether or not there was more than one author working on a play. Generally, the plot of the play would have been the first part of the writing process, although we do not know whether this would have been presented as a plot summary or an outline of five acts. This was read out, or summarized, to an interested acting company. Once commissioned by an acting company, playwrights would write the play out act by act. Sometimes the play would be delivered by the playwright in parts to the theatre company, sometimes it would be delivered in its entirety. The playhouse scribe, if the company had one (we know that for Shakespeare's company during the King's Men period it was Ralph Crane), would copy out a fair copy from the author's foul papers so that it made sense not only to the company but to the Master of the Revels. It was a very complex process and may have worked differently each time a play was written. Tiffany Stern's book, *Making Shakespeare from Stage to Page* provides probably the best summary of this process.

Audience positioning

The composition and structure of the audience in the original Globe is discussed in Chapter 2: *Context: Learning from the Globe*. When working on activities in this chapter it is also useful for students to understand that although we have no details on the precise location of different types of early modern theatre-goers, we do have some awareness of which social classes would be represented in different parts of the theatre.

The working men and women and the unemployed poor paid a penny to stand in the yard (the groundlings), while wealthier playgoers paid slightly more to enter the galleries. The wealthiest gentlemen paid significantly more to rent a gentlemen's room by, or lords' room behind, the stage. There are one or two contemporary references to the amounts paid by wealthy foreign visitors to partake of London's theatre scene: Giorgio Giustinian, the Venetian Ambassador in London from January 1606 to November 1608, invited a party of illustrious guests (which included the French Ambassador, his wife and the Secretary of the Florentine embassy) to see *Pericles* at the Globe. The party took over the lords' rooms over the stage, at a cost of more than twenty crowns. An entourage only slightly smaller went with Prince Frederick Lewis of Württemberg in 1610 to see *Othello* at the Globe.[10]

Warm-up activities

These are useful warm-ups for any group that is going on to explore performance and staging in a session. They encourage students to think about actor, audience and architecture and to consider how these elements work together in performance.

Oranges, cabbages and potatoes

Ask the whole group to form a circle. Divide the circle into three sections. Name one section oranges, one cabbages and the third potatoes.

Tell the group that you are going to read a speech. If someone cannot see your face at any time s/he should shout the name of his/her section. Stand in the middle of the circle and start to read the speech. Instantly one section, possibly more, will start calling oranges/cabbages/potatoes. Turn to the section that is calling loudest and continue reading. A different section will then start to call out; turn to address them and continue reading. Repeat this process for the remainder of the speech, or until you feel satisfied. You can ask a student to take this role, if more appropriate for your group.

Discuss what is happening during this process. What does it tell us about how an actor needs to work on the Globe stage? The discussion should cover the requirement of an actor on the Globe stage to make contact with different members of the audience and to be aware of the audience all around. The actor cannot deliver all of his/her lines from one place, but needs to move around the stage, connecting with different sections of the audience.

Group as director

Ask the group to form a circle and for a volunteer to be the actor for this activity. Explain that in this activity the students will explore the requirements of performing on the Globe stage and how the playing conditions in the theatre affect what an audience needs from staging and performance.

Explain that you will ask the volunteer to perform a speech in the middle of the circle. You will give him/her direction and will feed him/her the lines. The group should watch and listen carefully as their role will be to provide feedback on the performance.

Secretly give the volunteer his/her instructions: speak softly, do not look at anyone in the circle, look at the ground, do not move and be as boring as possible.

Use a speech from the play you are studying. If necessary, provide the group with a brief context of the moments leading up to the speech they are about to hear.

Feed the first line of the speech to the volunteer to deliver, repeat this process, one line at a time, for c 8–10 lines.

Ask the group for their comments about the performance. The comments need to be specific, e.g. 'it was terrible' is too general. Start with those members of the group behind the volunteer performer. Usually students make comments such as 'we couldn't see/ hear', 'the student's eyes were down'. Remind the students that in the Globe the lords' room was at the rear of the stage. Would this type of performance be acceptable to the lords and ladies?

Repeat this process for different parts of the circle, drawing comparisons between the audience/seating structure in the Globe. Finally, ask the group how this performance affects their understanding of what is happening in the play at that moment?

Tell the group that your volunteer did exactly as you directed. Now it is the group's opportunity to provide direction for the volunteer. Ask for specific suggestions. Students usually suggest the volunteer should speak up, make eye contact with the audience, move around and use gestures. Unpack these suggestions to ensure they are meaningful – e.g. gestures could mean anything, what is important is that any gestures the volunteer makes are produced by the words of the speech.

Repeat the process, feeding the lines one by one. Ask the volunteer to do as much as s/he possibly can to incorporate the group's suggestions into his/ her performance.

Discuss as before. How does this performance affect the group's understanding of the speech?

Actor, audience and architecture

This exercise follows on well from *Group as director*. It works well with the Prologue from Act 1 Scene 1 of *Henry V*, but could be used with a range of speeches and soliloquies. The aim of the exercise is simply to accustom students to thinking about actor, audience and architecture and how they are referenced, or work together in a speech. It can also give them a sense of how a speech might connect with different parts of the audience in different ways.

Divide the group into three. Label the groups 'actor', 'audience' and 'architecture'. A teacher or student should then read the selected speech. The task of each group is to listen for references to subjects or concepts related to their group name. When they hear a reference they should repeat the words or phrase. The reader should continue on, not pausing.

This gives a sense of how each of the three elements feature in a speech and when they may come together.

Key questions could include: What was mentioned most frequently? Were some groups mentioned together? Were there parts of the speech where some groups featured heavily? If so, what does this tell us about what is happening at that moment or the focus of the scene? What kind of language was used for each group? Did this change or develop throughout the speech? Why might that type of language have been used? Were all elements equally important? How did they elements work together in the speech?

Activities

A speech as duologue

Aims

This exercise was developed by Yolanda Vazquez as a way of helping students trace how a character's thoughts might change within a speech and to begin to think about the effect of the audience on our understanding of a long speech or soliloquy.

Practical considerations

Before beginning this exercise students should have completed either *Pointing on the Pronoun* or *Walking the Punctuation.* This activity works well in a larger space or in a classroom with desks.

Activity

In pairs, give students a long speech or soliloquy. The first reader should read up to the first punctuation mark. Their partner should then take over and read to the next punctuation mark. This process should be repeated for the whole speech.

At the end of the first reading, students should begin to identify the rhythm of the speech, the thoughts of the character, and places where these thoughts might be conflicting.

The pairs should read the speech again in the same way. This time they should really try to affect their partner with their lines. What do they find out about the character from this exercise? Can they divide the speech into sections and chart change or progression?

One member of the pair should now read the speech. At each punctuation mark their partner should respond with 'no'. S/he should say 'no' in as many different ways as s/he wishes: angry, as a put-down, gossipy (think Sybil in Fawlty Towers*). The speaker should react to the 'no': fighting, or working with it on their next line, as appropriate. This exercise should then be repeated, with 'yes'.*

Discuss in pairs and as a whole group how the tone of the 'no' or 'yes' affects what the character wants to achieve with their speech. Does it make their aims and desires clear and/or stronger?

In pairs, repeat the activity again. This time the partner responding with 'no' and 'yes' should choose which word is most appropriate for each interjection and which tone best suits the line or phrase. Discuss what each pair has found out about the speech through this process. If the students were to direct an actor playing the speech, what instructions would they give him or her?

Finally, bring the whole group into a circle and ask one person to stand in the middle and read the speech. At each punctuation mark the rest of the group should simultaneously respond with either 'no' or 'yes' in whatever tone they feel to be most appropriate. The person in the middle should try to direct their lines to different members of the group and really try to use the yes/no responses to shape their reading of the speech.

Ask the speaker why they spoke to different group members at different points of the speech. How did their responses help them play the lines? Which lines were hardest and why? Which lines became clearer through this process?

Extension: Globe audience

This extension activity works most effectively with a soliloquy.

Divide the group into four. Each group represents a section of the audience in the Globe theatre: Groundlings, Lower Gallery, Middle Gallery with Lords' and Gentlemen's rooms and Upper Gallery. Ensure that each group is familiar with the general characteristics of audience in their section. While it may not be possible to get the levels of the Globe in the classroom, arrange the groups in distinct tiers, with the Groundlings nearest the speaker, so that they correspond as far as possible to the Globe audience. This exercise can also be carried out in small groups of five, with one person representing each audience group. Small groups in this instance can often generate more discussion and experimentation.

Repeat the exercise. This time the speaker will need to direct their lines to different members of the audience. Discuss which audience group feels most appropriate for which lines and why.

Finally, the speaker should read the speech or soliloquy one last time, directing different lines to different areas of the audience, building in the points and directions gained from the last discussion. This time the rest of the group should not respond with 'yes' or 'no'; the speaker by now should be able to use the experience of their earlier responses to deliver the speech. If it is helpful to stop and try different ideas, students should do so. The speaker can be changed as desired.

How does this awareness of the audience add to our understanding of the soliloquy?

A

Thought units: Breaking down a speech

In Chapter 4: *Language: Inside out*, Giles Block talks about the importance of identifying units of thought. This is a key approach for actors when looking at language and exploring the progression of a character in a speech, scene or throughout a play.

Practical considerations

This activity works well with a soliloquy after *Speech as Duologue*. The first part can be completed by students individually, in pairs or in small groups. The later part of the activity requires small group work. All students can be given the same speech to work on, or speeches can be chosen from different parts of the play to enable the exploration of character development and/or changing language throughout the play.

Activity

Ask the students to read through the chosen speech or soliloquy and divide it into three parts. These parts should reflect the character's journey through the speech. They do not have to be equal. Most soliloquies or longer speeches fall naturally into three parts.

The students should look at each third of the speech and decide what they think is the dominant emotion in that section. It is worth noting that actors do not play an emotion, but often identify it to inform their playing of a situation.

In small groups, students should discuss the three emotions they chose and, if the first stages of the activity were completed individually/in pairs, reach a group consensus on which three emotions they wish to continue to work with. Arguments for chosen emotions must be rooted in the language of the speech.

Each group should now create three pictures, one for each emotion. Each group should share their pictures with the whole group. Discuss different choices (if the same speech) or what the emotions chosen tell us about the development of the character and language.

Individually or in groups, ask students to look at each third of the speech again. This time they should break each third into units. Each unit should deal with the same idea or subject matter. Compare and discuss choices as a whole group. (At this stage in the exercise, if the whole group is working with the same speech, it works well to give each small group a different unit of the speech and put together findings at the end of the exercise.)

Students should then take each unit and break it down again into different segments. Each segment should represent a thought or idea. An example taken from Juliet's speech in Act 3 Scene 2 of Romeo and Juliet *is given below with suggested section, unit and segment divisions. Students should discuss choices and give reasons for dividing the speech as they have.*

When they are happy with their divided speech, students should choose a verb for each segment. This verb should capture what is happening in the segment. This should be written next to the segment.

In small groups or individually, ask the students to create a still image for each verb. They should then put these together in the order they appear in the script and share them, if appropriate, with the rest of the group. When they are happy with the images they should turn these into a movement which uses their whole bodies to depict the verb. Again these can be shown to other groups.

There is much potential here, depending on the needs of the group and focus of the session. At this point the students are effectively dancing the speech and, if desired, this could be developed further into a performance piece.

For most groups, however, the next step is for students to experiment with speaking the speech, putting all the energy and emotion of the movement into the way they perform the words. This can be performed to small groups or the whole group, as desired. Students should think about where they want to be onstage, where they should move and which parts of the speech they feel connect with the audience.

At the end of the process, discuss what has been learnt about the speech and the character's journey through it. Focus on relating what has been learnt about the character to the language the character uses. This exercise feeds well into a developed written analysis of the speech.

T
***Romeo and Juliet:* Act 4 Scene 3, lines 14–59**

Section 1
Unit 1 Segment 1 Farewell!
Segment 2 God knows when we shall meet again.
Unit 2 Segment 3
I have a faint cold fear thrills through my veins,
That almost freezes up the heat of life:
Unit 3 Segment 4
I'll call them back again to comfort me:
Nurse!
Segment 5 What should she do here?
Segment 6 My dismal scene I needs must act alone.
Unit 4
Segment 7
Come, vial.
Segment 8 What if this mixture do not work at all?
Segment 9 Shall I be married then to-morrow morning?
Segment 10 No, no: this shall forbid it: lie thou there.
Lays down a knife

Section 2
What if it be a poison, which the friar
Subtly hath minister'd to have me dead,
Lest in this marriage he should be dishonour'd,
Because he married me before to Romeo?
I fear it is: and yet, methinks, it should not,
For he hath still been tried a holy man.

How if, when I am laid into the tomb,
I wake before the time that Romeo
Come to redeem me? there's a fearful point!
Shall I not, then, be stifled in the vault,
To whose foul mouth no healthsome air breathes in,
And there die strangled ere my Romeo comes?
Or, if I live, is it not very like,
The horrible conceit of death and night,
Together with the terror of the place,–
As in a vault, an ancient receptacle,
Where, for these many hundred years, the bones
Of all my buried ancestors are packed:
Where bloody Tybalt, yet but green in earth,
Lies festering in his shroud; where, as they say,
At some hours in the night spirits resort;–
Alack, alack, is it not like that I,
So early waking, what with loathsome smells,
And shrieks like mandrakes' torn out of the earth,
That living mortals, hearing them, run mad:–
O, if I wake, shall I not be distraught,
Environed with all these hideous fears?
And madly play with my forefather's joints?
And pluck the mangled Tybalt from his shroud?
And, in this rage, with some great kinsman's bone,
As with a club, dash out my desperate brains?
O, look! methinks I see my cousin's ghost
Seeking out Romeo, that did spit his body
Upon a rapier's point: stay, Tybalt, stay!
Section 3
Romeo, Romeo, Romeo, here's drink. I drink to thee.

Character lists

Aims

To gather all known information about a character throughout a scene or play. To explore the discrepant levels of awareness that exist between characters and audience. To consider how this information might inform our understanding of the play's structure and to identify key points of plot development.

Practical considerations

This activity can be carried out anywhere. It works equally well for any play or character.

Activity

During performance, the only people who know everything about the play unfolding before them are the audience. They hold all the information, hear every character's thoughts and ideas and witness all plot developments. In rehearsal, actors often try to gather all the information the audience will receive about their character during the course of the play. Many of the actors that work at the Globe will, at some point, make character lists to help them achieve this. Character lists are a widely used rehearsal technique. Actors usually make lists that detail:

- *what their character says about his or herself*
- *what other characters say about their character*
- *what their character says about the other characters in the play.*

Some actors also list all the factual information that is known about the character. These have to be irrefutable. For example, if an actor were playing Hamlet his list might include: I am a student; my father has just died; my father was King; my mother has quickly married my uncle, who is now King.

The lists above are not exhaustive. Different actors will approach this exercise in different ways and produce less or more extensive lists. Another category some actors add is 'physical actions', i.e. what we know for certain the character does, moment by moment, scene by scene. This list can be added as an extension activity if appropriate.

In the classroom, character lists are a really useful tool and, once created, can be referred to throughout the study of a play.

Divide all the characters in the play among the group and ask them to produce their character lists. If you wish to break this task down further, it is possible to ask different group members to compile the list for a character for a specific scene or act. Students should include the text that provides the information as part of their lists. They should also take care to attribute comments about their character to the character that made them and give a scene and line reference.

When all the lists are complete, compare each character. What do we find out about the characters? Does a character's view of his or herself remain constant or does it change? Similarly, who says what about who and how do these comments change or develop throughout the play? Are there any surprises about how the audience receive information about a character? Explore and analyse how Shakespeare creates the audience's perception of a character, scene by scene. Are there crucial moments or turning points? How might this knowledge affect an actor's portrayal of a given role?

If desired, students can plot a timeline for their character throughout the play, using this information.

When looking at the lists of factual information it can be useful to ask students to represent each character and speak his or her list. Each item on the list can then be directly compared with the other characters. This helps students consider the experience of the characters and the dynamics between them. It provides a method of considering how the audience is given information and how this affects the audience's understanding and response. For example, if this exercise was completed for the factual information given in the first part of Hamlet *Act 1 Scene 2 lines 1–159, students could make statements along the following lines:*

> *Hamlet: My father has died and my mother has quickly remarried (Hamlet refers to both a two-month and one-month interlude) my uncle who is now King. I am still grieving for my father and am very unhappy about my mother's rapid remarriage.*
>
> *Gertrude: My husband, the King, died recently. I have just married his brother, Claudius, who is now King. I am concerned my son Hamlet is still mourning his father. I want him to remain in Denmark rather than return to university in Wittenberg.*
>
> *Claudius: I have recently succeeded my late brother to the throne of Denmark and have married his widow. I am concerned about the war-like threats being made towards Denmark by Fortinbras. I feel my nephew, now my stepson, still shows 'unmanly' grief for his father.*

The completed lists can also be compared and provide a timeline for plot and character development throughout the play. For example, at what point does the audience receive factual information about Old Hamlet's murder? Which other characters are aware of this and at what stage in the play do they find out? What do different characters say about Claudius and what does this tell us about his relationships within the play and his structural role in the drama?

This can also be delivered as a version of hot-seating, with the character in the middle and other students walking around the outside speaking the

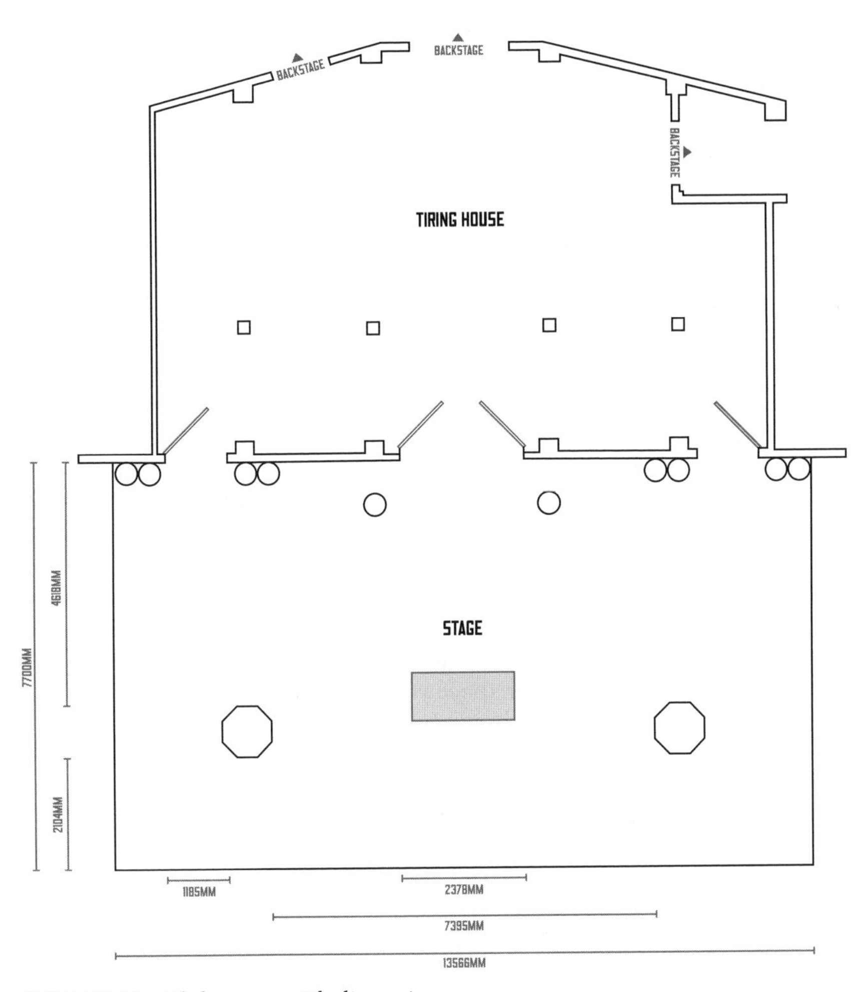

FIGURE 13 *Globe stage with dimensions.*

lines other characters say about the character to him/her. The character in the middle can also respond with lines they say about themselves or about others, as most appropriate.

Performing the soliloquy

Aims

This is an activity developed by Chris Stafford to explore the effect of staging a soliloquy and the impact of the relationship between actor, audience and staging on our understanding of a speech.

Practical considerations

This activity is an extension of the soliloquy work in Chapter 3: *Core approaches to Creative Shakespeare*. Students should have undertaken that sequence before commencing this activity. A space large enough to hold the whole group standing on a rough, mainly visualized, set-up of the Globe stage is required. As for *Four word soliloquy* a numbered print-out of the whole soliloquy is helpful. Every student should have a line and should be aware of who has the line before and after them. Exploration in the earlier activity should have given them a very good sense of the structure of the speech and engaged them in interrogating possible interpretations.

Create a space in the room that can represent the Globe stage (see the diagram above). This stage can be as basic (a chair or coat to mark the pillars and the shape of the space indicated) or as developed (a measured mark-up of the stage in a larger space with blocks as pillars) as fits with the space and time available for this exercise.

Activity

Give each student a line from the soliloquy. This can be the line they worked with in Four word soliloquy *or a different one. As before, if there are more students in the group than lines in the soliloquy, students can double lines (lines next to each other in the speech, on this occasion), or the soliloquy can be cut.*

Go through your mock-up of the Globe stage with the students. If appropriate students can set this up themselves, identifying important factors. Alternatively this can be pre-set for them and a run-through of the stage given. Ensure that students are aware of the position of the audience, impact of the position of the pillars and of the ideas around audience make-up and social verticality explored in Chapter 2: Context: Learning From the Globe.

With this knowledge, ask each student to choose the position on stage that s/he feels is the most appropriate place to deliver his or her line. Students do not need to be standing near the student who has the line before them. Make sure that everyone has memorized their line. It should be possible to put any print-outs away at this stage.

Go through the soliloquy for the first time, making sure the lines run in order and everyone knows when to speak. Afterwards ask the students to think about:

What part of the audience did they most connect with during their line?

Is it a strong connection?

Do they feel they are in the right position? If not they should move.

What physical position/stance have they taken?

Experiment with standing up, sitting down, leaning (if by a pillar). The stance should complement the line.

How might each student physicalize his or her line? Experiment with ideas developed in the Four word soliloquy *sequence.*

Which student/s has lines in the speech that they most connect with? Which lines (words, images etc.) resonate with their own? Students should experiment, reflecting that resonance by physically reacting to other lines in the speech.

Perform the soliloquy, taking all of the above into consideration and incorporating it, where appropriate, into the performance. At the end of the soliloquy each student should freeze in a position that physically represents his or her line.

Take a photograph of the final frozen image. If possible share it with the group.

Questions:

The purpose of these questions is to stimulate discussion and experimentation with the speech. Try it in as many different ways as desired.

What are the most powerful or pivotal lines in the speech?

Does the position of the students with those lines on stage reflect their importance? If not, identify why not and ask the students to move, to a position the group feel is appropriate.

Does this mean other students have to move?

How does this affect the overall picture and the group's telling of the soliloquy?

Which students feel their line has a very strong connection with the audience?

Does their position onstage reflect this and allow effective communication?

Are all members of the audience engaged by something in the speech?

Are there any lines that the group feel should be directed to particular sections of the audience? Change positions if necessary.

The group should give a final performance of the soliloquy incorporating their findings from their discussion and experiments. They should remember now that they need to communicate the story of the soliloquy to the audience. At the end, take another photograph. How is it different from the first one and what might it tell us about the soliloquy?

Final questions:

What journey has the character been on in the soliloquy?

What have the audience learnt about the character in the soliloquy?

How does the soliloquy affect what happens next in the play?

If desired, students can capture this exploration and use it to form the basis of a written analysis of the soliloquy and its dramatic function at that point in the play. This work can also form the starting point for a full-scale ensemble performance of the soliloquy, if appropriate for the group.

Variation

A possible variation on this exercise is to split the group in two at the beginning – one group for the first half of the soliloquy, one for the second. Carry out the activity with the group with the first half of the soliloquy. The second group should be the audience. They should think about where they are sitting or standing. Throughout the activity they should give feedback to the performing group and make suggestions.

The groups should then swap over and repeat the process. Finally the two halves should be put together, incorporating all relevant discussions and ideas.

A

Walk, freeze, sit

Aims

This exercise was developed by Chris Stafford as a quick way of enabling a group to focus on engagement with the audience and to examine physically the way in which language and actor can work together to communicate with the audience.

Practical considerations

This activity works well after the *Four word soliloquy* sequence in Chapter 3: *Core approaches to Creative Shakespeare* but can be carried out with a group who have not worked on that exercise, if they are confident with the text and play. It requires a space that is large enough for a group to walk around freely.

The activity works with any speech. If the speech is long it is best to work with pieces of it, around ten lines at a time, as longer sections can become quite laborious for the student reading. If space is limited, one small group can work with a ten-line segment at a time, while the rest of the group comment and advise. Another group can then work with the next ten lines of the speech and so on.

Activity

Nominate one of the group to read the ten lines of the speech. This should be someone who is confident to try different interpretations and to repeat the lines several times. The reader represents an actor in performance, so choose someone who is comfortable with this idea and happy to take direction from the rest of the group.

Ask the reader to read the speech while walking around the room. As s/he does so the rest of the group should also walk around the room. When each student moving feels s/he believes what the reader is saying they should freeze. When s/he feels the reader is communicating with them personally s/he should sit down. The objective for the reader is to get as many of the group frozen, then sitting down, as possible.

The reader can go up to students to 'work on' them and come back to any student still moving or standing as many times as s/he wishes.

It works well to pause the exercise midway, when some students are frozen and/or sitting down, and ask them when and why the reader's communication was successful. Gather tips for the reader to use and continue with the exercise.

At the end of the exercise, discuss what worked well. What was most effective about the language of the speech and why? What methods used by the reader were most effective? What can this tell us about the requirements of an actor and engaging with the audience? What tools or focus points might the exercise give us when we are looking at how the language of a speech might work in performance?

Cue scripts

A cue script exercise has been used by Globe Education since its inception. It gives us a way of exploring what may have been an original rehearsal practice. This approach is not used in Globe rehearsal rooms today. Working with this exercise enables students to identify the information Shakespeare provides to the actor from within his writing.

Aims

To explore how Shakespeare directs actors from within his writing. To use discoveries from working with cue scripts to deepen student understanding of structure, staging and character. To help students to contextualize Shakespeare's writing within what we know of early modern theatre practices.

Practical considerations

This activity requires a cue script for each member of the group. To make a cue script, simply separate each character's lines from the scene and place them on a piece of paper in the order they appear. Before each line or set of lines, place the three words that are spoken before the lines begin – these are the cue lines. Do not include the name of the character who speaks the lines. (See the example from *Julius Caesar* below.) Each character will have a different cue script. This work requires a space big enough for students to be able to act out a scene. The tasks at the end of the activity ideally require a space where students can stand in a circle. The *Julius Caesar* part of this activity works equally well with a group of fifteen or fifty, in a lecture hall or in a drama space. NB: 'cue script' is not an early modern theatre term.

Activity

This activity uses a three rehearsal structure.

The first part of this activity uses Julius Caesar *Act 3 Scene 2, see text below. It provides the simplest introduction to working in this way and provides a foundation for exploring other plays. This scene features Mark Antony, Julius Caesar (dead) and 4 Plebeians or citizens. The cue script below numbers all these parts. The Plebeians are numbered separately as parts 1, 2, 3 and 4. 'All' refers to the crowd and is labelled as number 5. The exercise works well if the teacher reads the part of Mark Antony as it is long and the students need to be able to focus on listening and responding rather than on speaking lots of lines. However the part can be given to a student if appropriate.*

Give out the parts and give everyone their individual cue scripts. Give parts 1, 2, 3 and 4 to individual students and part 5 (All) to everyone else in the group. Do not let the students know who has which part, or that many of them have the same part – they can then discover this and their relationships to each other on the first reading.

If the students are unfamiliar with Julius Caesar, *give them a brief context of what is happening in the scene they are about to read – e.g. Julius Caesar has been killed and his friend Mark Antony has come to talk to the crowd because he wants to explain what has happened, from his point of view.*

Ask the students to read through their cue scripts and to make sure they understand their lines.

First rehearsal: students should read through the scene listening for their cues (the three words that have been given on their script) and saying their lines. They should try to make what they feel is an appropriate response. It may be necessary to go through the scene twice to achieve a coherent reading. It is common at this stage for students to identify problems with overlapping or interrupting when reading. This is usually because the lines are constructed in this manner – some cue lines come before the character has finished speaking. The students should always start speaking immediately after their cue line whether the other character has finished speaking or not.

Key questions: What sort of people are you and how are you behaving in this scene? (e.g. a crowd, angry, impatient, displaying a crowd mentality, etc.) How do we know this information? (e.g. because the crowd interrupt, Mark Antony has to tell them to be patient, etc.) How does working with a cue script change the way we listen to a speech?

Second rehearsal: students should read the scene again, this time not only listening and responding but also doing whatever the text tells them to do. This rehearsal is about responding to the stage directions that are within the text. Students should move wherever necessary during the reading to carry out the stage directions. During this reading the scene will start to include movement. There is no director telling the group what to do. All the instructions are contained within the text.

Third rehearsal: ask the students to think of this as a dress rehearsal. They now know who they are speaking to and why. They also know where they need to be. This time, really think about those two elements and how they can be played to the greatest effect.

Discuss the group's findings from putting everything together in this rehearsal. Is everything as it should be? Are all the characters in the best possible places as indicated by the text? At this point students often notice that Mark Antony should start the scene above the crowd, as they later ask him to 'come down'. In the Globe theatre Mark Antony would most probably start the scene in the balcony above the stage.

Performance: when all the students are happy, perform the scene, putting everything the group have learnt together. What have the group discovered about the scene by performing it in this manner? How has Shakespeare structured his writing to create/develop character and to ensure maximum dramatic impact for the audience?

Having explored how cue scripts work in this scene, the group can now apply this knowledge to any play they are studying.

Divide the students into small groups, containing a corresponding number of students to parts in the cue script. Give them a cue script for a scene from the play they are studying. Cue scripts work for any scene. Examples of particularly effective scenes for a selection of plays are given below.

Ask the groups to work through their cue script employing the three rehearsal approach that they used for Julius Caesar. *They should find out as much about the scene as they can using this approach and think about the questions they explored after each rehearsal.*

Bring the whole group back together in a circle. Choose one student, each from a different small group, to play each character in the scene. The fact that all the groups have been exploring the play using the cue scripts mean that they should have all made similar discoveries and created a similar version of the scene. Ask the selected students to play the scene in the middle of the circle. Are the group happy with this interpretation of the scene? What have they learnt about the scene through using the cue scripts?

Repeat the exercise (with a different group of students if you wish). This time, the students should imagine that they are on the Globe stage. At this point it may be helpful if the group talk through the different parts of the stage and theatre, identifying one part of the circle as the front and back of the stage. This time, the students playing the scene should work on the premise that the audience are there to help them play the scene. They should make sure they play to and with them, factoring the audience into their performance as they feel most appropriate. The rest of the group, who are the audience, should look at their scripts again to see if there are any places where they feel the audience may help a particular character.

Example scenes

This activity works with any scene. Other good examples, of scenes rich in action/reaction are: *King Lear:* Act 1 Scene 1; *Othello:* Act 4 Scene 1; *Hamlet:* Act 3 Scene 4; *Romeo and Juliet:* Act 3 Scene 1; *Much Ado About Nothing:* Act 5 Scene 1 lines 46–105; *Macbeth:* Act 2 Scene 2 lines 14–55.

T

***Julius Caesar:* Act 3 Scene 2**

Complete script – lines 129–67

ANTONY
But here's a parchment with the seal of Caesar;
I found it in his closet, 'tis his will:
Let but the commons hear this testament–
Which, pardon me, I do not mean to read–
And they would go and kiss dead Caesar's wounds
And dip their napkins in his sacred blood,
Yea, beg a hair of him for memory,

And, dying, mention it within their wills,
Bequeathing it as a rich legacy
Unto their issue.

Fourth Citizen
We'll hear the will: read it, Mark Antony.

All
The will, the will! we will hear Caesar's will.

ANTONY
Have patience, gentle friends, I must not read it;
It is not meet you know how Caesar loved you.
You are not wood, you are not stones, but men;
And, being men, bearing the will of Caesar,
It will inflame you, it will make you mad:
'Tis good you know not that you are his heirs;
For, if you should, O, what would come of it!

Fourth Citizen
Read the will; we'll hear it, Antony;
You shall read us the will, Caesar's will.

ANTONY
Will you be patient? will you stay awhile?
I have o'ershot myself to tell you of it:
I fear I wrong the honourable men
Whose daggers have stabb'd Caesar; I do fear it.

Fourth Citizen
They were traitors: honourable men!

All
The will! the testament!

Second Citizen
They were villains, murderers: the will! read the will.

ANTONY
You will compel me, then, to read the will?
Then make a ring about the corpse of Caesar,
And let me show you him that made the will.
Shall I descend? and will you give me leave?

Several Citizens

Come down.

Second Citizen
Descend.

Third Citizen
You shall have leave.
ANTONY comes down

Fourth Citizen
A ring; stand round.

First Citizen
Stand from the hearse, stand from the body.

Second Citizen
Room for Antony, most noble Antony.

ANTONY
Nay, press not so upon me; stand far off.

Several Citizens
Stand back; room; bear back.

ANTONY
If you have tears, prepare to shed them now.

Cue Script: Fourth Citizen

Cue: Unto their issue
Fourth Citizen
We'll hear the will: read it, Mark Antony.
The will, the will! we will hear Caesar's will.

Cue: come of it!
Fourth Citizen
Read the will; we'll hear it, Antony;
You shall read us the will, Caesar's will.

Cue: do fear it.
Fourth Citizen
They were traitors: honourable men!
The will! the testament!

Cue: give me leave?

Fourth Citizen
Come down.

Cue: shall have leave.
ANTONY comes down
Fourth Citizen
A ring; stand round.

Cue: stand far off.
Fourth Citizen Stand back; room; bear back.

Cue Script: All

Cue: it, Mark Antony.
All
The will, the will! we will hear Caesar's will.

Cue: traitors: honourable men!
All
The will! the testament!

Cue: give me leave?
All
Come down.

Cue: stand far off.
All
Stand back; room; bear back.

Cue Script: Second Citizen

Cue: it, Mark Antony.
Second Citizen
The will, the will! we will hear Caesar's will.

Cue: traitors: honourable men!
Second Citizen
The will! the testament!
They were villains, murderers: the will! read the will.

Cue: give me leave?
Second Citizen
Come down. Descend.

Cue: from the body.

Second Citizen
Room for Antony, most noble Antony.

Cue: stand far off.
Second Citizen
Stand back; room; bear back.

Cue Script: Third Citizen

Cue: it, Mark Antony.
Third Citizen
The will, the will! we will hear Caesar's will.

Cue: traitors: honourable men!
Third citizen
The will! the testament!

Cue: give me leave?
Third citizen
Come down.

Cue: Descend.
Third Citizen
You shall have leave.
ANTONY comes down

Cue: stand far off.
Third Citizen
Stand back; room; bear back.

Cue Script: First Citizen

Cue: read it, Mark Antony.
First Citizen
The will, the will! we will hear Caesar's will.

Cue: traitors: honourable men!
First Citizen
The will! The testament!

Cue: will you give me leave?
First Citizen
Come down.

Cue: ring; stand round.

First Citizen
Stand from the hearse, stand from the body.

Cue: stand far off.
First Citizen
Stand back; room; bear back.

Cue Script: Antony
NB: If Antony is being read by a teacher s/he should keep the whole script for reference. Use this cue script only if Antony's part is being read by a student participating in the activity.

ANTONY
But here's a parchment with the seal of Caesar;
I found it in his closet, 'tis his will:
Let but the commons hear this testament–
Which, pardon me, I do not mean to read–
And they would go and kiss dead Caesar's wounds
And dip their napkins in his sacred blood,
Yea, beg a hair of him for memory,
And, dying, mention it within their wills,
Bequeathing it as a rich legacy
Unto their issue.

Cue: hear Caesar's will.
ANTONY
Have patience, gentle friends, I must not read it;
It is not meet you know how Caesar loved you.
You are not wood, you are not stones, but men;
And, being men, bearing the will of Caesar,
It will inflame you, it will make you mad:
'Tis good you know not that you are his heirs;
For, if you should, O, what would come of it!

Cue: will, Caesar's will.
ANTONY
Will you be patient? will you stay awhile?
I have o'ershot myself to tell you of it:
I fear I wrong the honourable men
Whose daggers have stabb'd Caesar;
I do fear it.

Cue: read the will.
ANTONY
You will compel me, then, to read the will?

Then make a ring about the corpse of Caesar,
And let me show you him that made the will.
Shall I descend? and will you give me leave?

Cue: most noble Antony.
ANTONY
Nay, press not so upon me; stand far off.

Cue: room; bear back.
ANTONY
If you have tears, prepare to shed them now.

A

Emotional journey

This activity is based on some of the work developed by Augusto Boal in his activities around 'The Rainbow of Desires'.[11]

Aims

To provide students with a method of identifying the key motivations for characters in a scene. To encourage them to consider the way in which the interpretative choices of actors and directors influence our understanding of a scene in performance. To provide students with a quick and accessible method of making these choices for themselves.

Practical considerations

This activity works with any scene, although it is most easily used with duologue. Space is helpful but not necessary and the activity can easily be carried out in a classroom with desks. It is best used towards the end of an activity sequence, when the whole group have explored thoroughly the piece of text.

Activity

Nominate two students to read each character in the scene. Ask them to read the scene putting all they have learnt from work in previous activities into their reading. The rest of the group should listen carefully and try to identify the emotions they feel are most important in the scene.

After the reading, ask the group to suggest the emotions they thought were important to each character. From their suggestions, ask the group to choose four emotions for each character. The four students who suggested each emotion should move to stand behind the relevant character. Their task is to physically embody the emotion when the scene is next read.

For example, if the scene chosen for the activity was Measure *for* Measure *Act 2 Scene 4, in which Angelo tells Isabella the terms under which he will pardon her brother, words for Angelo might be lust, anger, cunning, love, while Isabella's might be fear, love, control and care. There are no right or wrong answers. The debate that takes place is as important as the chosen words.*

The group should arrange the four students who are embodying the emotions in what they believe to be the order of importance of the emotions in the scene, with the student portraying the most important emotion nearest to the character. Students can imagine they are on the Globe stage and position the students playing emotions in the place they feel to be most appropriate in relation to the character – e.g. is fear close to Isabella or on the other side of the stage? They should make clear justifications for their decisions.

Read the scene again; students playing emotions should physicalize them, in any way they wish, when they feel their emotion appears in the scene.

Discuss what we find out about the way the scene develops/is structured through this exercise.

Ask the two students playing the characters to identify which emotion they wish to work with further. Repeat the reading of the scene, this time using one emotion per character. What does the scene gain and lose in this process? Do all the group agree with the emotion chosen? If not, why? If desired, this process can be repeated with other emotions.

At any point in this exercise students making suggestions can take the place of those currently embodying an emotion or character, to try out their ideas.

Reach a group consensus about which and how many emotions to include in the final reading. The group should position the students playing the emotions where they feel most appropriate.

Repeat the reading. Discuss what has been learnt about each character and the changes they go through in the scene. How can looking at the changing emotions deepen understanding of character and scene?

Tips

Adam: *Character lists* are really useful, but I like to remind students that Shakespeare's actors would have been unlikely to do this, as we believe they probably only had their parts. It's worth taking time before using *Cue Scripts* to make sure you are really comfortable with the material. Students needs very simple clear instructions for this to work, then it can be very exciting.

Bill: I like using *Character lists*. I also like to ask students to make a list of all the imagery a character uses. This idea was introduced to me by director Mike Alfreds. *Cue Scripts* are useful. I like the way they force students to just 'dive in' and think on their feet, this can often lead to great discoveries.

Chris: After I have worked through *Speech as duologue* I like to repeat the exercise but this time asking students to read to the end of of each unit of thought. This exercise is a good precursor to *Thought Units*.

Colin: I like to work using the three circles of concentration that I've been introduced to in rehearsals when looking at performing soliloquies. The first circle is about yourself – e.g. 'I'm thinking about what I'm going to have for dinner'; the second circle includes direct communication with someone else – e.g. 'do you have any ideas about what I could have for dinner?'; the third circle is universal – e.g. 'please anyone send me some dinner ideas'. I like to look at soliloquy and go through it identifying which each line is in which circle and to think about how the circles change throughout the speech. I like to start *Speech as duologue* working with verse lines, then move to dividing by punctuation and discussing the difference. This is a good activity for a more advanced group. I don't work with *Cue Scripts* – I simply find them too difficult for me!

Patricia: *Cue Scripts* is a good exercise to do with a group who are new to working together. They have to work collaboratively in this exercise and it takes them into a different space in their approach to the play. They realize quickly that everything is in the text. It makes them listen to each other. It is also a good approach for a group who are working on a performance as it reminds them they are a group putting on a play and that they need to work together for the performance to be effective.

Yolanda: If more advanced students want to be really efficient with *Character lists* they should go through the whole play each time for each individual list. This is a great way of developing familiarity with the play and of seeing the play from different perspectives. When working on *Cue Scripts* I find that students often need to be reminded that nobody is going to tell them what to do! If they read a piece of text that says they are moving, that means they have to move! The doing is up to the individual.

CHAPTER SIX

Performance

In this chapter we examine the ways in which young people can experience performance – as actor and audience. Shakespeare's plays are simply that: plays. We are accustomed to phrases such as 'page to stage' and 'text into performance', but for Shakespeare's early modern audiences the plays existed only on stage as performances. The plays were not published in the form we would recognize today during Shakespeare's lifetime. The intervening years have seen a reversal of this situation. We commonly refer to Shakespeare's plays as texts and students are accustomed to meeting the plays as words on a page. All of the ideas explored in this book seek to encourage and enable engagement with Shakespeare's plays as theatre – as drama that is incomplete without performance, actors and audience. This chapter focuses on performance: how we can create performance with young people and, in turn, how we can enable them to experience performance as a critical, engaged audience member.

Young people as performers: *Let me entertain you...*

When we work with a group to create a performance, the focus initially moves from analysing or understanding a scene to physicalizing the scene. We concentrate on how to interpret the words, how to make them 'dramatic', and how to present them to an audience. In rehearsal the focus moves from understanding the text to playing the text. We ask students to rehearse different ways of saying the words, to think about how they are standing and to convey how their character is feeling to the audience. We ask them to become actors playing for a contemporary audience, rather than students of a piece of early modern drama regarded as 'great' literature. The primary focus in this exercise is entertainment. Will the performance work? Will it engage the audience? Will it look good? The process of rehearsal is a process of familiarization. We often ask students to perform a line over and over, experimenting, trying to find the 'best' way of performing that moment. At the end of the rehearsal period, the task of any company of actors is to take the play they now know so well onto the stage and share it with an audience as if it were happening for the first time: to tell the story of the play as if it were taking place at that very moment.

The process of creating a performance therefore positions students very differently in relationship to a play than if they are simply studying it in a classroom. Whether a rehearsal period lasts for six weeks or an hour, by the end of it students are experts on the particular piece of text they are rehearsing. Performing for an audience gives them status. They have the authority. They are the interpreters of the play and have shaped their version of the story to share with the audience. Nobody knows this version of the play as well as they do. This is the opposite of the situation when they meet a play as something to study, when their primary relationship to the text is as something that they need to understand, analyse, then demonstrate that understanding to a third party, usually in writing.

This is one of the reasons why all of the activities in this book are creative, actor-based activities. Working in this way can enable students to 'get inside' the text to experience the play as performers do. Working as a performer on all, or a small part, of a play takes this process to another level. When focus moves from analysis to entertainment, learning often appears to take a back seat. The reality, however, could not be more different. Ask any group of students who have been rehearsing a play about the scene, characters, construction of the drama etc. and they will inevitably be able to discuss it in great detail, demonstrating a developed level of understanding. They also tend to display great confidence and are able to answer questions and discuss the scene or play thoughtfully and with insight. The old maxim that you never understand something so well as when you go through the process of teaching it to others is proved true here. You never understand a play so well as when you have been through the process of interpreting that play for an audience.

Performance draws on emotional intelligence, although of course all of the other intelligences are in play as well. Interestingly, while there is often a perception among students that to understand Shakespeare you have to be 'clever', very few of them would give 'cleverness' as a prerequisite for being a good actor. Thus the act of performing Shakespeare takes away some of the perceived barriers to the plays. These barriers are false, of course; Shakespeare is potentially one of the most accessible writers to all students, regardless of perceived academic ability, just as there is a long list actors who are Oxbridge graduates.

These are the positives. The main challenges of creating performance with young people are often time and space. The work in this chapter does require space for a group to stand together and move. Any empty space, or space that can be cleared, will work. The ideas in this chapter cover creating performance in a short space of time, with activities that will produce performances with a teaching group in as little as an hour. There are also ideas and suggestions for working to produce performances of a larger scale (with a much larger number of students), over a longer period.

What is a performance?

Any piece of work that involves rehearsal, with the objective of creating a piece of work to share with others, or another, is a type of performance. Performance can take place anywhere – from a classroom in front of fellow group members or a teacher, to a designated theatre space in front of a ticketed audience. Performance can be site-specific – the corridors of a school can be the anterooms at Elsinore, a playground a market square in Verona. The possibilities are limitless.

Performances can involve students working as performers in many different ways. Some performances will feature one student taking one part, while others can feature large numbers of students in one scene, working as an ensemble company to create their version of the play. Performance does not require costume or lighting, although if desired it can successfully utilize both those elements. Boys do not have to play boys and girls girls. It's always worth reminding students that in early modern theatre there were no women actors, with boys taking all female roles. Performance can be multimodal, combining elements of film, art, design, music and dance to create a whole. In short, performance can be anything you and your group would like it to be.

Creating performance: Key considerations

When creating any kind of performance with young people, Globe Education always begins by asking the following questions:

What is the objective of the performance?

How will it serve the needs of the group?

Who is the audience for the performance?

How many students will take part in the performance and in what capacity?

How long do you have to create the performance?

What space is available for a) rehearsal, b) performance?

What financial and human resources are available to create the performance?

All of the considerations above will determine the type of performance created. No type of performance is intrinsically superior to another. All that is important is to create a type of performance that responds to the needs of the students and the environment in which the performance is to be created.

It is also important that the group engage with the performance, develop it and feel ownership of it. Someone needs to clearly lead the process as director, whether it be a teacher or one of the students. The best productions, though, are usually ones that are a genuine collaboration between all participants. There is a delicate balance to strike, which will be different according to the needs of the particular group. All theatre companies need clear leadership and direction, but all participants need to be enabled to make a significant contribution to the creative process. Performances where young people simply repeat words they have been drilled in, but in which they have no investment, in a production in which they have been told where to stand, but have played no part in the creation of the scene and staging, tend to appear one-dimensional and can be unsatisfactory for all involved. For learning to take place it is important that the process is organic and collaborative. This does not mean that it should not be structured, but that the rehearsal structure allows room for experimentation and exploration and that the performance created comes from the young people involved.

When rehearsing, it is important to consider the relationship between process and performance. An exploratory, inclusive process usually leads to the best performance. A process that only values the end product is likely to provide less learning opportunities for students. A rehearsal process in which learning and process is valued, that leads to a performance that is a positive experience for all concerned, is an ideal outcome. It is important to recognize that no two performances or rehearsal processes are the same. Sometimes the process may be important to share directly with the audience. Providing the audience with an insight into the process of rehearsal can become part of the performance, if desired. On other occasions the performance may be very formal. When planning a performance it is important to consider the factors that influence your planned performance and evaluate how best to achieve a productive and positive equilibrium between process and performance.

Cutting text for performance

In Chapter 3: *Core approaches to Creative Shakespeare* we looked at cutting text for use in everyday activities. This section focuses on cutting text for performance, although many of the general principles outlined in Chapter 3 still hold true. It is very rare to see a Shakespeare play in performance that has not been cut in some way. Many Shakespeare plays would run well in excess of 3½ hours if they were not cut. How a play is cut always depends on the type of performance or production. Certainly each director of productions at the Globe will choose different lines to cut. Cuts are always influenced by the type of production that the director wishes to create. Sometimes characters can be cut completely if this serves the story a director wants to tell. There are very few rules; artistic interpretation is what drives the process of cutting. When cutting text for performance with young people it is, however, useful to consider the following areas:

- The story you wish to tell is paramount. The story must remain clear and easy to follow in the final cut. Obviously it is important to keep meaning as it is in the uncut text.
- The needs of the group and the type of performance you wish to create should drive the process of cutting.
- Look for repetition of information, in short cuts this can easily be removed.
- The director should first cut a version for his or herself, that serves the needs of group and production. It is important that cutting is carried out after the director has worked with the group. Never cut without knowledge of the group and their response to the play or scene for performance.
- It works well to make a fairly accurate cut initially. If in doubt, take lines out rather than leave them in. It is far easier to give a student another line than it is to take one away. Even young children will make sustained arguments to prevent favourite lines from being cut. Actors do the same! There is a balance to strike here, as group discussion about cuts and/or asking students to make an argument for a particular line provides a good learning opportunity. Again, it all depends on the group and the objective of the performance.
- Be ruthless and do not worry about cutting favourite or famous lines.
- Roughly 1 page of text (containing up to 20 lines in the Arden format) = 1 minute of performance. Think about how much time is available for the performance and cut accordingly.
- Roughly, it takes 1 hour to rehearse 1 page of text with a group of young people. This obviously varies from group to group and scene to scene, but generally we have found this to be a realistic expectation, particularly if you are creating ensemble performance

with a large group. Cut in consideration of the rehearsal time available.

- Generally, with young people, it takes more time to rehearse prose than verse. This is generally because the rhythm of the verse helps students to speak and feel the sense of the lines.
- Sometimes it is easiest to cut in stages – e.g. start with a two-page cut then take it to one. Your final cut needs to be made once the initial cut has been rehearsed. This provides an opportunity for students to contribute and for the cut to reflect discoveries in rehearsal. It also allows the director to respond to the students: can some students manage more text, would others be happier with less? Develop the final cut to reflect such needs.
- Never underestimate, in a school, the possible disruptions to the rehearsal process. I once observed an hour-long rehearsal for an ensemble performance in which there were 36 different interruptions, culminating in the entrance of an adult dressed as a pixie. Prepare for your possible pixies and plan and time the rehearsal process accordingly. The length of the cut needs to reflect realistically the time available to rehearse. It is far better to have a short, powerful performance than a long, underprepared, unfocused performance.

Everyday small-scale performance

One of the most useful and immediate ways to create performance with young people is with pieces that can be put together in around an hour in an average (cleared) classroom-sized space. This is often the best type of performance to use when the group are new to performance and when you wish to reach all students, many of whom may not participate in performance in any other circumstances. In this way, performance can also be easily integrated into the study of any Shakespeare play. Many of the activities in this book can be developed and combined to lead into a performance. Some ways of doing this are explored in Chapter 5: *Actor, Stage and Audience*. The activities which follow are simple complete ways of creating performance in a short space of time with a group of c 30 students, although they can be adapted for smaller and larger groups.

Adam's 10 point plan to performance

I always feel very nervous about saying an activity always delivers, but as far as it is possible to guarantee success with anything ... this activity always works – with a diverse range of groups. As the name suggests, it has been developed by Globe Education's Senior Practitioner, Adam Coleman. The plan has evolved over a period of approximately ten years. I've never seen Adam deliver it in quite the same way twice and it is the most current evolution we share here. It is a clear, straightforward way of creating a performance in a limited time frame. It also provides an effective first step into into a longer rehearsal process, leading to a more developed performance.

Aims

To provide a clear and varied method of rehearsal for students. To offer a straightforward way into rehearsal of a text. Adam developed the *10 Point Plan* because he saw that young people found it difficult to engage with the process of repeating a scene or moment in rehearsal. When rehearsing plays, he had found that the best directors always gave him a different focus, new ideas, to try every time he rehearsed a scene. Adam wanted to create an easy way of engaging young people in the rehearsal process and mirrored the techniques that worked for him as an actor.

Practical considerations

This activity requires a space where students can stand and move, initially in two groups. It requires copies of an edited script (see below for an example from Act 1 Scene 1 of *Romeo and Juliet* and other suggested scenes). The version of the activity here supposes a group of c 30 students, but the activity can work with smaller or larger groups, by simply adjusting the edit length and parts. It works for all dramatic scenes where action takes place. It does not work well with large sections of duologue or parts of a play which convey lots of information. The activity is structured to naturally prepare the students for performance and to create a version of the scene that they can perform at the end of the process.

Each point of the plan should be carried out in strict order, as each stage builds on the one before. The first time you deliver the plan, it works well to do so exactly as it is set down here. After that, develop it and make your own adjustments to suit students and environment – this is exactly how Adam works with the plan and it is part of its strength and versatility. The activity can be completed quickly, in approximately 1 hour, although it can take much longer, depending on the needs of the group and the desired depth of exploration at each stage of the plan.

Activity

Although this activity is about creating a performance, when we use it we do not mention the idea of performance until the last stage. We make students aware that they are trying different ways of performing a scene, but do not tell them that they are going to create a performance of the scene. Generally this is effective in taking the pressure off the process and enables students to engage with the task in the spirit of rehearsal rather than worrying about a potential end product.

Divide the students into two equal groups. Ask each group to form a circle in a space on opposite sides of the room. Give each student an edit of the scene, with clear parts, one for each student. (See the example below.) All students should have the whole edited script of the scene. Ask a student in each group (who feels confident with a little more text) to act as director. S/he should then take the longest part (in the case of this example, the Prince). S/he should help the group cast themselves in the other parts and should be responsible for telling the group leader or teacher when their group has completed each stage of the plan.

Ask each group to cast themselves, with the help of their director. Edits work well when most parts are around one or two lines in length. When this is complete, the students are ready to begin the plan. They should all stand for the duration of the exercise.

Each group should start each stage of the plan at the same time at a given signal. At the beginning of the activity they will tend to take different lengths of time to complete each stage. By the end of plan the two groups are usually naturally finishing the exercise together.

Stage 1: Robot voice

Ask the students to read through the scene in a robot voice (think calm dalek). They should annunciate every syllable but should not put any expression into their voice, it should be monotone. It helps to model this for the students before they begin.

Through this step students become familiar with the text without worrying at all about meaning or expression. They discover the syllable breakdowns and therefore the rhythm of the text and usually naturally discover where they need to breathe in their speech.

Stage 2: Whispering

Ask the students to read through the scene whispering the lines. They should speak clearly, as if they are confiding a secret. All the words should be whispered, with no exceptions, even though this may feel as if it is working against the words in places.

The act of whispering encourages students to connect emotionally with the scene and language. Whispering has associations with secrecy, conspiracy and excitement. We do not tend to whisper factual information, but often whisper when we gossip, have a tale to tell, or should not be speaking. While stage 1 of this process asks students to disconnect from the meaning of the language and discover its rhythm, stage 2 encourages emotional connection and intimacy with the language and scene.

Stage 3: Radio voice

Explain that for this stage the students should imagine they are actors recording a radio drama. When recording for radio there needs to be an intensity and clarity in an actor's voice. Remind students that this is different from a high level of volume. Ask them to imagine they are in a recording studio, standing in front of a large disk microphone. They should think about all they have learnt from the first two stages and try to put their discoveries into this reading. Count the students down before they begin the scene: '3, 2, 1 – on air...'. Vocal intensity and trying out discoveries made so far are the key focus of this stage.

Stage 4: Theatre voice: Actor and audience

Ask students, if they haven't done so already, to identify who they say their line to and why. Each group can have a short group discussion about this if required. The discussion and decisions do not need to be shared at this stage with the whole group.

Give the group a rough outline idea of the stage they will be working on, or, if desired, the Globe stage. This can be done simply by discussing the shape, front/back of the stage and position of the audience. Indicate where these points correspond to in the room. *(See page 151 for a diagram of the Globe stage if desired.)*

Ask each student from group A to stand at the place on the imagined stage that s/he believes is the best place to say his or her line. Group B should then do the same. The two groups will now be mixed up in different places across the stage/room.

When the students have done this, each student should locate visually the member of their group that they speak their line to. Students should remember that the group member they are looking for now might be standing on the other side of the stage/room. There will be students from the other group in between them and the person they are speaking to. If a student thinks his or her line is directed to the audience in any way, s/he should also make sure s/he is clear about where the imaginary audience are in the room.

At the given signal, the groups should begin the scene, putting everything they have learnt so far into the performance. They need to ensure they can be heard clearly by the other members of their group and should speak clearly to the person to whom their line is directed. All students will also need to listen carefully for their cue, from their group member who speaks before them. All students should be aware of where the audience is and if their line is directed to the audience in any way.

This is the most complicated part of the exercise so far. It may be helpful to repeat this stage a second time after the group have worked their way through it once. If you feel combining the groups around the room may be too challenging for the particular group, this stage can work well with each group performing their scene in turn, scattered around the room, while the other group act as audience.

The focus of this stage is to clarify who is being spoken to and when and to encourage precise vocal projection and an awareness of staging and audience. If desired, each group can discuss why they chose to stand where they did on the stage and compare this with the choices of their opposite number in the other group. Were choices similar or different? Why did each student make their particular staging choice? Which approaches or choices were successful and what challenges remain for the students?

Stage 5: Overlapping

Ask each group to return to their original position in the room. For the next stages of the activity the groups work separately, as for stages 1–3.

The groups should perform the scene again, incorporating their discoveries from stage 4. This time the students should not wait for the person before them to finish speaking but should interrupt them, starting their line at the point during the previous line that they feel is most appropriate – each student interrupting the speaker before them. Each student should complete his or her line, even though s/he is being interrupted.

This activity will naturally lead to an increase in the volume of students' speech. It also heightens the need and desire to really communicate the line to fellow actor/s and audience. The activity starts to focus the group on the energy and timing of the scene and the dramatic arc of the action. All of these factors should be highlighted naturally through the process of interrupting.

Stage 6: Hitting the paper

This stage builds on the emotional intensity and drama that students start to discover in stage 5.

Ask the students to read through the scene again. This time each student should hit his/her piece of paper during their line whenever they feel the impulse to do so. This might be on the words they feel are most important, or that sound most interesting. It is important for students not to over-think this too much and simply go with their instincts. It is equally important, however, that students do not hit the paper on every word as then no word will have impact.

This exercise helps students to focus on finding the emotional beat or rhythm of the scene. Sometimes students naturally hit the paper on the stressed syllables of the iambic pentameter. It can also highlight the rhythm of their character in the scene. Quite often the paper tears at this point. It is this type of intensity that we try to encourage students to put into their speaking of the language and the gestures which follow in stage 7.

Stage 7: Gesture

Ask the students to read through the scene again. This time they should replace the moments where they hit the paper with a gesture. Ideally the gesture they make should come from the emotional response to the word or moment that made the student want to hit the paper at that point in the previous stage. The gesture can be anything that seems appropriate to the students. If desired, gestures can also reflect any discoveries made in earlier stages of the exercise. By this point the students are fairly familiar with the scene and usually begin to naturally assimilate their learning from the process so far into each new stage.

Stage 8: Silent movie

Tell the students that they are now going to tell the story of the scene without words, using gesture only. They should think of this as a silent movie version of the scene. Ask the students to put their piece of paper down away from them, somewhere they will not slip on it. Encourage them to move during this version of the scene, if they feel that their gesture demands movement.

At this point students are often concerned that they will not be able to remember what's in their line or their cue. It is good if they can remember these things, but not essential. It is primarily important that they convey the emotion of their line and express their intentions physically to the other characters. If appropriate for the group, ask them to think about Yolanda's 7 important questions *(see Chapter 3 pages 36–7) and put their ideas about the character derived from this process into their silent playing of the scene.*

Stage 9: Outward circle

Ask the students, in their circle, to turn around so that they are facing outward. They will now have their backs to the other members of the group at varying degrees around the circle. Ask them to read the scene again, incorporating the movement or gesture they found in the previous stage.

While stage 8 deprives students of voice in order to encourage them to focus on gesture and movement, stage 9 deprives them of visual contact and communication in order to encourage them to listen to their fellow actors.

This stage of the activity is also designed to encourage the dual awareness an actor must have on stage, of both their fellow actors and the audience. When facing outward, all the students can see are students in the other group. The activity encourages awareness of the whole at the same time as focused listening between fellow group members.

Stage 10: Performance

Tell the students that they are now going to put everything they have discovered in stages 1–9 of the activity together to create a performance of the scene. Each group will perform the scene while the other group act as audience. The teacher/group leader and the other group will offer direction and ideas to be discussed and, where appropriate, incorporated into each group's performance.

Ask the group to imagine themselves on your chosen stage (see stage 3) and position themselves on the stage with Montagues facing Capulets. This can be in two lines to start with. Decide where the Prince should stand and when and where s/he should enter the scene.

Where students had an impulse to interrupt or gesture in earlier stages, they should take a movement towards the opposing Montague/Capulet. This scene is about confrontation, but students also need to be aware of the audience and that they need to play the scene to them as well as with their fellow actors.

Run the scene. Students can often remember the words without their paper at this stage, although they can use it if necessary. Ask for feedback from the group who are the audience at this point. The teacher as director should also make suggestions and the group should think about and develop their performances, staging and blocking of the scene. Run the scene again. Repeat as many times as desired.

Swap the groups over and repeat the process.

Both groups will now have a performance of the scene. It is usually quite developed after going through the plan. How much you rehearse and develop the performance from this point depends on individual objectives and the groups concerned.

If desired, it is possible to combine both groups for stage 10 of the activity. Two students (one from each group) play the same part and speak at the same time. This work can be developed into an ensemble performance. It is most straightforward, however, and probably most beneficial for individual students to adopt the single group method.

T
Romeo and Juliet Act 1 Scene 1 cut from lines 43–101
Capulet 1 bites his thumb at the Montagues

Montague 1
Do you bite your thumb sir?

Capulet 1
I do bite my thumb, sir.

Montague 2&3
Do you bite your thumb *at us* sir?

Capulet 1
Is the law on our side if I say ay?

Capulet 2
No

Capulet 1
No, sir, I do not bite my thumb at you, sir,

Capulet 3
But I bite my thumb, sir.

Capulet 4
Do you quarrel, sir?

Montague 4
Quarrel sir? No, sir.

Capulet 5
I serve as good a man as you.

Montague 5
No better

Capulet 5
Yes better sir

Montague 6
You lie!

Capulet 6
Draw if you be men!

Benvolio
Part fools!

Tybalt
Turn thee, Benvolio, look upon thy death.

Benvolio
I do but keep the peace.

Tybalt
Peace? I hate the word,
As I hate hell, all Montagues, and thee.
They fight

Montague's
Down with the Capulets! Down with the Capulets!

Capulet's
Down with the Montagues! Down with the Montagues!
Enter Prince

Prince
Rebellious subjects, enemies to peace,
You men, you beasts
Throw your weapons to the ground,
If ever you disturb our streets again,
Your lives shall pay the forfeit of the peace.
Once more, on pain of death, all men depart.

Other good scene examples: *Hamlet* Act 1 Scene 1 lines 1–45; *A Midsummer Night's Dream:* Act 5 Scene 1 lines 154–313; *Macbeth* Act 1 Scene 1 lines 1–11; *The Tempest* Act 1 Scene 1 lines 1–69.

All scene examples given, with the exception of *Macbeth*, require considerable cutting to create a script for this activity. Compare the original from *Romeo and Juliet* with the example given to gain a sense of the type of cut required. See also *Cutting Text for Performance* on pages 172–4.

The endgame

This activity is so called because the whole sequence builds to a final ensemble performance, the 'endgame' of the session. It was created by Adam Coleman, who wanted to devise a process that could lead to performance quickly and give students an experience that was as close to performance as possible within a short time frame. This activity is about more than the end product though. The performance uses students' learning throughout the session – without it the performance could not take place.

Aims

To create a short ensemble performance of a section of a play, or a whole play in overview. To encourage confidence with text and performance.

Practical considerations

This activity requires a space where the group can work in a circle with some break-out space within the room to develop ideas, if required. It requires a cut of the scene that serves the learning objectives of the performance. The cut for this activity is usually very short, but will vary from group to group and play to play. Two examples are given below. Act 1 Scene 5 from *Hamlet* provides an example of the use of this activity with a scene, while the cut from *Macbeth* gives an overview of the whole play. The sequence for *Hamlet* works well for more experienced students, while the example from *Macbeth* is the most prescribed version of this activity and works well as an introduction for a group that are new to a play and/or performance. Many of the activities in Chapter 3: *Core approaches to Creative Shakespeare* work well to develop students' responses to the scene and can be incorporated into the performance. The *Pointing on the Pronoun* sequence and *Archetypes* are particularly useful. Many of the steps below can be completed in a short time frame – e.g. 30 seconds to create a still image. This activity can be driven through quickly (the brevity of the cut helps this approach) but there are real possibilities for development and peer discussion and evaluations of work if there is time available. The activity often requires several students to play the same character at the same time. For the *Macbeth Endgame*, use a circle as the basis for the activity. Students can step in and out of the circle if desired, or stay in their circle positions throughout to say their lines. Staging can be developed further if desired and appropriate for the group.

Activity

Cutting the text – an optional first stage

If the group know the play or scene chosen for this activity it can work well to begin by asking the group to make a cut of the text, to use for their performance. They should be clear about the objectives for the cut and of the issues and considerations explored in Cutting Text *above. Remind them to focus on the essence of the story when they are cutting. In the case of the example from Act 1 Scene 5 given below, the scene between Hamlet and the ghost of his father, the story is one of murder and a request for revenge. It can work well to ask small groups to make their own cut and then discuss and compare choices. The whole group should then agree which cut version they wish to work with for performance. Alternatively, each small group can be given a section of the scene to cut, with a suggested word limit. These cuts can then be put together to create a whole script for performance of the scene. It works well for a short version of this activity if the cut is short, as then students can then remember their line/s and experience performance, as actors do, without a piece of paper in their hand. They can then fully commit to the performance physically without the barrier of the paper between them and the audience.*

Creating performance

Divide the cut you are working with into sections. Divide the group into a corresponding number of small groups and give each one a section of the scene to work with.

Ask each group to begin by creating a still image of their section of the scene. Their physical representation should be based on the language of the scene at this stage. These can be shared with the whole group and discussed, if desired. It is quite useful to do this as it helps each group to think about audience and how their interpretation of the scene is most effectively communicated to an audience.

Each group should next add movement to their image. This movement should stem from the image and should draw on the rhythm in the language. The group should think about the start and end point of their movement. It needs to be the equivalent of a punctuated piece of writing so that the audience can see what is most important in the line. Again, share and discuss if desired. What does adding the movement bring to our understanding of this moment?

The next step is to think about the sounds of the scene. Each group should experiment with their lines and explore the sounds within them. The Vowels and Consonants *activity on pages 131–2 works well at this stage. When they have tried different interpretations of the lines, the group should decide which sounds and words they wish to emphasize for their performance. Devices such as echoing a line, repeating a line or whispering a line can be incorporated into their performance at this point, if appropriate. Again it can help to share with the other groups (either two groups together or a whole group sharing) and get feed back.*

The students should remember that they are trying to make the scene dramatic – it should work for an audience in a theatre. The language is their main method of creating this drama; the language should be communicated physically as well as verbally.

Bring the whole group together and ask them to run their created scenes in order without stopping to create the whole scene. Take immediate feedback and comments from the group.

Ask each group to decide what or who is their point of focus for the scene. In the case of this example, it would be Hamlet. The whole group should run the scene again, incorporating their point of focus into the performance.

Decide on what kind of stage the scene is being performed. Provide students with either a rough physical or imaginary representation of the stage. This can be as rudimentary or developed as space and time available. It is only important that the students understand the shape of the stage and position of the audience. Ask each group to choose a position for their line on the stage. They can move around the stage if they wish. The whole group should then perform the scene again, incorporating their point of focus in the scene and remembering that they will also need to have a point of focus with the audience.

It often helps at this stage to run the whole scene a few times so that the students can play with movement and focus. Different groups will have different points of focus at different times and this can provide a rich source of discussion, if desired.

The group will by now be familiar with the whole scene. Where they feel it is appropriate, they can echo words or phrases from other groups. They can also physically react to lines from other groups. Run the scene incorporating this echoing.

Ask the whole group to consider the structure of the scene. Where is it at its most dramatic? How can the group show how the scene builds and where the pace of the scene changes? What lines or words are key to this understanding and how can they most effectively be communicated to the audience?

The scene can now be run and the features developed. When the group are happy, they should make a final performance together of the whole scene. This can be an 'endgame' in itself, or the performance can then be built on in any way desired. More text can be added. Movement can be extended. The possibilities are numerous.

This is a simple version of this activity. Many of the activities featured throughout this book could be used as stages to performance and if there is a larger time frame for this activity it can work well to move through each chosen activity, putting them together to create a performance at the end of the process – e.g. another possible sequence could be Archetypes *pages 38–47;* Pointing on the Pronoun *sequence pages 57–63;* Tactics *pages 47–57;* Vowels and Consonants *pages 131–2.*

T
Hamlet: Act 5 Scene 1 lines 9–39

Ghost 1
I am thy father's spirit,
Doomed for a certain term to walk the night

Ghost 2
And for the day confined to fast in fires
Til the foul crimes done in my days of nature
Are burnt and purged away.

Ghost 3
.....................................List, list O list,
If thou didst ever thy dear father love –
Revenge his foul and most unnatural murder!

Hamlet
Murder!

Ghost 3
Murder most foul – as in the best it is

Ghost 4
'Tis given out that, sleeping in my orchard,
A serpent stung me.

Ghost 5
The serpent that did sting thy father's life!
Now wears his crown.

Hamlet
O my prophetic soul!
My uncle!

NB: it does not matter if groups have lines of unequal length. This can provide a useful method of differentiation if appropriate.

Macbeth: A very simple whole group approach to ensemble performance

This version of *Endgame* is most suitable for a group in the very early stages of experiencing and exploring performance. It is one of the most controlled activities we use. Its particular aim is to provide a group with a safe, positive initial experience of performance that introduces them to some of the key tools they will use in more developed work. If the group are not familiar with the play it is possible to fill in the gaps of the story as the activity progresses. In fact this activity can sometimes work well as a quick introduction to the play. If a group know the play well they may wish to create their own edit of the whole play and create their own notes on how it could be played.

The notes below are quite detailed, to provide an idea of how the activity can work in a short time frame – c 1 hour. They are suggestions only of possibilities.

Ask the group to stand in a circle. They should stay in this position throughout the exercise. During the activity the whole group will work through the script below. Do not give the script to the group but teach them the words, line by line, as they work through the activity. You can lead/prompt them if necessary in the final performance. Throughout the activity the students will play a variety of different parts. The whole group will together play a variety of characters. There are also moments where a single student can be asked to play a particular character. Throughout the activity students should be questioned and asked to contribute ideas. Some suggestions are given below, but obviously the nature and level of discussion will vary from group to group.

The whole group begin as witches. Use the line '...withered and wild in their attire' (Act 1 Scene 3 line 40) and ask the group to think of a creature that this line suggests. It works well to avoid mentioning the word 'witch' before this as it tends to lead to lots of stereotypical 'witchy' acting! The idea of withered and wild creatures produces physical work that is more interesting and thoughtful.

Choose a student to play Macbeth and ask him/her to kneel in a ball-type pose in the middle of the circle

Macbeth: Whole play ensemble performance edit

T
Witches: **Macbeth [x 5]**

In their chosen physical shape for the witches, the whole group should begin by chanting 'Macbeth' x 5. It should start softly and build to a crescendo on number 5. Individual movement can be added if desired. They should act as if they are conjuring Macbeth to them – drawing him from the heath towards them. Ask the students how they should say 'Macbeth' and how this might change or develop on each of the 5 chants of the name. How should they gesture towards the Macbeth in the middle of the circle?

On each of the chants the student playing Macbeth should rise a little more, so that by the end of the chanting s/he is standing in the middle of the circle. Macbeth is a warrior at the beginning of the play, so the group should explore how Macbeth should stand. The student playing Macbeth should then adopt the chosen stance.

Witches: **All hail Macbeth that shall be king.**

How would the witches treat a king? As a group, agree a gesture to signify kingship and the significance of the prophecy – e.g. the whole group bow to Macbeth and mime placing a crown on his head. In what tone of voice would the witches speak to Macbeth and why?

Witches: **King! [x 3]**

As before, discuss how this can build to a crescendo and the different ways the group could say 'king' each time. How might Macbeth react to this prophecy? Try out some ideas. Macbeth should then adopt the chosen reaction or stance.

Lady Macbeth: **He brings great news.** (from the side of the circle)

A single student should be asked to play Lady Macbeth. This line is a reaction to the news she receives from Macbeth that the King is on the way to their castle. In this version of the play, who might she say this to? How does she feel about this news and what are her plans? Ask all of the group to suggest ways for Lady Macbeth to deliver this line.

All: **He brings great news. [x 2]** (echoing Lady Macbeth)

Discuss how this could be said. How should each repetition build upon the other? This is not a naturalistic interpretation of the play, so how might these lines give a foreshadowing of the murder to come?

> *Macbeth*: **I have done the deed – this is a sorry sight.** [x 2] (holding the two daggers)

This is the moment after Duncan's murder. As above, discuss how the repetition can be used to develop the drama of the scene. How does the Macbeth we see here differ from the warrior at the beginning of the piece? Who is he talking to?

> *All*: **I have done the deed – this is a sorry sight.** [x 2]

> *Lady Macbeth*: **A foolish thought to say a sorry sight.**

> *All*: **A foolish thought to say a sorry sight.**

As above, discuss the role of the echoing and differing tone of each repetition. Who is the strongest at this moment, Macbeth or Lady Macbeth? How can the students show this physically?

> *Lady Macbeth*: **Out damn spot, out I say.**

> *All*: **Out damn spot, out I say.** [x 2]

These lines are taken from Lady Macbeth's sleepwalking scene. How has her character changed and how can this be shown to the audience? What physical gestures need to accompany these lines? How can the repetition by the whole group be used to create atmosphere? Experiment with different levels of sound. Getting the whole group to join in with the line repetition gradually until the level builds to a frenzy works well here. The group may wish to repeat the line more that 2 times if this works well.

> *Macduff*: **Turn hell hound turn.** (a single student on the centre of the circle; where does the student playing Macduff stand in relationship to the student playing Macbeth?)

> *All*: **Turn hell hound turn.**

These lines are from the final battle. How does Macduff appear? How is he different from Macbeth? Where does he need to be standing in relation to the student playing Macbeth for the line to work? How can the group make the most of the words 'hell hound'?

Macbeth: **I will not yield.**

All (as Macduff): **My voice is in my sword.** [x 3] (all slay him)

Ask the group to think about how physically they can slay Macbeth without actually touching him. How can the group move together to heighten the impact? How should the delivery of the lines vary and build? How should Macbeth react?

Macduff (to Malcolm): **Hail, King of Scotland!** (a single student should play Malcolm)

All: **Hail, King of Scotland!** [x 2]

This is the end of the play and Malcolm is crowned King. Who are the group at this point and how might they react to the news? How should Malcolm stand and behave?

Once the group have worked through the activity it can be repeated as many times as desired, developing the performance each time.

FIGURE 14 *Endgame*

Tips

Adam: *Endgame* works for any play. Try to use work from other activities in the book to feed into the performance; it can be a great way for a group to put their discoveries about a character into a performance.

Bill: Students can do a lot with one line in this type of performance. It is also helpful for them to work with one line as they can learn it and experiment with confidence. I often work with *Archetypes* as a precursor to creating this type of performance.

Chris: I try to make *Endgame* as inclusive and theatrical as possible. It works well to incorporate work from other activities such as *Archetypes* into the performance. I also like to build an awareness of the Globe stage into this performance, if I am going on to rehearse it in more detail with the group.

Yolanda: Many of the stages of *Adam's ten point plan* use activities explored in other chapters. I find it works well to think about which activities will work well for the particular group and performance context and combine them to form my own version of the plan. It is particularly helpful if the group have worked on these activities in greater depth in other sessions. Ironically I find *Endgame* a very good way of starting work on a play, or of starting a session. It is a great warm-up, as well as potentially a session in its own right.

Larger-scale, developed performance

Historically, Shakespeare plays, have been widely used for school productions. There are many books that deal very well with this subject and with directing in general. For this reason I do not plan to discuss further this type of production. Since its inception Globe Education has sought to develop methods that include as many young people as possible in productions of Shakespeare, largely through the use of ensemble playing and by sharing out scenes of one play among different groups. It is these methods that are discussed in greater detail in this section.

Sometimes Shakespeare plays do not appear an attractive option for performances on a bigger scale with a large group of students. This is often because the numbers of parts do not seem to work well for a large group. This section looks at the possibilities offered by ensemble performance and offers a model for a large-scale ensemble production.There are also sometimes concerns about language complexity and the effect of working with Shakespeare's language within a limited rehearsal period. In practice, once students are immersed in the rehearsal process and the story of the play this is not an issue. In fact, the rhythms of the verse can be positively helpful to students when learning lines, exploring pace and creating the drama of a scene in performance.

A good cut of the play, tailored to the needs of the group, is key to a successful production and can go a long way to address the needs of the particular group and performance. Casting can experiment with gender roles. The Globe has staged all-male and all-female productions. Ensemble playing lends itself to casting across gender, as it creates a version of the play that is not influenced by expectations of naturalism. Shakespeare wrote for all-male companies and this further liberates us when we start the process of casting young people. We should feel able to cast regardless of gender, in the way we feel is most appropriate for the particular production.

Globe Education has created large-scale productions of a Shakespeare play with whole schools, casts of 400-plus students from c 16 different schools and classes of c 30 students. Basically anything is possible. It is important when considering a larger-scale production of a Shakespeare play to begin by evaluating your needs and aims, then developing the type of production and cutting the text to meet those aims. This is true of any production, of course – not just Shakespeare. In many ways Shakespeare is more flexible than a piece of modern drama or a musical. There are no copyright considerations and it is possible to do anything you wish with the play. There are endless possibilities for multimodal productions, ensemble productions and productions with a large cast. The production can really be the group's interpretation of the play. This can provide an excellent opportunity for students to feel real ownership of the production and to create a performance that is a reflection of their particular response to the play.

Ensemble performance

Ensemble performance involves a large group in the creation of a scene. In ensemble performance each student can play multiple roles, although some students may take a very clear role throughout the production. It is an effective way of involving lots of students, not just on stage in a scene, but actively contributing to that scene at all times. All students contribute to a whole piece. The story of the scene is not told naturalistically. It is possible for lots of different students to play Macbeth, for example, at different moments, or for the whole group to speak some of Macbeth's lines together. In this type of work, the physicality of the scene becomes important. The group can create images for key moments and at different points in the scene students can work in varying ways. For example, a student can work individually – e.g. speaking Macbeth's lines – in a small group physically representing Macbeth's reaction to the witches and repeating the key line/s at this moment, or as a whole, creating a image or speaking a line. An ensemble scene can be anything the scene director wants it to be. Two examples of possible ways into ensemble playing are given in the *Endgame* exercise above.

When introducing the idea of ensemble playing to students, a football analogy can be useful. As footballers, actors involved in ensemble playing work as a team, playing together at all times, but all have individual roles to play in the scene. For a teacher, ensemble playing offers an opportunity to engage a group of students in playing a scene or moment that enables them all to be actively involved in the process. It can also provide a method for scaffolding student involvement, enabling less confident students to take part fully in a performance without the pressure of individual lines. Equally it provides an opportunity to challenge more confident students, with individual lines or a predominant physical role.

Adam Coleman, pioneer of much of Globe Education's ensemble work, comments:

> I always start an ensemble rehearsal process with clear ideas and exercises, but I also try to let the scene evolve from the ideas of the group. Students often gain confidence during the process and it is always rewarding to be able to give a student who was less confident initially more to do as rehearsals progress. For this reason I try to remain as flexible as possible, although obviously there is a balance to achieve between openness to new ideas and the production of a finished scene of which students and group leader feel proud ... although I find one usually leads to the other.
>
> It is important to make sure that each student is clear about what s/he is doing and who s/he is playing at all times, particularly if this changes throughout the scene. The scene director should identify where the key dramatic moments come in the scene and consider how these will be built up to, marked and moved on from. S/he should consider what levels of vocal sound should be used and when to use a lone student voice and when all should speak together. Experimenting with levels of sound in this manner can provide a powerful score to the scene. The sounds and rhythms of the words are particularly important. Physically students can effectively represent the key imagery of the scene .This can work in almost a dance-like way. The group can also physically represent place and set, if appropriate. Physical and vocal work together tell the story of the scene. The scene director's job is to balance all of these elements. Telling the story of the scene clearly is always my primary focus. If I feel a scene is too busy I simply cut text or action.

Our Theatre – *a model for large cast ensemble production*

Every year since Shakespeare's Globe opened in 1997 Globe Education has worked with Southwark schools on the *Our Theatre* project, funded each year by PwC. Between 12 and 16 schools rehearse a different scene from the same Shakespeare play separately for around ten weeks, then put the scenes together to create their own version of a Shakespeare play, performed on the Globe stage. Each group works with their own Globe Education Practitioner and teacher to create their performance. This model works well across a year group, a school, or a collection of schools. It enables a large group of students to be involved in a production of a Shakespeare play, but does not put pressure on a single group of students or group leader. It allows individual groups to work separately to their own time frames and needs but unites them in a common goal. As such, it is a really useful model for creating a large-scale school production of a Shakespeare play. The numbers of students involved are determined simply by the desired outcome of the production.

The 'Our Theatre' process -key considerations:
When creating this type of production Globe Education considers and works through the following elements. Their importance will vary according to the scale and aims of the production. They are offered here as a possible template for work in and across schools and as a possible stimulus for individuals to create their own model for large-scale productions of Shakespeare plays.

- Consider who is the production for and what are its aims.
- Decide how many young people will be involved. Do they belong to existing group (such as a class or club) who will all take part, or will new groups be formed?
- Identify a member of staff to act as project director with overall artistic responsibility for the production.
- Assign one (or more, if available) member of staff to each group. Each group can then have its own rehearsal time. The member of staff will act as director for the group. Older/more experienced students can provide support as assistant directors if appropriate
- All members of staff should meet regularly throughout the process, under the leadership of the project director. At these meetings they should discuss the progress of their groups and agree on key production elements such as costumes and props.
- The project director should divide the play (uncut at this stage)

into sections or blocks, with one block per group taking part in the production. The blocks should be a complete section of the story. They do not have to be complete scenes, although sometimes this will be the case. They do not need to be equal in length. It is important that the story remains clear and that each group is able to tell a clear section of the story in their performance. The project director should assign each group a block of the play, using their knowledge of the group to choose the most appropriate section of the story to serve the group's needs.

- After a workshop with the group to explore the story of their block, the group director should make an initial cut – see *Cutting text for performance* above for further details. S/he should meet with the project director to go through this cut. This ensures parity across the production as a whole.
- Each group should then rehearse separately for the allotted time period.
- Throughout the rehearsal period the group leaders and project director should meet on a regular basis. They should agree common threads for the production, such as set and props, that can be used in all scenes. They should also focus on scene transitions. Group

FIGURE 15 *Our Theatre. The Tempest, 2011*

leaders with blocks following each other should discuss how one ends and the next begins

- Ensure that groups are aware of the performance space and have a rehearsal in the space.
- The day before the performance, or on the day itself, if time allows, hold a dress rehearsal in the performance space, where the play is put together. Each block is run one after the other, in order, so that the whole play is performed. Ensure that each group is ready to take the stage immediately the block before them finishes. Experiment with creative ways of doing this during the rehearsal period.
- Groups performing in the play can also be audience. Logistically they simply need to be moved discreetly from the auditorium to backstage, or their entrance point, in plenty of time for their performance. They can return to the auditorium again after their performance.
- Consider other factors that will make the individual blocks work together to make a whole performance. Music is a useful unifying tool and can be composed and played by a different group of students, if desired. Common costume elements can also have a unifying effect. This can be as simple as groups or characters wearing the same colour shirt.
- Consider the end of the performance and how each group can be thanked and/or applauded without all having to return to the stage.

Performing Shakespeare can seem challenging for young people, but it is a challenge they invariably meet and in which they often exceed their expectations and sometimes that of their teachers and group leaders. An experience of performing Shakespeare puts young people the other side of the text they are often asked to study and gives them a first-hand experience of the way Shakespeare and his company would have known the plays – as actors performing a story for an audience.

Young people as audience

The other way in which young people can 'meet' Shakespeare's plays in performance is as audience. In Globe Education's *Playing Shakespeare with Deutsche Bank* production of *Macbeth* there was a pre-show in which two young actors dressed in school uniform walked around a theatre full of school children, asking for help to find their group. Students and teachers alike were, for the most part, enormously helpful. Conversations were had, solutions found, a connection was made. Moments later, at the beginning of the show there was a loud explosion. The two young actors 'magically' emerged bloodied from body bags on the stage to become two of the witches in the opening scene. There was a moment where the young audience, many of whom had never been to a theatre before, instantly understood what theatre is about. That it is live, that each performance is unique, that it is not only for the audience but that theatre, particularly at the Globe, is made through the interaction of actor and audience. In the words of one young Globe audience member, 'in the theatre there is no glass'. Experiencing theatre in this way – being part of a live event – was commonplace for Shakespeare's audiences. In the Globe theatre, how an audience reacts to a line can affect the way in which the next line is said. Being part of an audience, like performing, can empower students. If they feel engaged with a performance and form feelings and opinions about their experience they are instantly theatre critics. They need simply then to learn a vocabulary through which to express their feelings and reactions both verbally and in writing.

When young people 'hear' a play they encounter it as Shakespeare intended. Literally hearing the words can make them accessible. I know a production is successful if a young audience ask why it wasn't performed in Shakespeare's language. It always is, but when the words are spoken, a scene given a context and a character's emotions and dilemmas played out before them, a play that can appear inaccessible on a page becomes simply a story shared between actor and audience.

Planning a theatre visit

The logistical considerations when planning a theatre visit can be considerable. The pressure on financial, human and curriculum resources can be significant. For these reasons alone it is vital that the visit is worthwhile and facilitates maximum learning. It is also important that the visit is a socially and culturally positive experience for the young people concerned. The act of going to a theatre can provide learning of social and cultural significance that is as important as any learning about the play itself. This is particularly true if the group contains students who are new to theatre. A touring production visiting your school or organization, however, can be equally valuable. It all depends on the needs and previous experience of the young people concerned.

As ever, it is important to place knowledge of your group at the centre of all planning. Not all Shakespeare productions are necessarily suitable for young people. Again, this is especially true if the group is relatively new to theatre-going. Young people need to build their experience as audience members just as they would build their experience in any other area. It is a progressive journey. Therefore it is important to choose productions that meet the needs of your students on their particular stage of the journey. Length is a key factor, as is setting, production style and theatre environment. Theatre companies are usually very happy to discuss this information (to the best of their current knowledge) in advance of booking.

Bill Buckhurst, Director of four Globe Education *Playing Shakespeare with Deutsche Bank* productions, shares his key considerations for planning productions for young people new, or relatively new, to theatre.

> I always try to think back to my experience of going to see Shakespeare from eleven onwards. I'm afraid it wasn't always very positive. That was because I simply was not engaged. I always try to think of ways in which a young audience can engage with the material. I think the first way of doing this is to make sure the production has a clear story that everybody can understand. Some of Shakespeare's stories are very complex, so this can be a challenge. The main challenge for young people, though, is often the language, so I focus on ways of making the language clear and live for the audience. If the story is not clear the audience is less likely to want to go on the journey with you; this is particularly important in the Globe when the audience are so important and are, in effect, an extra character in the story. I do a lot of work in the rehearsal room on the language. If we as a company are not clear about what we mean with every line, the audience will not understand it. I think I have an advantage at the Globe as the audience are engaged with the actual story-telling. Words are not spoken into a dark auditorium. I try and find as many opportunities as I can to make the audience feel part of the production.
>
> Young people are used to edited films, video games, things happening very quickly. I try to be aware of this but not in any way to produce theatre that patronizes its audience. I try to make sure the language is fresh and new. I put action in the yard of the theatre. I really try to make sure the actors are sharing the play with the audience. Period costume can sometimes be an obstacle. It doesn't have to be, by any means, but I have always gone down a more contemporary route with design because it is a way of enabling young people to make a connection. If an actor looks as if they have just stepped out of the crowd it is an immediate way of enabling young people to connect with the play. The actors may be speaking language that is four hundred years old but they are recognizably people going on a journey. I try to make the young audience feel that they are part of the story and that they 'own' that performance.

Preparing for a theatre visit

Preparing for a visit to a theatre to see a Shakespeare play is a combination of three factors: preparing students for the process of being an audience for live theatre; preparing them to see or 'hear' (as Shakespeare's contemporaries would have said) a specific Shakespeare play; and finally, preparing them for a specific production of that play. How this is done and the importance of each element depends entirely on the particular group.

If a group are not experienced theatre-goers its important to consider whether they have an existing schema through which to process the production. Find out their perceptions of being a theatre audience and build from that point. In the theatre there may be 'no glass' but there is also no pause button. Both actors and fellow audience can hear the comments of those around them and will be affected by their tone and content. Young people willingly suspend disbelief and engage with the performance but sometimes the subtleties of the interface between the 'real' world and the world of the play can be confusing. This is particularly true in a theatre such as the Globe that sometimes plays with the relationship and interface between actor and audience. It can be helpful to run through what to expect at the particular venue staging the production and to discuss similarities and differences between other audience experience. Cinema, pop concerts and football matches can be useful points of comparison.

The students should be prepared to engage with the story of the play. This does not necessarily mean that they should know the whole story of the play. Sometimes this can be detrimental and take away the excitement

FIGURE 16 *Playing Shakespeare with Deutsche Bank*

of finding out what happens next. In reality, the timing of the theatre visit in relation to the period in which the play is studied will determine how much of the story students know. There are pros and cons at whichever point a theatre visit takes place. A visit early in the study of the play can be beneficial in exciting students and, for less experienced groups, locating the play clearly as a script for theatrical interpretation and performance. It is important, however, that students understand the production is simply one interpretation of the play rather than the definitive version.

Chris Stafford, Producer of *Playing Shakespeare with Deutsche Bank* comments:

> It is helpful for a group to have a sense of part of the story; sometimes knowing the whole story really well can take away part of the experience. However in most cases the extent to which the group know the story will depend on the point they have reached in their study of a play. I never want to know how a film will end before going to see it, so where possible apply this principle when preparing groups for theatre productions. Working on a specific scene can be a good way to prepare. Choose one that you know is key to the play and is unlikely to be cut in the production. Remember that the group is going to see a specific production, not a definitive version of the play. The story told in the production may be the result of artistic decisions taken in rehearsal. The story seen on stage may not be identical to the story in the text of the play. For example, in our recent production of *Romeo and Juliet* the cut of the play resulted in Paris's story ending at the death of Juliet – the audience did not see him die at the end of the play. It's helpful for students to understand the context in which the play was written. Also for them to have specific aspects of the play or production to think about. In the Globe, for example, it's useful to ask students to think about the way the audience are involved in soliloquies. Preparation is all about striking the right balance for the group. We want students to feel prepared enough to be able to engage with the show, but not to know so much information that there is little left for them to discover moment by moment in the performance. Wanting to find out what happens next, or how it happens, is a key part of any audience experience. It's important to ask: Do you and your group want the spoilers?

Preparation that focuses on a specific scene or moments between characters is particularly effective. Working through any of the exercises in Chapter 3: *Core approaches to Creative Shakespeare* can provide a useful method of familiarizing students with characters and key ideas in the play. Give students moments to look out for and questions to consider that are pertinent to your particular study of the play. Ensure that they are equipped enough to be able to engage with what is happening and to gain maximum benefit from the experience. As before, the most effective method of achieving this result will vary from group to group.

Many theatre companies produce websites to support their plays. These can provide a good starting point when preparing to see that particular production. Remind students that the director and producers have chosen to tell the story of the play in a particular way – the production is their interpretation only. Encourage students to think about the elements that make up a production such as casting, cuts to the text, staging, setting, design (costume, props, lighting), music, particular characterization or performances, and the presentation of key moments in the play. They should consider their response to the creative choices made for each of these areas. Reading theatre reviews and breaking down the key considerations for each reviewer can be useful preparation and provide a focus for the performance. At whatever level they are working it is important that the group are equipped to be critical interpreters of the production.

After the visit it is important that students respond to their experience. Discuss and explore their response to the production, in a way that is most appropriate to the group. Writing reviews is one obvious approach. Challenging students to create small group interpretations and performances of a scene in response to the way in which it was staged in the production is equally effective and stimulates much debate. Simply discussing the production, starting from the students' immediate response and progressing to the discussion of the use and combination of key production elements, is a simple but highly effective way to develop critical interpretation skills.

Using performances of Shakespeare on film

Visits to a theatre, or the visit of a theatre company to school, are not always physically or financially viable. Film here has a vital role to play in giving access to Shakespeare in performance to all students. These issues aside, screen drama is a key part of our culture and film interpretations of Shakespeare's plays are plentiful. Therefore analysis of film interpretations of Shakespeare's plays have an important role to play in our contemporary understanding and analysis of Shakespeare in performance.

Globe Education has been working with Professor Tony Howard from Warwick University's School of English and Comparative Literary Studies on the use of Shakespeare on film since the early 1990s.[1] Here he describes his rationale and approaches for using filmed Shakespeare with young people.

Professor Tony Howard

One of the reasons I started using filmed versions of Shakespeare in my teaching was as a way of putting an actor in the room. I couldn't snap my fingers and bring an actor physically into my sessions every day, but I could show a film clip and put a range of different actors in front of my students. It provided me with an easy way to engage students actively with the play.

Film is a medium that everyone is used to. We grow up watching television and film from our early years. The impact is immediate and the play can become instantly accessible – it lifts the play from the page. Everyone, of whatever age, is accustomed to reading film images and scenes. As a result film can defamiliarize Shakespeare.

All students are already film critics without necessarily knowing it. They engage in a critical process every time they turn on the television or watch a DVD. As a result of this, performance of Shakespeare on film can be more accessible to them than it is on stage. Film directors work a lot in close-up, so it is easy for young people to become more emotionally involved with characters on film. This in turn enables emotional engagement with the language. One of the key strengths of film, of course, is the strong visual element, but one of the potential hazards with this is that a film can be taken by students as the definitive interpretation of the play. However, as soon as students are asked to compare different film versions of the same scene, this issue disappears. A comparative approach is therefore key to the effective use of Shakespeare on film as a teaching tool.

Just as young people are accustomed to reading and interpreting screen images, they are also experienced debaters about the film or television they view. Viewing and debating two or three different film extracts from the same Shakespeare play is an instant method of engaging students in developed critical analysis. It also enables students to view the play in a variety of contexts: historical, cultural and social.

Film is a very flexible tool. We speak of looking at a screen as a passive activity, but actually it isn't: the spectator's mind is active, it's the screen that is inert, it can't engage with the students' responses as an actor at the Globe does. This is why comparative analysis is vital, and why the teacher is all-important if film is to function as a successful method for students to engage with Shakespeare in performance. It is the role of the teacher to provide the means of interaction that actors can provoke in the Globe theatre, to react to their students' responses in the moment and to ensure that there is a conversation between student audience and screen performance.

A film performance can be available to your students any time you wish. The action can be paused and discussed at any point. This can create an intimate experience for students. It is not possible to stop an actor mid-performance in the theatre and debate student reactions to the play. Film provides us with this powerful opportunity.

Tony Howard's advice for using Shakespeare on film in the classroom

1. As stated above, it is important to always use film comparatively. Three or four clips of film are a good number to work with for an hour session. If possible, have some extra clips prepared in case the clips you selected for some reason do not engage the group. Choose extracts that you believe will 'speak to' the particular group. Finding and preparing film clips can be time-consuming. There are many DVDs available now and YouTube is a valuable and very convenient resource. Searching for a play on YouTube can produce some interesting results. Organizations such as the BFI and Film Club have a wealth of resources and comparative material.
2. Which clips you choose, and the objective of the session, will depend on the needs of the group. Consider whether to provide students with a focus for viewing the clips before they watch them or whether to introduce that after viewing.
3. Comparing text with film version is an important part of this process. Consider whether students should look at the text before or after viewing the film. It can also be useful for them to consider what is not in the text. The Battle of Agincourt in *Henry V*, for example, has very few lines within it. The battle as staged in films of *Henry V* usually contains far more action. It is the director's way of fulfilling the Chorus's request to 'Let us ... on your imaginary forces work' (*Henry V* Prologue line 18).
4. Choose moments from the play to work on that are particularly interesting or that are relevant to the group's study focus. Beginnings of films work well as they are the point at which the audience enters the world of the play. Showing students three different film openings provides them with three disagreements to discuss – three different directorial views of the beginning of the play and its meaning. Endings of films are equally useful. All openings and endings provide an editorial statement on the play. Comparison of two or more film endings facilitates detailed critical discussion about directorial choice and interpretations of a play.
5. Be aware that the clips you choose will suggest a particular interpretation of the play, which may not be the interpretation students would see if watching the film in its entirety. Teachers here play an editorial role and should be aware of the choices they are inevitably making.
6. It really does not matter if the film is not very 'good' (you are only

using a short clip and extracts need not be longer than one minute if desired). Sometimes these clips foster the most intense debate.

7. It is particularly important not to use clips from older films on their own, as this can result in Shakespeare appearing alien and distant. Comparatively, however, they are excellent tools and stimulate contextual discussions. Using film versions from different time periods can exemplify the flexibility of Shakespeare's language and the timelessness of the stories told in the plays.
8. Know the clips you use well but, as ever, be prepared to be flexible in response to students' comments. One of the great things about using film is that student responses are immediate and genuine.
9. Ensure that students are clear about what is interpretation and particular to the given film and what is in the play. Remember that their reaction to a film is not necessarily a reaction to the play.
10. Be aware of the potential of film to facilitate exploration of different cultures and social, political and historical contexts.
11. Clips from the recorded Globe theatre performances provide a good counterpoint with film clips, and an avenue through which to discuss the difference between theatre and film. Be aware, however, that filmed theatre performance is quite a different genre to film. It is a different type of study material. If used with this awareness, clips of both kinds can provide a useful tool for exploring specific moments of a play.
12. Encourage students to use the cinema in their head: allow them to respond creatively to the play on the page. Asking them to write a film script for an appropriate section of text can be a way of doing this. Students can also be given media resources to create their own response to the play and thus become film-makers themselves.

CHAPTER SEVEN

Learning through Shakespeare

Shakespeare's plays can provide a powerful tool for learning. The universal nature of the stories of the plays provides endless opportunities to explore a range of issues and ideas. In such work the primary objective is not to learn about the plays themselves (although this type of learning may also take place), but to use the plays as a frame to explore a specific issue. Shakespeare's plays depict worlds that are often alien to students, but the challenges and situations encountered by the characters in those worlds can resonate strongly with our lives today. They are simultaneously distant from our world, yet relevant to our humanity. It is this combination that makes the plays such wonderful vehicles for exploration and teaching. Students feel 'safe' discussing a character's situation and exploring their feelings because they belong to the specific world of the play, yet in doing so they are enabled to reflect on their own feelings and response to such a situation.

It is possible to build this type of reflection into our everyday teaching of Shakespeare. For example, students looking at Macbeth's 'If it were done...' (*Macbeth* Act 2 Scene 7 line 32) soliloquy can explore the process by which we make decisions and go to consider the impact of our decisions on our lives and future events. When planning sessions it is always worth considering the points which could facilitate broader learning; such learning can also benefit study of the play. Often if students can associate with dilemmas of the characters in a play and can relate these to their own lives, they find it easier to engage with the play or scene and to formulate detailed response and analysis.

Equally, though, Globe Education creates projects that focus specifically on learning through Shakespeare, in which the plays provide a framework for personal and social development. Such work might use a whole play or focus on part of a play. Sessions or projects can vary in length, depending on the group and aims and objectives for the work. Past projects have explored many different kinds of plays and situations: for example, *Coriolanus* to explore transition, *Romeo and Juliet* to address conflict between two newly merged teaching classes, *As You Like It* with young people undergoing treatment in hospital, and *King Lear* to build communication and literacy skills.

Patricia Kerrigan has always been motivated in her work for Globe Education by the potential of Shakespeare's plays to provide a tool for student learning about humanity and the wider world. Patricia comments:

> As an actor playing and rehearsing a character in a Shakespeare play, you have to find an emotional connection with that character and his or her situation. I've always found that, in making that connection, you begin to learn something more about yourself. You are not just learning about words and their meaning, you are learning about human nature, about what it means to be a human being. Connecting with Shakespeare's characters can teach us so many things: what it means to be a part of society, what it means to be in a relationship, how an individual might react to good fortune and, in turn, adversity. The list is endless.
>
> The splendour of teaching Shakespeare for me is that my focus might be teaching a group about a play so they can write an essay or pass an exam, but an individual might walk away from the session understanding a little bit more about themselves, with new insights through which to process their own thoughts and feelings. There are basic fundamental ideas and 'truths' explored in these plays that can apply to every aspect of our lives.
>
> It is possible for a group to go on a collective journey through the exploration of a play that can challenge the status quo and create a new group dynamic, or set of behaviours.
>
> As a practitioner, the plays give me an opportunity to look at a group dynamic and to find ways of using the plays to address any issues. If appropriate, it can enable me to help individual students using the frame of the play. This can be as simple as considering the status of roles I ask a student to play or the particular scenes or moments I choose to explore. I can use my teaching of the play to achieve a better balance in the classroom dynamic. A young person may not be able to explore feelings of love as themselves, but they might be able to explore and discuss Romeo's feelings of love for Juliet and, in doing so, gain fresh insights into their own emotions.

The starting point for all such work is, as ever, the needs of the group and the desired outcomes of the project. A play, or part of a play, can then be chosen that mirrors the situation of the group and will provide a vehicle through which to explore relevant ideas and dilemmas. This type of work is often a gradual process. Each session can be structured to explore a specific issue, leading students to some form of discussion and decision-making that can then inform planning for the next session. It is important that there is space for students to explore and discover and for group leaders to recognize that this may lead the session in unforeseen directions. This is always true, of course, but never more so than when using the plays for this purpose. In role work and the use of drama, approaches such as those championed by Dorothy Heathcote and later Cecily O'Neil can be important tools in this process.

Learning through Shakespeare can take many forms. As it relies on the unique interaction between all involved, it will never take exactly the same form twice. The accounts of the projects which follow below simply provide an overview of some programmes devised and delivered by Globe Education in collaboration with two different project partners. Their aims are different, but both seek to use Shakespeare as a means through which to explore issues and achieve aims relevant to the group in question. Together they provide an insight into what is possible and highlight some of the different ways in which Shakespeare might be used as a tool for learning.

A ten-week project for Evelina Hospital School, London

In May 2010 Globe Education was approached by the Evelina Hospital School, part of St Thomas's Hospital London, to create a piece of work with their day and longer-term students, all patients at the hospital. They wanted to use Shakespeare as a means of exploring some of the challenges that faced their young people: building their confidence and sense of self during a difficult period for both them and their families. Extensive consultation with teachers and hospital staff resulted in a ten-week project using *As You Like It* as a frame. Multimodal approaches and ensemble performance techniques were combined to create a final promenade performance on the school floor of the hospital.

Secondary school teacher and freelance journalist Isobel Durrant reflects on her experience of the project.

'To liberty, and not to banishment': Isobel Durrant

It's surprising how many conversations can include the words 'with his eyes full of anger' in a small classroom of teenagers. A few summers ago, along with 'thou diest' and 'to liberty, and not to banishment', it became a classroom catchphrase. Pupils and staff delivering the words as punchlines to all manner of conversations and situations.

We were high on Shakespeare's *As You Like It* at the time, caught up in the excitement of an inspiring project with Globe Education that culminated in a thrilling afternoon of drama, music and installation.

The project ran across all areas of our hospital school, from Early Years to Secondary, reaching pupils receiving dialysis and those too unwell to leave the wards. In the Secondary Classroom, where I still teach, I remember it as a magical, joyous few weeks, and a lot of hard work. We ate, drank and dreamt *As You Like It*. The Globe Education Practitioners who came in and worked alongside us each brought different skills and made different demands on us and our pupils. Their expectations were high. Pupils had to work hard to meet them. So did we. We used our classroom blog to share ideas and keep an open discussion going with the Globe Education Practitioners when they weren't with us. That way the pupils were in on all the thinking and decisions and knew their opinions were valued and taken seriously.

Three of the long-term pupils had speaking parts, performing scenes from the play. They were expected to learn their lines. I asked them one morning how they were getting on and suddenly realized they had no experience of learning speeches and no idea how. One of them had dyslexia. So we all had copies in front of us and read repeatedly from them, prompting the players, until they – and everyone else – were word perfect. That's when we really began to play with the lines, building on the sessions we had enjoyed with the practitioners. One boy's encyclopaedic knowledge of soap operas and sitcoms came into its own. He seamlessly drew parallels between Shakespeare's story and programmes familiar to his peers, dextrously analysing motives and behaviour while the adults listened open-mouthed.

Celia, Rosalind, Orlando and Duke Frederick moved into the classroom with us. They were as vivid to us as any celebrity in *Heat* magazine. We discussed them: their feelings, their motives, their problems, their desires.

Our theme was transformation. How the characters disguise themselves and in the process start to reveal truths about themselves, to find out who and what they are. We transformed our little section of the school into the Duke's court. We decided on colourschemes and made fans and slippers from card printed with excerpts from the play. We hung them around the room so they twirled and twisted like charms. We made kaleidoscopes from the same colours, used boxes with built-in microphones to deliver snatches of text and give the audience moments of discovery when the boxes were opened to reveal jewels, pearls, scraps of velvet and other fabrics, tissue paper hearts. We made masks to symbolize the characters' disguises – masks that not just our cast would use, but also the audience, who would equally be transformed by the experience.

Pupils listened to each other, all caught up in the spirit of the project. They grew in confidence, learned to speak their words with conviction, to stand up, to be proud of themselves and each other. They offered each other support and took risks. As a teacher I watched them move into that zone where they began to be independent of us, to take charge of what they were doing, of own their learning. That is what teachers want for our pupils, to see them take flight, to go to places we cannot take them. They discovered unsuspected talents and revelled in the journey. It was a learning curve for all of us and one I feel privileged to have been part of. Afterwards we were proud, but sad.

As one pupil wrote in her feedback: 'The whole five weeks was just amazing. When the Globe theatre first came in, and we did our first workshop with Kate, I didn't want to take part as I was shy and didn't want to look silly, but now I love doing the workshops and I'm quite upset that there ain't going to be anymore. I now want to join the Globe Youth Theatre group. I am hoping to join in September.'

A whole school cross-curricular project for children with complex learning difficulties

In 2003 Jon David, Headmaster of Gosden House School for children with complex learning difficulties, embarked on a ten-week project with Globe Education to produce a cross-curricular site-specific performance of *Romeo and Juliet* at his school. The project was to involve the whole school, both primary and secondary students, and culminate in a week in July in which the whole curriculum would be taught through the play, ending with the performance. Ten years on, after a decade of Gosden, Globe projects, Jon reflects on what made that initial project so effective that it stimulated a decade-long collaboration. Former Gosden House School student 'Ellen' * reflects on her personal journey each year, and what a decade of 'learning through Shakespeare' has contributed to her educational experience.

* Student names have been changed

Gosden and Globe: 'Two Households both alike in dignity...'
Jon David: Headmaster, Director/Trustee of Gosden Lighthouse Company

Gosden House School is a Surrey Local Authority residential school for children with complex learning difficulties. Gosden House is committed to experiential learning and an individualized programme of study designed to enhance students' learning and engagement through a multisensory approach. This project was jointly planned and carried out by Gosden staff and Globe Education Practitioners.

Our first project together was stimulated by a desire to challenge our students and to involve the whole school, working together through the arts to achieve a common goal. When Gosden and Globe staff first met to plan the project we discovered a shared ethos, probably best encapsulated in Gosden's mission statement: 'Children First and People Matter'. It was this and our ambition to provide the children with a powerful and empowering experience through exploring a Shakespeare play that guided our project planning. Globe Education Practitioners worked in the school for weekly sessions throughout the summer term and in its penultimate week took up residence at Gosden, becoming full-time residential members of the school community, to help guide our production of *Romeo and Juliet* to its performance.

Gosden House is a beautiful school set within 44 acres of parkland. There are about 110 children on roll ranging in age from 4 through to 16. The practitioners' aim was to work with the school's creative team to produce a site-specific promenade version of *Romeo and Juliet* in the Gosden House building and grounds, culminating in a final scene on the newly built stage in the school's Victorian walled garden.

Ellen's story starts in July 2003 as a little girl waving a flag and shouting 'Down with the Montagues'. It ends with Ellen, as a mature 16-year-old, successfully completing a three-week work experience based at Globe Education in London.

> **Ellen**
> I was six, I waved flags. I remember feeling excited, a bit scared. I waved a flag and shouted 'Down with the Montagues'. It was fun because I was a Capulet. I remember feeling safe, secure, excited. The whole school was there. More flags; hanging from our windows. Giant banners; all that colour. But most of all; the happiness.
>
> The walled garden, everyone crying as we watched the end. It was sad but lovely. I watched the film we made over and over. It helped me with my memories. I loved it. I loved the Globe actors; they are part of our Gosden family. Globe week has always been such fun. Lunchtimes – so noisy. You could always tell when the actors were in.
>
> Particularly Adam! He was such fun. We all love Adam. [Adam Coleman] He understands us; we always cheer when he comes into school.

What has become known as 'Globe Week' at Gosden fully integrates the practitioners into school life. The key issues are trust, respect and understanding. The Globe Education Practitioners are carefully selected in close co-operation between Gosden and Globe Education. We, as the receiving organization, have always insisted that even before they start there should be a clear understanding of purpose and the unique ethos of Gosden House. The planning for the week is meticulous. Practitioners are allocated to class teachers and scenes and work to a tight and focused timetable. The edit of plays concerned is a key factor in their successful delivery. As pressure grows towards the performance, staff and practitioners meet on a regular basis for collaborative work. To work effectively, trust must build very quickly. This can only happen if expectations from both organizations are clearly met and achieved. Performance is also key. Each performance is unique. It happens only once. The cycle of planning, practice, performance and active learning leads staff and students alike to that passing breathless moment of performance, a unique moment, that impacts on all who share it. In such a context learning becomes both individual and social. Education in its purest form through shared experience.

At the end of that first project week in July 2003, weeks of planning, editing, redrafting and – most importantly – listening to and reflecting the student voice and understanding of the text culminated in a whole school performance. There had been weeks of preparation. Nothing, though, could have prepared me for the impact that performance would have on my school. One hundred and ten students with complex learning difficulties performed this joint collaboration with such poignancy that the final scene in the school's walled garden shook the audience with emotion. The impact on everyone present was remarkable. Video capture at the time recorded the disbelief of what we had all experienced. Reality seemed stretched. Smiling, happy children. Many parents crying, overcome by the emotions of the moment. The power of such emotions lives on in the hearts of all those present.

'My child shone like a star today. I can't believe it.' (Gosden House School parent)

The Gosden, Globe creative partnership, established that day, encapsulates the very best in innovative, collaborative work which can transform children's lives forever.

Ellen moved year groups, time moved on. It was decided that the enormous success of our *Romeo and Juliet* should be followed by a more conventional stage performance of *The Tempest* but that we should use a whole range of artwork to create an aesthetic for our production. We endeavoured to extend our collaboration to local schools who joined our production.

The playhouse format created limitations and opportunities for performance. Parents were directly involved in the process rather than the performance and were welcomed in to witness workshops both in drama, music and creative arts. Ellen found more difficulty in remembering this production but she did remember the huge range of artwork that this production brought to the whole school environment. *'I was very impressed with the big boat that they brought into the school hall. It was a real one.'* The production confirmed our belief in the positive impact of the productions on our students and the desire of all to make the project a yearly occurrence. We decided to develop our collaboration and seek to explore the potential for the use of Shakespeare at Gosden as a long-term project. In this spirit of challenge and questioning, *Hamlet* seemed an obvious choice for our work in 2005.

Ellen

We started with a big bang. We had 10 children from Italy staying in the school and they played drums to start with. I was a grave digger. We really got into the zone. We played football with a skull and Mr David sang a really silly song with us all about graves! 'A pick axe and a spade. Four and a shrouding sheet.' I really enjoyed it. It was my first real part. The Globe people made the play really come to life. We all had red T shirts with skulls on.

This production was the best-attended performance yet. The practitioners, teachers and staff had all grown in confidence. The performance became fully inclusive, involving a whole range of community organizations.

In such an ambitious production, meticulous editing added to the challenge of creating a coherent performance – one that was not only true to the spirit of this most worthy of plays, but also entertained and stimulated the children's interests. The play culminated in all the participants singing 'To be, or not to be. That is the question', Shakespeare's famous soliloquy set to an anthem created by the school's choir and initially recorded in the school's recording studio.

The enigma that is Shakespeare the man was highlighted for the children in 2006 when, in combination with the Globe Education Practitioners, he decided to join with us in our production! One of the most dramatic moments in the school's history was his arrival. An actor fresh from the Globe (Colin Hurley) played a curious Shakespeare in search of a name for his 'Scottish play'. For Ellen, who was now 11, it was a moment of real engagement.

Ellen

Shakespeare arrived from the Globe. It was great. He arrived in a horse and carriage.

He asked us to think of a name for his new play. We all met him in the Coach House.

The horse was black and beautiful. I played a witch on the blasted heath. We worked with the actors in the wild field, built a camp of twigs, and charged the audience with gruesome cries and then we made spells. I have still got the thumb in my bedroom [the thumb was one of the props designed by the children to boil up their spells]: 'Round about the cauldron go, in the poisoned entrails throw.' We had some great songs in the play. I loved the scene in Birnam Wood. That happened in the orchard. Lots of trees running about.

The Gosden, Globe partnership was now developing into a seamless company of players. During the passage of the years new young Globe Education Practitioners were introduced, new children and Gosden staff. The relationship between the two organizations strengthened year on year and both organizations were able to train more Globe Education Practitioners and teachers in methods for positive interventions for Gosden students, through the use of creative approaches to learning – Shakespeare's plays providing the framework for all of our exploring. We were constantly revising and reflecting on our practice. This work became key to providing Globe Education Practitioners with the opportunity to understand a full range of special needs. The project was now a training ground for the practitioners and for Gosden House staff alike. We learnt from each other, constantly exploring and developing new skills. When we visited Shakespeare's Globe on Bankside with our students they took part in workshops led by practitioners that had been trained in SEN work at Gosden. My staff led training sessions at the Globe and thus the learning generated by the Gosden, Globe project infused all areas of Globe Education teaching for young people with SEN, whether it was in Southwark schools or in outreach programmes internationally.

In July 2007 Gosden celebrated its sixtieth birthday with the party to end all parties and a Gosden, Globe production of *A Midsummer Night's Dream.*

> **Ellen**
> It was fantastic. We called it *The Diamond Dream*. The school was full of fairies and rude mechanicals. We all learnt the song 'Is all our company here? I'd like to sing it now cos we are the rude mechanicals.' I played Titania and we learnt choral speaking. You could feel the rhythm of our words. We sung lots of songs. But the best bit for me was when students from Broadwater [a local school] joined us for their rap and dance.
> And the rude mechanicals were SO funny!

The company of practitioners worked closely with teachers to work with a wide range of props in site-specific scenes. We used the natural contours of the setting. Gosden is blessed with a full 40 acres of parkland and each year it is part of our creative brief to develop and create a new area. The dream-like quality of *A Midsummer Night's Dream* was further created by the construction of giant puppets. These puppets were built by the children. The play took on a personality all of its own. A key factor in all our productions is the music used to transport and set the narrative in the scene. Children of all ages singing to the wind in the open air, together with a wide range of acoustic instruments and drums.

> **Ellen**
> It all ended with a huge Greek dance like Zorba, the Greek. Patrick [Director, Globe Education] planted an olive tree and we all clapped. That tree is still growing strong today.

The metaphor of the olive tree is not lost in our partnership. In a world of symbols the peace we have achieved through our creative partnership strengthens with each passing year.

Ellen Sonnets 2008
We had a mega installation. A festival called GosFest. We had our own tents. And the audience came and looked at each tent. They were all different. Our own installation art.

We also had windbreakers and washing lines with socks. My job was quite different – I had to be the toilet tent. I was only needed for my feet and sound effects! It was a minor acting part really. I had to pretend I had had too many beans. This whole project was very different from anything we had done before. It was a lot quieter, not much singing, no parents, relaxed. Less manic and low stress. I really enjoyed GosFest. It's all I can remember apart from Sonnet 23 which is still written on the courtyard wall.

This particular project was a challenge to us all. A lot of sonnets were very difficult for us all to understand, apart from those most popular. The most interesting aspect of this year's project was the creation of tent town consisting of a fixed tenting area. Gosfest provided a really stimulating installation for all our visitors and students – each tent exquisitely fitted out, representing an individual sonnet theme. The practitioners and staff worked on a range of multisensory activities to emphasize not only the drama of the sonnets but their encompassing nature. The sonnets threw up more questions than they answered.

We looked for our next project to one of Shakespeare's masterpieces – a tale of revenge and jealousy, one that tracks the sick mind with breathtaking detail and explores how language can distort love into the green-eyed monster of jealousy.

Ellen *Othello* 2009
I played Othello and then Desdemona. Smothered, I was. I've never been killed in a scene before. It was on a big bed with drapes. It was a scene that really meant something to me. I really enjoyed playing Desdemona. I could understand it from her point of view. I really connected. This is not a nice story. Before *Othello* Shakespeare seemed just a nice thing to do. Something to do for your parents. It was now for me, that I really understood. I knew how Desdemona felt.

Othello is a really heavy play and we needed all the practitioners' skills and Gosden staff experience to make the play work for the children. To stage the scenes of murder, jealousy and revenge we used small groups of older students who were able to work together. Difficult and tortuous lines were shared. Murderous scenes were tempered with dance-like qualities. We cast four 'Othellos' and four 'Desdemonas'. But the end is just as brutal, even if diluted to the power of four. This production used a range of lyrical songs including a theme to highlight Othello's growing jealousy. The shifting scene and setting of *Othello* allowed great emphasis to be put on the site-specific performance within the school grounds. This created a range of cross-curricular opportunities. The school maintenance department created a gondola on wheels and the whole school worked on a project involving water, light and Venice. The production started with a full soundscape prologue created in the IT studio at Gosden. This was one of our most successful productions.

The Gosden, Globe alliance decided for the next year we would let the children choose their favourite moments and plays from earlier projects. To emphasize the low-key nature of the performance we called it *The No Show Show.*

> **Ellen** *The No Show Show* 2010
> *The No Show* brought back so many memories. It was a strange title. Each class picked their favourite track from the shows of the past. No laughing, everything quiet in the walled garden. Romeo kills Juliet's cousin, children not frightened, drawn in. If acted well the children will watch. We gained so much from watching other people. If there was not enough power children were looking outside at the airplanes. In the school during Globe Week we met new people, and learnt new techniques. They do it differently. I've never had a problem working with Globe people. Friendly and easy to get along with. Very clever. Not using difficult words. They do sometimes use complicated words but ones they knew we could cope with. They all seemed to be patient and kind. They take on Gosden values. The actors bring out the best in the children. *The No Show* featured all the songs I loved. 'Is all our company here?' is my favourite.

The No Show was a great celebration and reflection of the huge variety of plays explored during this extraordinary long and productive partnership. We decided that for the next production we would attempt the challenge of *The Tempest* again. This time, however, the production would be set within the wild surroundings of the school grounds. There had been a recent tsunami in Japan and the school had learnt about the impact of the tsunamis of 2005 on the Pacific basin. It was agreed that our 'Tempest' would be inspired by the impact of the tsunami on one community in Sri Lanka. The simplicity of *The No Show* was superseded by a very complex range of techniques and approaches, including a 6-projector multimedia sinking of the ship in the opening scene and manifestation of Ariel in the form of a free-spirited dolphin. The school was transformed into an undersea coral reef and the audience transported through an 'undersea cave' to the horrors of a tsunami-strewn playground and then into the haven of Prospero's island.

The impact of the tsunami was reflected though imaginative sets created across the grounds. The separate scenes were acted out in various places around the school and everyone gathered at the end to take part in a full Bollywood dance. The walled garden shook again, not with emotion, but with celebration and happiness. The whole performance was dedicated to the children and survivors of the Sri Lankan tsunami and money was raised and donated to them.

Ellen *The Tempest* 2011
I played Caliban. It was fun. A nice change from playing a hero. A real baddie. I was really transformed from being a small person. Kate was very good at teaching us how to act as men. Very inspirational. I had to act standing on a table. I pulled a silly face, trying to get a reaction from the audience. I played it for three different audiences. I had butterflies for the first. But as soon as I started I didn't want it to end. So many faces. Difficult to isolate any specific people. The part really helped my communication skills.

A good relationship with the audience is essential. All this helped my confidence.

If I didn't have the Gosden Globe productions I wouldn't have been confident or brave enough to do my work experience there. I couldn't replace it with anything else. It was so special. After *The Tempest* production I went to the classroom. A stranger came up and told me how good I was. Will the world be ready for me? I could go on and do more.

It gave me a buzz. I want that compliment again.

Ellen was in her final year at Gosden and was offered the chance of work experience at Shakespeare's Globe in London. She joined the Globe Education staff there as they prepared for the *Playing Shakespeare with Deutsche Bank* production at the Globe of *A Midsummer Night's Dream*.

Ellen Work experience
My placement was 3 days for 3 weeks. I worked in the Education building and in the Globe Theatre and studio working on *A Midsummer's Night Dream*. I went up with Dad. Commuting with Dad was cool. We caught the train at 8 for a 10 start. We went from Boxhill – nice and quiet, as we got further to London, crammed in. Chatted to Dad on way up. We got off the train at London Bridge and then walked past boats and the London Dungeon to Shakespeare's Globe's Education building. Bit nerve-wracking.

Places I hadn't been before. Went backstage and explored props in the attic. Spent my first day, testing lights for broken bulbs – as the plug went in there was a great spark – painters painting a balcony scene, plugged in and all the lights went off! Couldn't believe it! People at Globe – knew some, others not at all, Adam, David, Katherine and

> Fiona – rest new. Worked with the Production Team [Ellen gave a full description of them all!] making props. I had the job of making beards. Watched them rehearse. Met Bill, the Director and the actors. Watched and observed them. Same as we did at school. Warm-up beforehand – good to watch. My Headmaster came to visit. I showed him around. Not stressful because I knew him. No pressure. Showed him around the strange things in the props room. My favourite area. Never got a pass – a bit sad – borrowed lots of others. Good breaks and lunch breaks. Always someone to be with and talk to. Didn't treat me differently. Nice not to be treated like an outcast – accepted and not made to feel different. All very kind and nice. Respectful.
>
> Saw the last performance in the Globe of *A Midsummer Night's Dream*, where I had made all the props. Took my parents and my family. They had better use my beard, that's all I could think about! I kept watching – focused on the play and then a miracle happened. Hippolyta was getting married, she threw her bouquet high into the packed Globe theatre. I desperately wanted to catch it. No chance. And then something amazing happened. Dad rose up as if in slow motion and grasped the bouquet from the air and turned to me and said 'I think this is yours!' It was the cherry on top. The Globe Theatre and Globe Education have changed my life forever. It was a once in a lifetime thing to do.

Ellen's comments together with the message below that I received from a parent perhaps best sum up the impact of Gosden's collaboration with Globe Education. The journey has been personal to us but its impact highlights the potential for the use of Shakespeare as a tool for learning and the development of young people in any setting. If all involved commit to the project and take care to set up a creative environment that values children, people, imagination and sharing, anything is possible.

> I have two children at Gosden and watching them being involved in the summer performances of Shakespeare with the support of the Globe Theatre has just been amazing. The children absolutely love having the actors involved, they love working with them, copying them and performing with them. It gives them an incredible amount ofconfidence. It seems incredible, but my 6- and 8-year-old children, both with learning difficulties, actually said lines from *The Tempest*. I might have to repeat that. My children. With Learning Difficulties. Actually acted and quoted lines from a Shakespeare play. A Shakespeare Play! Amazing.

The whole performance teaches the children so much as they are involved in every aspect: they make and paint scenery; they glue and stick and sew costumes; they sing and dance and recite Shakespeare; they learn teamwork and performance skills. They enjoy their own moment of spotlight and then share the euphoria of the final group songs. Watching the whole school sing

'Is all our company here?' and then dance all together was awe-inspiring and very emotional.

Children I have known over the years at Gosden have progressed incredibly and watching them perform on their own with no support was fantastic. In the final scenes it is safe to say that there was not a dry eye or a throat un-lumped in that walled garden as we all sang together as a school.

FIGURE 17 *Gosden House School. Othello, 2009*

APPENDIX 1: MENUS

The lists below provide the equivalent of menu options in a cookery book – activities that work well together in a session or as a sequence. Most of the activity sequences, e.g. *Tactics* or *Soliloquy*, given in the book work well run together in a session. More frequently, however, we find ourselves taking activities from different sequences, putting them together to provide a structure for a session.

As ever, how this is done and what is included depends on the aims of the session and the needs of the group. The examples given below provide some possibilities but they are by no means exhaustive and illustrate generally how activities can work together. It is worth noting that there is one example of a menu in Chapter 6: *Performance: Adam's ten point plan* largely draws together activities found throughout the book. Each activity serves a particular purpose in the overall plan and progressively leads to the session goal – in this case, performance.

I have given an idea of the level of the menu. In reality, however, all of these activities can be used with any age, if it is appropriate for the group. We frequently change the amount of text used, depending on the level. This is one of the best ways of changing an activity to serve the needs of the group. The menus are broken down into types of work. It's important to stress that I believe most activities offer complete learning opportunities. Divisions such as character, language, etc. are to a large extent artificial. We do not see these elements separately on stage, they work together to create a moment of performance. It is obviously useful for students to be able to identify them separately, however, in their writing.

Complete scene analysis: including character, language and ideas. NB: rhythm is dealt with separately below.

Basic
Archetypes
Apply archetypes to an edited speech
Yes/No or Advance, retreat, manoeuvre
Hook, probe, deflect

More advanced
Archetypes

Apply archetypes to edited speech
Hook, probe, deflect
Pointing on the pronoun sequence

Basic
Status line up
Status pairs
Status improvisation
Hook, probe deflect

More advanced
Status line up
Status pairs
Sit, stand, kneel
Pointing on the pronoun (to find out where the power lies)

Basic
Yes/No
Yolanda's seven questions (less questions for a less experienced group)
Pointing on the pronoun sequence to interrupting

More advanced
Yes/No
Yolanda's seven questions (less questions for a less experienced group)
Pointing on the pronoun (whole sequence)
Speech as duologue

Rhythm
Basic
Atama, Abaccu, Laborena
Hakka 'We stress the words we want the world to hear'
Creating own lines
Cardiogram – in groups of four
Human cardiogram of the whole speech

More advanced
Atama, Abaccu, Laborena
Hakka 'We stress the words we want the world to hear'
Galloping and heartbeat
Creating own lines
Cardiogram – whole speech
Line sharing
Walking the punctuation

Staging

Basic

Oranges, Cabbages and Potatoes
Explanation of early modern theatre practices
Speech as duologue
Cue scripts

More advanced

Oranges, Cabbages and Potatoes
Explanation of early modern theatre practices
Speech as duologue
Cue scripts
Yes/No sequence to look at more modern theatre approaches to looking at character
Playing the scene as if on the Globe stage

Soliloquy

Basic

Whispering
Four word soliloquy
Small group story

More advanced

Hakka
Whispering
Four word soliloquy
Speech as duologue
Small group story
Cardiogram
Performing the soliloquy

NOTES

Chapter one

1. Rex Gibson *Teaching Shakespeare* (Cambridge, 1998), xii
2. World Shakespeare Festival research produced in conjunction with the BritishCouncil, 2012. http: // www.britishcouncil.org/society/worldshakespeare-festival-education (accessed 21.05.13)
3. Rex Gibson *Teaching Shakespeare* (Cambridge, 1998), 5

Chapter two

1. Christie Carson and Farah Karim-Cooper *Shakespeare's Globe A Theatrical Experiment* (Cambridge, 2008), 103
2. Christie Carson and Farah Karim-Cooper *Shakespeare's Globe A Theatrical Experiment* (Cambridge, 2008), 104
3. Andrew Gurr, *The Shakespearean Stage, 1574–1642* (Cambridge, 1992), 261
4. Robert Kruger (ed.) Epigrammes 17, 'In Cosmum,' *The Poems of Sir John Davies,* (Oxford, 1975), 136
5. Clare Williams (trans.) *Thomas Platter's Travels in England,* 1599, (London, 1959), 166–7
6. Christie Carson and Farah Karim-Cooper *Shakespeare's Globe A Theatrical Experiment* (Cambridge, 2008), 43
7. Christie Carson and Farah Karim-Cooper *Shakespeare's Globe A Theatrical Experiment* (Cambridge, 2008), 107

Chapter three

1. Max Stafford-Clark *Letters to George: The account of a Rehearsal* (London, 2004)

Chapter four

1. Giles expands upon these ideas in Giles Block *Speaking the Speech: An actor's guide to Shakespeare* (London, 2013)

Chapter five

1. Martin White *Renaissance Drama in Action: an introduction to aspects of theatre production and performance* (London, 1998), 28
2. Ibid p. 28
3. Ibid p. 28
4. Ibid p. 30
5. Ibid p. 32
6. Ibid p. 26
7. Ibid p. 28
8. Ibid p. 28
9. Ibid p. 28
10. Ibid p. 28
11. Developed in Augusto Boal *The Rainbow of Desires: The Boal Method of Theatre and Therapy* (London, Routledge, 1995)

Chapter six

1. Tony Howard teaches Shakespeare and film at Warwick University. His books include *Women as Hamlet: Performance as Interpretation in Theatre, Film and Fiction* (Cambridge University Press, 2007)

INDEX